Communication Media and Internet

Communication Media and Internet

Antra Arora

RANDOM PUBLICATIONS
NEW DELHI (INDIA)

Communication Media and Internet

ISBN 978-93-5111-506-9

Published in 2015 in India by

RANDOM PUBLICATIONS

4376-A/4B, Gali Murari Lal, Ansari Road
New Delhi-110 002
Phone : +9111-43580356, 011-23289044, 011-43142548
e-mail: sales@randompublications.com,
info@randompublications.com, randomexports@gmail.com

Reprint 2022

Type Setting by : Friends Media, Delhi-110089
Digitally Printed at: Replika Press Pvt. Ltd.

Preface

The Internet arose in the late 1960s out of efforts to share expensive computer resources provided by the military to universities across the United States. The initial network, called ARPAnet, went online for the first time in the fall of 1969. As the number of incompatible networks grew in the 1970s, Bob Kahn and Vint Cerf developed the TCP/IP protocols that would allow the networks to communicate with each other. In 1983 ARPAnet started using the TCP/IP protocols. This is commonly seen as the true beginning of the Internet.

The Internet is unique among the mass media in allowing interpersonal communication through e-mail and instant messaging; group communication through listservs, newsgroups, and discussion boards; and mass communication through the World Wide Web. The Web has turned the Internet into a major mass medium that provides news, entertainment, and community interaction. The Web offers a mix of content providers, including traditional media companies, new media companies offering publications available only on the Web, aggregator sites that offer help in navigating the Web, and individuals who have something they want to say.

Over the past several years, users have moved increasingly from slow dial-up connections to high-speed "always on" connections that have changed how people view and use the Internet. Media are making use of these high-speed connections to deliver content that includes a rich mix of video, audio, photos, and text.

This book provides a thorough overview to the modern media environment. It will be an incredibly useful resource for media professionals, online communities, webbloggers, teachers, students, researchers and anyone who is serious about learning how new technologies are changing the media landscape.

Author

Contents

1

Introduction to Communication Media

Communication is the activity of conveying information through the exchange of thoughts, messages, or information, as by speech, visuals, signals, writing, or behavior.

Communication requires a sender, a message, and a recipient, although the receiver need not be present or aware of the sender's intent to communicate at the time of communication; thus communication can occur across vast distances in time and space. Communication requires that the communicating parties share an area of communicative commonality. The communication process is complete once the receiver has understood the message of the sender.

Media are the storage and transmission channels or tools used to store and deliver information or data. It is often referred to as synonymous with mass media or news media, but may refer to a single medium used to communicate any data for any purpose.

Media has an important role to play in effective communication and with the IT revolution it has now been of inevitable use and vitality. In adult learning from building up environment or motivating people for literacy to sensitizing people about population explosion, girl child education, health awareness, etc. visual media have played a significant role. Communication system refers to dissemination of information. Communication is part of networking. Communication strategy in adult learning is significant to achieve effective transfer of information so that adult learners achieve the purpose of coming to the adult learning setup.

Some of the earlier methods used for communication have been visual and audio in the form of gestures, sound and pictures/drawings. Technology today has transformed these sounds and gestures to produce speech, videos, films, posters and theatre. The evolution of different means has opened up a vast potential for communication. With a plethora of tools and methods to use, the communicator may find it difficult to choose an appropriate one. How is this choice to be made? Answer to this question depends on our understanding of the impact of information technology on our everyday life.

Electronic Media Revolution

In the last century, a revolution in telecommunications has greatly altered communication by providing new media for long distance communication. The first transatlantic two-way radio broadcast occurred in 1906 and led to common communication via analogue and digital media:

- Analog telecommunications include traditional telephony, radio, and TV broadcasts.
- Digital telecommunications allow for computer-mediated communication, telegraphy, and computer networks.

Modern communication media now allow for intense long-distance exchanges between larger numbers of people (many-to-many communication via e-mail, Internet forums, and teleportation). On the other hand, many traditional broadcast media and mass media favor one-to-many communication (television, cinema, radio, newspaper, magazines, and also facebook).

In recent years there has been an information technology (IT) revolution. While paper-based manual systems for processing information and communicating are still very much evident, computer-based technology is increasingly undertaking most office functions and procedures. The implications of IT on communication methods cannot be ignored. However, technology will always require people, and in communication it is the input of the human agency that will ensure effective communication (or otherwise).

The fundamental skills of structure, tone and composition will always be of vital importance in ensuring effective communication. As originators of printed communications, people have control over these factors. However, while technological developments are making their role more interesting and challenging, the basic presentation techniques conventions should not be allowed to suffer. High standards must be set and maintained in order to ensure that your communications are not only appropriately worded and logically structured, but are also consistently and attractively presented.

Electronic media is enjoying broader use every day with an increase in electronic devices being made. The meaning of electronic media, as it is known in various spheres, has changed with the passage of time. The term media has achieved a broader meaning nowadays as compared to that given it a decade ago. Earlier, there was multimedia, once only a piece of software (application software) used to play audio (sound) and video (visual object with or without sound). Following this, it was CD (Compact Disc) and DVD (Digital Versatile Disc), then camera of 3G (Third Generation) applications in the field. In modern terms, the media includes all the software which are used in PC (Computer) or Laptop or Mobile Phone installed for normal or better performance of the system; today, however, hard discs of computer is an example of electronic media. This type of hard disc is becoming increasingly smaller in size.

The latest inclusion in the field is magnetic media (magnetic stripe) whose application is common, in the fastest growing Information Technology field. Modern day IT media is commonly used in the banking sector and by the Income Tax Department for the purpose of providing the easiest and fastest possible services to the consumers. In this magnetic strip all the data relating to a particular consumer is stored. Credit card, Debit card , ATM card, High end travel card are comprised within the term Media as it is known today. The main feature of these types of media is these are prepared unrecorded (blank form) and data is normally stored at a later stage as per the requirement of its user or consumer.

Visual Communication

Visuals are used effectively to strengthen communication. Visuals help people remember what they hear. The trick is in relating what you hear to a picture. For a majority of people it is easier to remember pictures than to remember just words. People like to put into pictures what they are hearing. You can say that visuals play the following key roles in our life.

Relevance

Visuals can give accurate representation of ideas: visuals help to define facts and information easily and precisely. They can identify and describe in concrete terms giving meaning to words. However, it is important to remember that to give accurate information the visuals must also be accurate. So if it is necessary, take the help of skilled artists or use photographs.

ii) *Visuals save time Imagine that as a communicator you are talking about some common diseases.* You want to give a description about the digestive system in humans. Suppose you have to use only words to describe what happens to the food, if we consider only the time factor, the time taken will certainly be much more than if you had a visual of the digestive system.

iii) *Visuals help memory.* As we have already described earlier, visuals help people to remember and recall much better. Most adults, we find, will be able to recall things they had seen in their youth, than a talk heard just a day or two before.

vi) *Visuals can stimulate the imagination.* Pictures can often be used as a starting point for discussions and debates. Visuals are not only a quick way of acquiring facts but also of using them. Details presented in a picture can make people think and react.

v) *Visuals provide a shared experience* We have seen that when the communicator and the audience share a common experience, communication becomes much easier. Visuals get two people thinking on similar lines about the same subject. It cuts down the possibility of there being ambiguity about the subject under discussion.

Examples of Visual Media

It is relevant to learn about various examples of visual media in more detail because you as a professional adult educator would have many occasions to use them at different forums.

The following seven categories of visual media have their own purposes, advantages and disadvantages and it is a good idea to be aware of strengths and weaknesses of each category. Hopefully the following discussion would make explicit these aspects of each of the examples of visual media discussed here.

a) Pictures

b) Puppets

c) Dramas, street plays and roles plays

d) Audio Cassettes
e) Videos
f) Broadcast media
g) Teleconferencing

a) Pictures

Pictures are the common factor in video, posters, charts, flip charts, slides and so on. For any of these tools to be understood we have to understand the basic principle of the tool that is the picture. The pictures that we select must be appropriate to the purpose of the communication, the viewer (audience) and the subject (content) of the communication.

Besides understanding the purpose of using pictures to communicate ideas, it is necessary to keep in mind the profile of the audience or the viewer and you would obviously select the pictures appropriate to the theme of the message you want to communicate. Some pictures can communicate more than what words can convey. In this sense, adult educator have a very good tool by way of pictures to communicate unusual messages. Hope that you will make use of this tool in your professional work.

Using any means of communication has its advantages and disadvantages and it is important that we fully appreciate this dimension before deciding to use a particular tool of communication.

b) Puppets

One of the best used forms of rural communication in India has been the puppet. For ages this method of communication has held centre stage. Puppetry has evolved as an art form and in many regions of India it is a way of livelihood for many artisans. Rajasthan is particularly famous for its puppets.

c) Dramas, Role-Plays and Street Plays

Drama is used in many countries, not just for entertainment but as a media for giving social messages. In India the street play or the nukkad natak is a common form of drama that is used for transmitting social messages.

The use of drama is an educative experience for both the performers as well as the audience. Many social activists have also used the formal theatre regularly. Drama takes many forms. Besides the role-play and street play, one also comes across the pantomime plays that do not use language but only facial expressions and body gestures. Dance is also one form of drama. The classical dances in Odissi, Kathakali, Rabindra natya, etc. have been used effectively in communication social messages.

To help us simplify the different forms of drama we can club it in the following categories.

1. The formal drama with written scripts, rehearsals, actors, etc.
2. Impromptu dramatization where the situation and story are suggested and people make up actions and use their own words.
3. Informal theatre with a flexible script, interactions with the audiences and absence of costumes or props.

In different regions of India, adult educators have made efforts to use folk media to impart social messages.

d) Audio cassettes

Almost everywhere in the world, audio cassettes and nowadays compressed discs (CDs) have been used by adult educators as very effective tools of communication.

e) Videos

Videos have been largely used as a mass media and dissemination tool. Many projects today have a separate unit for production of videos that can help in development work. The role of video in development communication has been to educate, helping to spread messages prepared by professional producers. It is necessary to have a better understanding of the advantages and disadvantages of the videography.

f) Broadcast Media

Television and Radio In India, a high percentage of people have access to radio and slightly less percentage have access to television. Both these media are powerful channels of communication and have been used under many circumstances to spread developmental messages.

Both TV and radio programs can be used by a trainer in developmental work. In using the television, the communicator needs to know the content and timing of the program and how the program can be used. As we have said earlier, the TV can be used with other media, like posters or charts and other printed material. A communicator can also use a lecture or discussion mode coupled with TV viewing.

g) Teleconferencing

Teleconferencing is an interactive mode of communication, where high quality multi-media links and satellites are used to establish links between the trainer and trainee.

Advantages

Teleconferencing is good option to provide uniform training to all the field functionaries.

Through Teleconferencing a good strategy can make all the project partners feel linked and involved directly. This is an important medium to provide a quick and uniform training to all field functionaries and it minimizes distortion and time lag in messages.

Disadvantages

It is a highly technical medium and requires basic electronic media facilities like telephone, fax, etc., that are not easily available in rural areas. A trainer-trainee live interaction is absent because of the distances separating both.

When there are too many calls to attend, trainers may miss out some queries or may not be able to answer them satisfactorily.

The above description of various examples of visual media leads us to the quest for learning in detail about communication systems and strategy most suitable for adult educators and adult learners.

Communication Systems

A system for communicating is generally called communication system that is often a facility comprising the structures set up for disseminating information. In other words, you could also describe a communication system as a facility to provide information transfer between persons and equipment.

Communicating as a Part of Networks

The system may be a collection of individual communication networks,transmission systems and relay stations and terminal equipment for interconnecting and interoperating so as to make an integrated whole. The individual components of such a system possess a common purpose and employ common procedures and operate as a unified organizational structure. Often, nowadays a communication system is recognized as a telephone, radio, television, data transmission, or other system in which information-bearing signals originate at one place and arereproduced at a distant point. We are here going to talk about communication systems in a more general and broad sense of the term.

Various Forms Communication

Organization charts make it easier to see how communication can take place vertically (between levels), horizontally (between sections) and diagonally (between different levels and sections). It is important to keep all communication routes as open and as effective as possible. Let us briefly discuss the various communication systems in the following paragraphs.

Downward communication This is by far the most frequent form of communication within an organization, where higher levels communicate with staff below them. In this category are communications like memos, notices, in-house newsletters, company handbook, procedure manuals.

Upward communication

The upward communication flow is equally important as the downward flow. Communications are directed upwards to managers, supervisors or directors by using memos, reports, meetings, informal discussions.

Horizontal communication

This occurs between people of the same status - sales staff, departmental heads, directors, supervisors. As well as memos and reports, horizontal communication could include committee meetings, seminars and conferences.

Diagonal communication

Tasks frequently arise which involve more than one department and there is often no obvious line of authority. Diagonal communication often relies largely on cooperation, goodwill and respect between the parties concerned.

Unofficial communication

When the correct lines of communication are not used, the grapevine often results. This term describes an unofficial communication system, which is constantly changing. The grapevine is a vehicle for distortions of the truth; it is basically a kind of rumor and gossip. An active grapevine can cause much damage to an organization by spreading incomplete, false or exaggerated information. It results in low morale, cynicism, fear and an unsettled workforce. Although the grapevine may never be completely eradicated, one should take steps to reduce its influence by considering carefully ways in which information is communicated, particularly in times of uncertainty within the organization. The confidence of an organization's employees is vitally important, and adequate and accurate information should always be made available to the people concerned at the earliest possible opportunity, through the correct channels.

Communication Strategy

In the overall communication strategy, we need to address five major questions which will help us define the communication strategy for our community.

- What is the message that we are communicating?
- Who is the target audience for our message?
- What behaviors should we promote among the target audience?
- What message concepts will promote perceived benefits of the new behavior?
- What channels of communication will reach our targets audiences as often and as affordably as possible?

Why, How and What of Communicating

Why do we need to communicate?

This need was felt because of a variety of factors. As a useful exercise, perhaps you could write some of the reasons why working with the poor rural women is necessary or is a need based activity that arises from your assessment of the situation and your understanding of the goals of adult learning.

How do we assess and prioritize the needs?

First, we have to assess what the women want to know and then prioritize what should be communicated first. For example, women may want to know how to cultivate fodder in wastelands, they may want to know how to improve the breed of their cattle and they may want to know how a motion picture is made.Now each of the needs is a topic for communication.

Deciding on what to communicate

After having understood the needs of the women, we now need to pick and choose what we have to communicate. There is a plethora of information available on any given subject, but as communicators we assess the level of understanding of the women and then decide what they will understand. Communication should always be targeted at the middle level so that it is not too simple, neither too technical. Suppose we are communicating about growing vegetables and kitchen gardening to a group of women belonging to the farming community. Then we presume that they will know the basics of growing vegetables. What we need to focus on in this case may be composting, varieties that can be grown, improving production or introducing new methods in horticulture.

Selection of Tools and Methods

We have spoken at length about this in the previous section. Based on the input to be given we can select the appropriate tools and methods for delivering the communication package. There are already many tools available to us through the Project. Many of the materials developed like posters, flip charts, handbooks, video-films can help us. In addition we can use programs on radio and television where such facilities are available.

Process of Communication

Once the needs are understood, the content of communication decided and the tools and methods selected, we can work on the process of communication. This simply means who will communicate what - using what tools - to whom -when - and - with what effect. When we answer these questions for each of our communications we are in addition focusing on two things.

i) What is the time that we are setting for our communication - when?

ii) What is the outcome that we expect from our communication - with what effect?

Deciding on the time to communicate is important. Suppose we organize an exposure visit for a community involved in farming and it is harvesting time, then people may join us but not participate fully.

Monitoring and Evaluation

What is the outcome that we expect from the communication? What is the objective of our communication in creating awareness? Is it only giving information? Is it providing skills? Does it aim to change behaviors? Depending on these objectives, we need to look for the impact of the communication and also measure the impact.

Restructuring the Message

In a long-term communication process, monitoring and evaluation helps us in restructuring messages that we give. This means that when we find gaps that exist in our communication - in terms of content, tools, delivery, place and time - we must make adjustments before going in for another round of communication. Communication is a process of constant learning and innovation. We must understand that evaluating the communication cannot be done in isolation.

Social Impact of Media

Media technology has made communicating increasingly easier as time has passed throughout history. Today, children are encouraged to use media tools in school and are expected to have a general understanding of the various technologies available. The internet is arguably one of the most effective tools in media for communication. Tools such as e-mail, Skype, Facebook etc., have brought people closer together and created new online communities. However, some may argue that certain types of media can hinder face-to-face communication and therefore can result in complications like identity fraud.

In a large consumer-driven society, electronic media (such as television) and print media (such as newspapers) are important for distributing advertisement media. More technologically advanced societies have access to goods and services through newer media than less technologically advanced societies.

Media, through media and communications psychology, has helped to connect diverse people from far and near geographical location. It has also helped in the aspect of on- line/ internet business and other activities that has an on-line version. All media intended to affect human behavior is initiatied through communication and the intended behavior is coached in psychology. Therefore, understanding media and communications psychology is fundamental in understanding the social and individual effects of media. The expanding field of media and communications psychology combines these established disciplines in a new way.

Timing change based on innovation and efficiency may not have a direct correlation with technology. The information revolution is based on modern advancements. During the 19th century, the information "boom" rapidly advanced because of postal systems, increase in newspaper accessibility, as well as schools "modernizing". These advancements were made due to the increase of people becoming literate and educated. The methodology of communication although has changed and dispersed in numerous directions based on the source of its sociocultural impact.

References

Biagi, S. (2004). *Media Impact.* Wadsworth Pub Co, 7th edition.

Caron, A. H. and Caronia, L. (2007). *Moving cultures: mobile communication in everyday life*. McGill-Queen's University Press.

Long, Paul; Wall, Tim (2009). *Media Studies: Text, Production and Context*. Pearson Education.

McQuail, Denis (2000) *McQuail's Mass Communication Theory* (fourth edition), Sage, London, pp. 16–34. MAS

2

Telegraph and Telephone

Telegraph

A telegraph that uses electrical signals, usually conveyed via telecommunication lines or radio. The electromagnetic telegraph is a device for human-to-human transmission of coded text messages.

The telegraph, superseded optical semaphore telegraph systems, such as those designed by Claude Chappe for the French military, and Friedrich Clemens Gerke for the Prussian military, thus becoming the first form of electrical telecommunications. In a matter of decades after their creation, electrical telegraph networks permitted people and commerce to almost instantly transmit messages across both continents and oceans, with widespread social and economic impacts.

From early studies of electricity, electrical phenomena were known to travel with great speed, and many experimenters worked on the application of electricity to communications at a distance.

All the known effects of electricity - such as sparks, electrostatic attraction, chemical changes, electric shocks, and later electromagnetism - were applied to the problems of detecting controlled transmissions of electricity at various distances.

In 1746 the French scientist and abbé Jean-Antoine Nollet, gathered about two hundred monks into a circle about a mile (1.6 km) in circumference, with pieces of iron wire connecting them. He then discharged a battery of Leyden jars through the human chain and observed that each man reacted at substantially the same time to the electric shock, showing that the speed of electricity's propagation was very high.

In 1753 an anonymous writer in the Scots Magazine suggested an electrostatic telegraph. Using one wire for each letter of the alphabet, a message could be transmitted by connecting the wire terminals in turn to an electrostatic machine, and observing the deflection of pith balls at the far end. Telegraphs employing electrostatic attraction were the basis of early experiments in electrical telegraphy in Europe, but were abandoned as being impractical and were never developed into a useful communication system.

In 1800 Alessandro Volta invented the Voltaic Pile, allowing for a continuous current of electricity for experimentation. This became a source of a low-voltage current that could be used to produce more distinct effects, and which was far less limited than the momentary discharge of an electrostatic machine, which with Leyden jars were the only previously known man-made sources of electricity.

Another very early experiment in electrical telegraphy was an electrochemical telegraph created by the German physician, anatomist and inventor Samuel Thomas von Sömmering in 1809, based on an earlier, less robust design of 1804 by Catalan polymath and scientist Francisco Salva Campillo. Both their designs employed multiple wires (up to 35) to represent almost all Latin letters and numerals. Thus, messages could be conveyed electrically up to a few kilometers (in von Sömmering's design), with each of the telegraph receiver's wires immersed in a separate glass tube of acid. An electric current was sequentially applied by the sender through the various wires representing each digit of a message; at the recipient's end the currents electrolysed the acid in the tubes in sequence, releasing streams of hydrogen bubbles next to each associated letter or numeral. The telegraph receiver's operator would watch the bubbles and could then record the transmitted message, albeit at a very low baud rate. The principal disadvantage to the system was its prohibitive cost, due to having to manufacture and string-up the multiple wire circuits it employed, as opposed to the single wire (with ground return) used by later telegraphs.

In 1816, Francis Ronalds set up a primitive telegraph. He ran eight miles (13 km) of cable (encased in glass tubing) through his back garden suspending it from two wooden lattices. and succeeded in getting an electrical signal along the full length using static high voltage electricity.

At both ends there were clockwork operated dials with numbers and letters of the alphabet.

Hans Christian Ørsted discovered in 1820 that an electric current produces a magnetic field which will deflect a compass needle. In the same year Johann Schweigger invented the galvanometer, with a coil of wire around a compass, which could be used as a sensitive indicator for an electric current.

In 1821, André-Marie Ampère suggested that telegraphy could be done by a system of galvanometers, with one wire per galvanometer to indicate each letter, and said he had experimented successfully with such a system. In 1824, Peter Barlow said that such a system only worked to a distance of about 200 feet (61 m), and so was impractical.

In 1825 William Sturgeon invented the electromagnet, with a single winding of uninsulated wire on a piece of varnished iron, which increased the magnetic force produced by electric current. Joseph Henry improved it in 1828 by placing several windings of insulated wire around the bar, creating a much more powerful electromagnet which could operate a telegraph through the high resistance of long telegraph wires.

In 1832 an electromagnetic telegraph was created by Baron Schilling in Russia, and in 1833 Carl Friedrich Gauss and Wilhelm Weber invented their own code to communicate over a distance of 1200 m within Göttingen, Germany.

Then in 1835 Joseph Henry invented the critical electrical relay, by which a weak current could operate a powerful local electromagnet over very long distances.

Schilling Telegraph

The telegraph invented by Baron Schilling von Canstatt in 1832 had a transmitting device which consisted of a keyboard with 16 black-and-white keys. These served for switching the electric current. The receiving instrument consisted of six galvanometers with magnetic needles, suspended from the silk threads. Both stations of Shilling's telegraph were connected by eight wires; six were connected with the galvanometers, one served for the return current and one - for a signal bell. When at the starting station the operator pressed a key, the corresponding pointer was deflected at the receiving station. Different positions of black and white flags on different disks gave combinations which corresponded to the letters or numbers. Pavel Shilling subsequently improved its apparatus. He reduced the number of connecting wires from eight to two.

On October 21, 1832, Schilling managed a short-distance transmission of signals between two telegraphs in different rooms of his apartment. In 1836 the British government attempted to buy the design but Schilling instead accepted overtures from Nicholas I of Russia. Schilling's telegraph was tested on a 5 kilometres (3.1 mi) experimental underground and underwater cable, laid around the building of the main Admiralty in Saint Petersburg and was approved for a telegraph between the imperial palace at Peterhof and the naval base at Kronstadt. However, the project was cancelled following Schilling's death in 1837. Schilling was also one of the first to put into practice the idea of the binary system of signal transmission.

William Fothergill Cooke studied anatomy in Heidelberg in 1834-6, where the physics professor introduced him to the Schilling telegraph in 1836.

Gauss-Weber telegraph and Carl Steinheil

Carl Friedrich Gauss, one of the most influential mathematicians of the early 19th century, developed a new theory of the Earth's magnetism in 1831, together with the physics professor Wilhelm Weber in Göttingen. Among the most important inventions of the time was the unifilar and bifilar magnetometer, enabling them to measure even the smallest deflections of the needle. In 1833 they installed a 1,200 metres (3,900 ft) long wire above the town's roofs. Gauss combined the Poggendorff-Schweigger multiplicator with his magnetometer to build a more sensitive device, the galvanometer. To change the direction of the electric current, he constructed a commutator of his own. As a result, he was able to make the distant needle move in the direction set by the commutator on the other end of the line.

At first, they used the telegraph to coordinate time, but soon they developed other signals; finally, their own alphabet. The alphabet was encoded in a binary code which was transmitted by positive or negative voltage pulses which were generated by means of moving an induction coil up and down over a permanent magnet and connecting the coil with the transmission wires by means of the commutator. The page of Gauss' laboratory notebook containing both his code and the first message transmitted, as well as a replica of the telegraph made in the 1850s under the instructions of Weber are kept in the faculty of physics of Göttingen University.

Gauss was convinced that this communication would be a help to his kingdom's towns.

Later in the same year, instead of a Voltaic pile, Gauss used an induction pulse, enabling him to transmit seven letters a minute instead of two. The inventors and university were too poor to develop the telegraph on their own, but they received funding from Alexander von Humboldt. Carl August Steinheil in Munich was able to build a telegraph network within the city in 1835-6. He installed a telegraph line along the first German railroad in 1835.

Alter and the Elderton Telegraph

Across the Atlantic, in 1836 an American scientist, Dr. David Alter, invented the first known American electric telegraph, in Elderton, Pennsylvania, one year before the Morse telegraph. Alter demonstrated it to witnesses but never developed the idea into a practical system. He was interviewed later for the book Biographical and Historical Cyclopedia of Indiana and Armstrong Counties, in which he said: "I may say that there is no connection at all between the telegraph of Morse and others and that of myself.... Professor Morse most probably never heard of me or my Elderton telegraph."

Cooke & Wheatstone

The first commercial electrical telegraph was co-developed by Sir William Fothergill Cooke and Charles Wheatstone. Cooke and Wheatstone patented it in May 1837 as an alarm system, and it was first successfully demonstrated on 25 July 1837 between Euston and Camden Town in London. It entered commercial use on the Great Western Railway over the 13 miles (21 km) from Paddington station to West Drayton on 9 April 1839. John Tawell was apprehended following the use of a needle telegraph message from Slough to Paddington on 1 January 1845. This is thought to be the first use of the telegraph to catch a murderer. The message was:

> A MURDER HAS GUST BEEN COMMITTED AT SALT HILL AND THE SUSPECTED MURDERER WAS SEEN TO TAKE A FIRST CLASS TICKET TO LONDON BY THE TRAIN WHICH LEFT SLOUGH AT 742 PM HE IS IN THE GARB OF A KWAKER WITH A GREAT COAT ON WHICH REACHES NEARLY DOWN TO HIS FEET HE IS IN THE LAST COMPARTMENT OF THE SECOND CLASS COMPARTMENT

The Cooke-Wheatstone system did not support punctuation, lower case, or the letters J, Q, and Z; hence the misspelling of 'just' and 'Quaker'. "Second class compartment" should also probably read "second first-class carriage"; this information was not significant, however, as Tawell was not arrested at the station, but at a nearby coffee shop.

Morse Telegraphs

In the United States, the telegraph was developed by Samuel Morse and Alfred Vail. Samuel F. B. Morse independently developed an electrical telegraph in 1836, an alternative design that was capable of transmitting over long distances using poor quality wire. His assistant, Alfred Vail, developed the Morse code signaling alphabet with Morse.

On 6 January 1838 Morse first successfully tested the device at the Speedwell Ironworks near Morristown, New Jersey, and on 8 February he publicly demonstrated it to a scientific committee at the Franklin Institute in Philadelphia, Pennsylvania.

In 1843 the U.S. Congress appropriated $30,000 to fund an experimental telegraph line from Washington, D.C. to Baltimore. By 1 May 1844, the line had been completed from the U.S. Capitol to Annapolis Junction in Maryland. That day the Whig Party nominated Henry Clay at its national convention in Baltimore. News of the nomination was hand-carried by railroad to Annapolis Junction where Vail wired it to Morse in the Capitol. On 24 May 1844, after the line was completed, Morse made the first public demonstration of his telegraph by sending a message from the Supreme Court Chamber in the U.S. Capitol in Washington, D.C. to the B&O Railroad "outer depot" (now the B&O Railroad Museum) in Baltimore. The famous message was: What hath God wrought (from the Biblical Book of Numbers 23:23: Surely there is no enchantment against Jacob, neither is there any divination against Israel: according to this time it shall be said of Jacob and of Israel, What hath God wrought!).

The Morse-Vail telegraph was quickly deployed in the following two decades. Morse failed to properly credit Vail for the powerful electromagnets used in his telegraph. The original Morse design, without the relay or the "intensity" and "quantity" electromagnets invented by Vail, only worked to a distance of 40 feet (12 m).

This was a practical electrical telegraph system, and subsequently electrical telegraph came to refer to a signaling telegram - a system where an operator makes and breaks an electrical contact with a telegraph key, which results in an audible signal at the other end produced by a telegraph sounder, which is interpreted and transcribed by a human. Morse and Vail's first telegraphs used a pen and paper system to record the marks of the Morse Code, and interpreted the marks visually, but operators soon realized that they could "read" the clicking of the receiver directly by ear. Systems which automatically read the signals and print formed characters are generally called teleprinters rather than telegraph systems. Some electrical telegraphs used indicators which were read visually rather than by ear. The most notable of these was the early transatlantic telegraph cable.

According to a Pennsylvania Historical and Museum Commission heritage marker installed along Pennsylvania Route 230 near Elizabethtown, Pennsylvania in 1947, the first commercial telegraph line in the United States ran along a railroad right-of-way (currently part of Amtrak's Keystone Corridor) between Lancaster, Pennsylvania and Harrisburg, Pennsylvania in 1845. The first message, received on January 8, 1846, was "Why don't you write, you rascals?"

Earth batteries were used by early experimenters as energy sources for telegraphy. Such devices were used for telegraph systems in the United States as far back as 1859.

On 24 October 1861, the first transcontinental telegraph system was established. Spanning North America, an existing network in the eastern United States was connected to the small network in California by a link between Omaha and Carson City via Salt Lake City. The first telegram on that line was sent by Brigham Young, then governor of Utah which affirmed that the Territory had not seceded. It read "Utah has not seceded but is firm for the Constitution and the laws of our once happy country." The slower Pony Express system ceased operation two days later. Carson City has another claim in the history of telegraphs for the largest and costliest transmission ever sent came from there.

As the transcontinental telegraph was laid it passed through Nebraska where Republican sympathizers prior to the American Civil War were eager to gain statehood for Nevada before the next presidential election so that Abraham Lincoln would have enough votes to win. They rushed to send the entire state constitution by telegraph to the United States Congress, which approved it and sent it to the President for signature. They did not believe sending it by train would guarantee it would arrive on time. The constitution was sent on 31 October, just eight days before the election on 7 November 1864.

Transatlantic Era

Submarine transatlantic cables installed in 1857 and 1858 operated for only a few days or weeks before they failed. This drove the study of underwater telegraph cables and accelerated interest in mathematical analysis of electromagnetic transmission lines. The first successful transatlantic telegraph cable was completed on 27 July 1866. The lasting connections were achieved by the ship SS Great Eastern, captained by Sir James Anderson.

In 1867, David Brooks (while working for the Central Pacific Railroad) was awarded U.S. Patent 63,206 and U.S. Patent 69,622 for his improvements to telegraph insulators. He was also awarded reissue number 2,717 in 1867, for U.S. Patent 45,221, which had originally been awarded to him in 1864, for his insulator design. Brooks' patents allowed the Central Pacific to communicate more easily with construction crews building the First Transcontinental Railroad in America; news of the completion of the railroad was broadcast by telegraph on 10 May 1869, with the telegrapher striking his key in unison with the strikes on the Golden Spike during the completion ceremony.

Global Communication

The miles of American telegraph grew from 40 in 1846 to 12,000 in 1850 to 23,000 in 1852. In Europe it increased from 2,000 in 1849 to 110,000 in 1869. The cost of sending 10 words was $1.55 in 1850, $1 in 1870, 40¢ in 1890. Within 29 years of its first installation at Euston Station, the telegraph network crossed the oceans to every continent but Antarctica, making instant global communication possible for the first time. The telegraph's greatest accomplishment was to expand information boundaries, allowing data to reach its destination before its usefulness expired to a decisively higher degree than before, particularly in trade. Regarding information about events at significant distances, the telegraph for the first time allowed one to be informed about what had happened before this sank down into the realm of the historic. Thus the telegraph liberated information transfer from transportation. The impetus of this was war, which created the need of expanding the telegraph's service. Its effects were immediate, reducing more than a day off delivery time.

News through newspapers also evolved due to the telegraph's inception. The telegraph could carry information, but there was a need for someone to obtain information to begin with at the distant source of the news and to deliver it to the telegraph office. Newspapers could not use their own reporters as they would obstruct other reporters, jamming the telegraph line. The solution was co-operation. In New York, the six major newspapers established an association for foreign news and a separate one for other sources - the first wire service. Ultimately this resulted in the proliferation of news with competition breaking out between the original six papers and other rivals. Thus the telegraph did not only transport news but also played a dominant role in establishing the industry and the profession of journalism.

Applications

In many instances, applications of the electrical telegraph in the long period between its invention and demise as a significant carrier of information were similar to the Internet. Telegraphy allowed applications such as message routing, social networking (between Morse operators—with gossiping and even marriages among operators being celebrated via telegraph), instant messaging, cryptography and text coding, abbreviated language slang, network security experts, hackers, wire fraud, mailing lists, spamming, e-commerce, stock exchange minute-by-minute reports (via the ticker tape machine invented by Edison), and many others. These points of comparisons have spurred modern commentators, such as Tom Standage, to refer to the 19th Century telegraphic network as the "Victorian Internet".

Submarine Communications Cable

A submarine communications cable is a cable laid on the sea bed between land-based stations to carry telecommunication signals across stretches of ocean. The first submarine communications cables, laid in the 1850s, carried telegraphy traffic. Subsequent generations of cables carried telephone traffic, then data communications traffic. Modern cables use optical fiber technology to carry digital data, which includes telephone, Internet and private data traffic.

Modern cables are typically 69 millimetres (2.7 in) in diameter and weigh around 10 kilograms per metre (7 lb/ft), although thinner and lighter cables are used for deep-water sections. As of 2010, submarine cables link all the world's continents except Antarctica.

Trials

After William Cooke and Charles Wheatstone had introduced their working telegraph in 1839, the idea of a submarine line across the Atlantic Ocean began to be thought of as a possible triumph of the future. Samuel Morse proclaimed his faith in it as early as 1840, and in 1842, he submerged a wire, insulated with tarred hemp and India rubber, in the water of New York Harbor, and telegraphed through it. The following autumn, Wheatstone performed a similar experiment in Swansea Bay. A good insulator to cover the wire and prevent the electric current from leaking into the water was necessary for the success of a long submarine line. India rubber had been tried by Moritz von Jacobi, the Prussian electrical engineer, as far back as the early 19th century.

Another insulating gum which could be melted by heat and readily applied to wire made its appearance in 1842. Gutta-percha, the adhesive juice of the Palaquium gutta tree, was introduced to Europe by William Montgomerie, a Scottish surgeon in the service of the British East India Company. Twenty years earlier, he had seen whips made of it in Singapore, and he believed that it would be useful in the fabrication of surgical apparatuses. Michael Faraday and Wheatstone soon discovered the merits of gutta-percha as an insulator, and in 1845, the latter suggested that it should be employed to cover the wire which was proposed to be laid from Dover to Calais. It was tried on a wire laid across the Rhine between Deutz and Cologne. In 1849, C.V. Walker, electrician to the South Eastern Railway, submerged a wire coated with gutta-percha along the coast off Dover.

The First Commercial Cables

In August 1850, John Watkins Brett's Anglo-French Telegraph Company laid the first line across the English Channel. It was simply a copper wire coated with gutta-percha, without any other protection. The experiment served to keep alive the concession, and the next year, on November 13, 1851, a protected core, or true cable, was laid from a government hulk, the Blazer, which was towed across the Channel. The next year, Great Britain and Ireland were linked together. In 1852, a cable laid by the Submarine Telegraph Company linked London to Paris. In May, 1853, England was joined to the Netherlands by a cable across the North Sea, from Orford Ness to The Hague. It was laid by the Monarch, a paddle steamer which had been fitted for the work.

Transatlantic Telegraph Cable

The first attempt at laying a transatlantic telegraph cable was promoted by Cyrus West Field, who persuaded British industrialists to fund and lay one in 1858. However, the technology of the day was not capable of supporting the project; it was plagued with problems from the outset, and was in operation for only a month. Subsequent attempts in 1865 and 1866 with the world's largest steamship, the SS Great Eastern, used a more advanced technology and produced the first successful transatlantic cable. The Great Eastern later went on to lay the first cable reaching to India from Aden, Yemen, in 1870.

British Dominance of Early Cable

From the 1850s until 1911, British submarine cable systems dominated the most important market, the North Atlantic Ocean. The British had both supply side and demand side advantages. In terms of supply, Britain had entrepreneurs willing to put forth enormous amounts of capital necessary to build, lay and maintain these cables. In terms of demand, Britain's vast colonial empire led to business for the cable companies from news agencies, trading and shipping companies, and the British government. Many of Britain's colonies had significant populations of European settlers, making news about them of interest to the general public in the home country.

British officials believed that depending on telegraph lines that passed through non-British territory posed a security risk, as lines could be cut and messages could be interrupted during wartime. They sought the creation of a worldwide network within the empire, which became known as the All Red Line, and conversely prepared strategies to quickly interrupt enemy communications. Britain's very first action after declaring war on Germany in World War I was to have the cable ship Teleconia cut the five cables linking Germany with North America. Thereafter the only way Germany could communicate was by wireless, and that meant that Room 40 could listen in.

The submarine cables were an economic boon to trading companies because owners of ships could communicate with captains when they reached their destination on the other side of the ocean and even give directions as to where to go next to pick up more cargo based on reported pricing and supply information. The British government had obvious uses for the cables in maintaining administrative communications with governors throughout its empire as well as in engaging other nations diplomatically and communicating with its military units in wartime. The geographic location of British territory was also an advantage as it included both Ireland on the east side of the Atlantic ocean and Newfoundland in North America on the west side, making for the shortest route across the ocean, which reduced costs significantly.

A few facts put this dominance of the industry in perspective. In 1896, there were thirty cable laying ships in the world and twenty-four of them were owned by British companies. In 1892, British companies owned and operated two-thirds of the world's cables and by 1923, their share was still 42.7 percent. During World War I, Britain's telegraph communications were almost completely uninterrupted, while it was able to quickly cut Germany's cables worldwide.

An 1863 cable to Bombay, India (now Mumbai) provided a crucial link to Saudi Arabia. In 1870, Bombay was linked to London via submarine cable in a combined operation by four cable companies, at the behest of the British Government. In 1872, these four companies were combined to form the mammoth globespanning Eastern Telegraph Company, owned by John Pender. A spin-off from Eastern Telegraph Company was a second sister company, the Eastern Extension, China and Australasia Telegraph Company, commonly known simply as "the Extension". In 1872, Australia was linked by cable to Bombay via Singapore and China and in 1876, the cable linked the British Empire from London to New Zealand.

The first trans-pacific cables were completed in 1902–03, linking the US mainland to Hawaii in 1902 and Guam to the Philippines in 1903. Canada, Australia, New Zealand and Fiji were also linked in 1902.

88 years later, the North Pacific Cable system was the first regenerative (repeatered) system to completely cross the Pacific from the US mainland to Japan. The US portion of NPC was manufactured in Portland, Oregon, from 1989 to 1991 at STC Submarine Systems, and later Alcatel Submarine Networks. The system was laid by Cable & Wireless Marine on the CS Cable Venture in 1991.

Construction

Transatlantic cables of the 19th century consisted of an outer layer of iron and later steel wire, wrapping India rubber, wrapping gutta-percha, which surrounded a multi-stranded copper wire at the core. The portions closest to each shore landing had additional protective armor wires. Gutta-percha, a natural polymer similar to rubber, had nearly ideal properties for insulating submarine cables, with the exception of a rather high dielectric constant which made cable capacitance high. Gutta-percha was not replaced as a cable insulation until polyethylene was introduced in the 1930s. In the 1920s, the American military experimented with rubber-insulated cables as an alternative to gutta-percha, since American interests controlled significant supplies of rubber but no gutta-percha manufacturers.

Bandwidth Problems

Early long-distance submarine telegraph cables exhibited formidable electrical problems. Unlike modern cables, the technology of the 19th century did not allow for in-line repeater amplifiers in the cable. Large voltages were used to attempt to overcome the electrical resistance of their tremendous length but the cables' distributed capacitance and inductance combined to distort the telegraph pulses in the line, reducing the cable's bandwidth, severely limiting the data rate for telegraph operation to 10–12 words per minute.

As early as 1823, Francis Ronalds had observed that electric signals were retarded in passing through an insulated wire or core laid underground, and the same effect was noticed by Latimer Clark (1853) on cores immersed in water, and particularly on the lengthy cable between England and The Hague. Michael Faraday showed that the effect was caused by capacitance between the wire and the earth (or water) surrounding it. Faraday had noticed that when a wire is charged from a battery (for example when pressing a telegraph key), the electric charge in the wire induces an opposite charge in the water as it travels along. In 1831, Faraday described this effect in what is now referred to as Faraday's law of induction. As the two charges attract each other, the exciting charge is retarded. The core acts as a capacitor distributed along the length of the cable which, coupled with the resistance and inductance of the cable limits the speed at which a signal travels through the conductor of the cable.

Early cable designs failed to analyze these effects correctly. Famously, E.O.W. Whitehouse had dismissed the problems and insisted that a transatlantic cable was feasible. When he subsequently became electrician of the Atlantic Telegraph Company, he became involved in a public dispute with William Thomson. Whitehouse believed that, with enough voltage, any cable could be driven. Because of the excessive voltages recommended by Whitehouse, Cyrus West Field's first transatlantic cable never worked reliably, and eventually short circuited to the ocean when Whitehouse increased the voltage beyond the cable design limit.

Thomson designed a complex electric-field generator that minimized current by resonating the cable, and a sensitive light-beam mirror galvanometer for detecting the faint telegraph signals. Thomson became wealthy on the royalties of these, and several related inventions. Thomson was elevated to Lord Kelvin for his contributions in this area, chiefly an accurate mathematical model of the cable, which permitted design of the equipment for accurate telegraphy. The effects of atmospheric electricity and the geomagnetic field on submarine cables also motivated many of the early polar expeditions.

Thomson had produced a mathematical analysis of propagation of electrical signals into telegraph cables based on their capacitance and resistance, but since long submarine cables operated at slow rates, he did not include the effects of inductance. By the 1890s, Oliver Heaviside had produced the modern general form of the telegrapher's equations which included the effects of inductance and which were essential to extending the theory of transmission lines to higher frequencies required for high-speed data and voice.

Transatlantic Telephony

While laying a transatlantic telephone cable was seriously considered from the 1920s, the technology required for economically feasible telecommunications was not developed until the 1940s. A first attempt to lay a pupinized telephone cable failed in the early 1930s due to the Great Depression.

In 1942, Siemens Brothers of New Charlton, London in conjunction with the United Kingdom National Physical Laboratory, adapted submarine communications cable technology to create the world's first submarine oil pipeline in Operation Pluto during World War II.

TAT-1 (Transatlantic No. 1) was the first transatlantic telephone cable system. Between 1955 and 1956, cable was laid between Gallanach Bay, near Oban, Scotland and Clarenville, Newfoundland and Labrador. It was inaugurated on September 25, 1956, initially carrying 36 telephone channels.

In the 1960s, transoceanic cables were coaxial cables that transmitted frequency-multiplexed voiceband signals. A high voltage direct current on the inner conductor powered repeaters (two-way amplifiers placed at intervals along the cable). The first-generation repeaters remain among the most reliable vacuum tube amplifiers ever designed. Later ones were transistorized. Many of these cables are still usable, but have been abandoned because their capacity is too small to be commercially viable. Some have been used as scientific instruments to measure earthquake waves and other geomagnetic events.

Optical Telephone Cables

In the 1980s, fiber optic cables were developed. The first transatlantic telephone cable to use optical fiber was TAT-8, which went into operation in 1988. A fiber-optic cable comprises multiple pairs of fibers. Each pair has one fiber in each direction. TAT-8 had two operational pairs and one backup pair.

Modern optical fiber repeaters use a solid-state optical amplifier, usually an Erbium-doped fiber amplifier. Each repeater contains separate equipment for each fiber. These comprise signal reforming, error measurement and controls. A solid-state laser dispatches the signal into the next length of fiber. The solid-state laser excites a short length of doped fiber that itself acts as a laser amplifier. As the light passes through the fiber, it is amplified. This system also permits wavelength-division multiplexing, which dramatically increases the capacity of the fiber.

Repeaters are powered by a constant direct current passed down the conductor near the center of the cable, so all repeaters in a cable are in series. Power feed equipment is installed at the terminal stations. Typically both ends share the current generation with one end providing a positive voltage and the other a negative voltage. A virtual earth point exists roughly halfway along the cable under normal operation. The amplifiers or repeaters derive their power from the potential difference across them.

The optic fiber used in undersea cables is chosen for its exceptional clarity, permitting runs of more than 100 kilometers between repeaters to minimize the number of amplifiers and the distortion they cause.

The rising demand for these fiber-optic cables outpaced the capacity of providers such as AT&T. Having to shift traffic to satellites resulted in poorer quality signals. To address this issue, AT&T had to improve its cable laying abilities. It invested $100 million in producing two specialized fiber-optic cable laying vessels. These included laboratories in the ships for splicing cable and testing its electrical properties. Such field monitoring is important because the glass of fiber-optic cable is less malleable than the copper cable that had been formerly used. The ships are equipped with additional propellers that increase maneuverability. This capability is important because fiber-optic cable must be laid straight from the stern (another factor copper cable laying ships did not have to contend with).

Originally, submarine cables were simple point-to-point connections. With the development of submarine branching units (SBUs), more than one destination could be served by a single cable system. Modern cable systems now usually have their fibers arranged in a self-healing ring to increase their redundancy, with the submarine sections following different paths on the ocean floor. One driver for this development was that the capacity of cable systems had become so large that it was not possible to completely back-up a cable system with satellite capacity, so it became necessary to provide sufficient terrestrial back-up capability. Not all telecommunications organizations wish to take advantage of this capability, so modern cable systems may have dual landing points in some countries (where back-up capability is required) and only single landing points in other countries where back-up capability is either not required, the capacity to the country is small enough to be backed up by other means, or having back-up is regarded as too expensive.

A further redundant-path development over and above the self-healing rings approach is the "Mesh Network" whereby fast switching equipment is used to transfer services between network paths with little to no effect on higher-level protocols if a path becomes inoperable. As more paths become available to use between two points, the less likely it is that one or two simultaneous failures will prevent end-to-end service.

As of 2012, operators had "successfully demonstrated long-term, error-free transmission at 100 Gbps across Atlantic Ocean" routes of up to 6,000 km (3,700 mi), meaning a typical cable can move tens of terabits per second overseas. Speeds improved rapidly in the last few years, with 40 Gbit/s having been offered on that route only three years earlier in August 2009.

Switching and all-by-sea routing commonly increases the distance and thus the round trip latency by more than 50%. For example, the round trip delay (RTD) or latency of the fastest transatlantic connections is under 60 ms, close to the theoretical maximum for an all-sea route. While in theory, a great circle route between London and New York City is only 5,600 km (3,500 mi), this requires several land masses (Ireland, Newfoundland, Prince Edward Island and the isthmus connecting New Brunswick to Nova Scotia) to be traversed, as well as the extremely tidal Bay of Fundy and a land route along Massachusetts' north shore from Gloucester to Boston and through fairly built up areas to Manhattan itself. In theory, using this partly land route could result in round trip times below 40 ms, not counting switching. Along routes with less land in the way, speeds can approach speed of light minimums in the long term.

Importance of Submarine Cables

As of 2006, overseas satellite links accounted for only 1 percent of international traffic, while the remainder was carried by undersea cable. The reliability of submarine cables is high, especially when (as noted above) multiple paths are available in the event of a cable break. Also, the total carrying capacity of submarine cables is in the terabits per second, while satellites typically offer only megabits per second and display higher latency. However, a typical multi-terabit, transoceanic submarine cable system costs several hundred million dollars to construct.

As a result of these cables' cost and usefulness, they are highly valued not only by the corporations building and operating them for profit, but also by national governments. For instance, the Australian government considers its submarine cable systems to be "vital to the national economy". Accordingly, the Australian Communications and Media Authority (ACMA) has created protection zones that restrict activities that could potentially damage cables linking Australia to the rest of the world. The ACMA also regulates all projects to install new submarine cables.

Investment in and Financing of Submarine Cables

Almost all fiber optic cables from TAT-8 in 1988 until approximately 1997 were constructed by "consortia" of operators. For example, TAT-8 counted 35 participants including most major international carriers at the time such as AT&T Corporation. Two privately financed, non-consortium cables were constructed in the late 1990s, which preceded a massive, speculative rush to construct privately financed cables that peaked in more than $22 billion worth of investment between 1999 and 2001. This was followed by the bankruptcy and reorganization of cable operators such as Global Crossing, 360networks, FLAG, Worldcom, and Asia Global Crossing.

There has been an increasing tendency in recent years to expand submarine cable capacity in the Pacific Ocean (the previous bias always having been to lay communications cable across the Atlantic Ocean which separates the United States and Europe). For example, between 1998 and 2003, approximately 70% of undersea fiber-optic cable was laid in the Pacific. This is in part a response to the emerging significance of Asian markets in the global economy.

Although much of the investment in submarine cables has been directed toward developed markets such as the transatlantic and transpacific routes, in recent years there has been an increased effort to expand the submarine cable network to serve the developing world. For instance, in July 2009, an underwater fiber optic cable line plugged East Africa into the broader Internet. The company that provided this new cable was SEACOM, which is 75% owned by Africans. The project is based on the hope that new information technology will reduce the cost of doing business in Africa and between Africa and other international parties. Still, the project was delayed by a month due to increased piracy along the coast, a reminder that the developing world faces other struggles that new technologies such as this may not necessarily solve.

Out of Range

Antarctica is the only continent yet to be reached by a submarine telecommunications cable. All phone, video, and e-mail traffic must be relayed to the rest of the world via satellite, which is still quite unreliable. Bases on the continent itself are able to communicate with one another via radio, but this is only a local network. To be a viable alternative, a fiber-optic cable would have to be able to withstand temperatures of -80° C as well as massive strain from ice flowing up to 10 meters per year. Thus, plugging into the larger Internet backbone with the high bandwidth afforded by fiber-optic cable is still an as yet infeasible economic and technical challenge in the Antarctic.

Cable Repair

Cables can be broken by fishing trawlers, anchors, earthquakes, turbidity currents and even shark bites. Based on surveying breaks in the Atlantic

Ocean and the Caribbean Sea, it was found that between 1959 and 1996, fewer than 9% were due to natural events. In response to this threat to the communications network, the practice of cable burial has developed. The average incidence of cable faults was 3.7 per 1,000 km (620 mi) per year from 1959 to 1979. That rate was reduced to 0.44 faults per 1000 km per year after 1985, due to widespread burial of cable starting in 1980. Still, cable breaks are by no means a thing of the past, with more than 50 repairs a year in the Atlantic alone, and significant breaks in 2006, 2008 and 2009.

The propensity for fishing trawler nets to cause cable faults may well have been exploited during the Cold War. For example, in February 1959, a series of 12 breaks occurred in five American trans-Atlantic communications cables. In response, a United States naval vessel, the U.S.S. Roy O. Hale detained and investigated the Soviet trawler Novorosiysk. A review of the ship's log indicated it had been in the region of each of the cables when they broke. Broken sections of cable were also found on the deck of the Novorosiysk. It appeared that the cables had been dragged along by the ship's nets, and then cut once they were pulled up onto the deck to release the nets. The Soviet Union's stance on the investigation was that it was unjustified, but the United States cited the Convention for the Protection of Submarine Telegraph Cables of 1884 to which Russia had been committed (prior to the formation of the Soviet Union) as evidence of violation of international protocol.

Shore stations can locate a break in a cable by electrical measurements, such as through spread-spectrum time-domain reflectometry (SSTDR). SSTDR is a type of time domain reflectometry that can be used in live environments very quickly. Presently, SSTDR can collect a complete data set in 20 ms. Spread spectrum signals are sent down the wire and then the reflected signal is observed. It is then correlated with the copy of the sent signal and mathematical algorithms are applied to the shape and timing of the signals to locate the break.

A cable repair ship will be sent to the location to drop a marker buoy near the break. Several types of grapples are used depending on the situation. If the sea bed in question is sandy, a grapple with rigid prongs is used to plough under the surface and catch the cable. If the cable is on a rocky sea surface, the grapple is more flexible, with hooks along its length so that it can adjust to the changing surface. In especially deep water, the cable may not be strong enough to lift as a single unit, so a special grapple that cuts the cable soon after it has been hooked is used and only one length of cable is brought to the surface at a time, whereupon a new section is spliced in. The repaired cable is longer than the original, so the excess is deliberately laid in a 'U' shape on the seabed. A submersible can be used to repair cables that lie in shallower waters.

A number of ports near important cable routes became homes to specialised cable repair ships. Halifax, Nova Scotia was home to a half dozen such vessels for most of the 20th century including long-lived vessels such as the CS Cyrus West Field, CS Minia and CS Mackay-Bennett. The latter two were contracted to recover victims from the sinking of the RMS Titanic. The crews of these vessels developed many new techniques and devices to repair and improve cable laying, such as the "plough".

Intelligence Gathering

Underwater cables, which cannot be kept under constant surveillance, have tempted intelligence-gathering organizations since the late 19th century. Frequently at the beginning of wars, nations have cut the cables of the other sides to shape the information flows into cables that were being monitored. The most ambitious efforts occurred in World War I, when British and German forces systematically attempted to destroy the others' worldwide communications systems by cutting their cables with surface ships or submarines. During the Cold War, the United States Navy and National Security Agency (NSA) succeeded in placing wire taps on Soviet underwater communication lines in Operation Ivy Bells.

Environmental Impact

The main point of interaction of cables with marine life is in the benthic zone of the oceans where the majority of cable lies. Recent studies (in 2003 and 2006) have indicated that cables pose minimal impacts on life in these environments. In sampling sediment cores around cables and in areas removed from cables, there were few statistically significant differences in organism diversity or abundance. The main difference was that the cables provided an attachment point for anemones that typically could not grow in soft sediment areas. Data from 1877 to 1955 showed a total of 16 cable faults caused by the entanglement of various whales, but such deadly entanglements have entirely ceased after the transition from telegraph cables to coaxial cables and then fiber-optic cables (the new cables are better designed in terms of torsional balance so that they have less of a tendency to coil).

Telephone

The telephone, or phone, is a telecommunications device that transmits and receives sounds, usually the human voice. Telephones are a point-to-point communication system whose most basic function is to allow two people separated by large distances to talk to each other. Developed in the mid-1870s by Alexander Graham Bell and others, the telephone has long been considered indispensable to businesses, households and governments, is now one of the most common appliances in the developed world. The word "telephone" has been adapted to many languages and is now recognized around the world.

All modern telephones have a microphone to speak into, an earphone (or 'speaker') which reproduces the voice of the other person, a ringer which makes a sound to alert the owner when a call is coming in, and a keypad (or on older phones a telephone dial) to enter the telephone number of the telephone to be called. The microphone and earphone are usually built into a handset which is held up to the face to talk. The keypad may be part of the handset or of a base unit to which the handset would be connected. A landline telephone is connected by a pair of wires to the telephone network, while a mobile phone is portable and communicates with the telephone network by radio. A cordless telephone has a portable handset which communicates by radio transmission with the handset owners base station which is connected by wire to the telephone network, and can only be used within about 50 feet from the base station.

The microphone converts the sound waves to electrical signals and then these are sent through the telephone network to the other phone and there converted by an earphone, or speaker, back into sound waves. Telephones are a duplex communications medium, meaning they allow the people on both ends to talk simultaneously. The telephone network, consisting of a worldwide net of telephone lines, fiberoptic cables, microwave transmission, cellular networks, communications satellites, and undersea telephone cables connected by switching centers, allows any telephone in the world to communicate with any other. Each telephone line has an identifying number called its telephone number. To initiate a telephone call the user enters the other telephone's number into a numeric keypad on the phone.

Although originally designed for simple voice communications, most modern telephones have many additional capabilities. They may be able to record spoken messages, send and receive text messages, take and display photographs or video, play music, and surf the Internet. A current trend is phones that integrate all mobile communication and computing needs; these are called smartphones.

Invention of Telephone

Credit for the invention of the electric telephone is frequently disputed, and new controversies over the issue have arisen from time to time. As with other influential inventions such as radio, television, the light bulb, and the computer, there were several inventors who did pioneering experimental work on voice transmission over a wire and improved on each other's ideas. Innocenzo Manzetti, Antonio Meucci, Johann Philipp Reis, Elisha Gray, Alexander Graham Bell, and Thomas Edison, among others, have all been credited with pioneering work on the telephone. An undisputed fact is that Alexander Graham Bell was the first to be awarded a patent for the electric telephone by the United States Patent and Trademark Office (USPTO) in March 1876. That first patent by Bell was the master patent of the telephone, from which other patents for electric telephone devices and features flowed.

The early history of the telephone became and still remains a confusing morass of claims and counterclaims, which were not clarified by the large number of lawsuits that hoped to resolve the patent claims of many individuals and commercial competitors. The Bell and Edison patents, however, were forensically victorious and commercially decisive.

A Hungarian engineer, Tivadar Puskás, quickly invented the telephone switchboard in 1876, which allowed for the formation of telephone exchanges, and eventually networks.

Basic Principles

A traditional landline telephone system, also known as "plain old telephone service" (POTS), commonly carries both control and audio signals on the same twisted pair (C) of insulated wires: the telephone line. The signaling equipment, or ringer, consists of a bell, beeper, light or other device (A7) to alert the user to incoming calls, and number buttons or a rotary dial (A4) to enter a telephone number for outgoing calls. Most of the expense of wire-line telephone service is the wires, so telephones transmit both the incoming and outgoing voice channels on a single pair of wires. A twisted pair line rejects electromagnetic interference (EMI) and crosstalk better than a single wire or an untwisted pair. The strong outgoing voice signal from the microphone does not overpower the weaker incoming speaker signal with a sidetone because a hybrid coil (A3) subtracts the microphone's signal from the signal sent to the local speaker. The junction box (B) arrests lightning (B2) and adjusts the line's resistance (B1) to maximize the signal power for the line's length. Telephones have similar adjustments for inside line lengths (A8). The wire's voltages are negative compared to earth, to reduce galvanic corrosion. Negative voltage attracts positive metal ions toward the wires.

Details of Operation

The landline telephone contains a switchhook (A4) and an alerting device, usually a ringer (A7), that remains connected to the phone line whenever the phone is "on hook" (i.e. the switch (A4) is open), and other components which are connected when the phone is "off hook". The off-hook components include a transmitter (microphone, A2), a receiver (speaker, A1), and other circuits for dialing, filtering (A3), and amplification.

A calling party wishing to speak to another party will pick up the telephone's handset, thereby operating a lever which closes the switchhook (A4), which powers the telephone by connecting the transmitter (microphone), receiver (speaker), and related audio components to the line. The off-hook circuitry has a low resistance (less than 300 ohms) which causes a direct current (DC), which comes down the line (C) from the telephone exchange. The exchange detects this current, attaches a digit receiver circuit to the line, and sends a dial tone to indicate readiness. On a modern push-button telephone, the caller then presses the number keys to send the telephone number of the called party. The keys control a tone generator circuit (not shown) that makes DTMF tones that the exchange receives. A rotary-dial telephone uses pulse dialing, sending electrical pulses, that the exchange can count to get the telephone number (as of 2010 many exchanges were still equipped to handle pulse dialing). If the called party's line is available, the exchange sends an intermittent ringing signal (about 90 volts alternating current (AC) in North America and UK and 60 volts in Germany) to alert the called party to an incoming call. If the called party's line is in use, the exchange returns a busy signal to the calling party.

However, if the called party's line is in use but has call waiting installed, the exchange sends an intermittent audible tone to the called party to indicate an incoming call.

The phone's ringer (A7) is connected to the line through a capacitor (A6), a device which blocks direct current but passes alternating current. So, the phone draws no current when it is on hook (a DC voltage is continually connected to the line), but exchange circuitry (D2) can send an AC voltage down the line to ring for an incoming call. (When there is no exchange, telephones often have hand-cranked magnetos to make the ringing voltage.) When a landline phone is inactive or "on hook", the circuitry at the telephone exchange detects the absence of direct current and therefore "knows" that the phone is on hook (therefore, only AC current will go through) with only the alerting device electrically connected to the line. When a party initiates a call to this line, the exchange sends the ringing signal. When the called party picks up the handset, they actuate a double-circuit switchhook (not shown) which simultaneously disconnects the alerting device and connects the audio circuitry to the line. This, in turn, draws direct current through the line, confirming that the called phone is now active. The exchange circuitry turns off the ring signal, and both phones are now active and connected through the exchange. The parties may now converse as long as both phones remain off hook. When a party "hangs up", placing the handset back on the cradle or hook, direct current ceases in that line, signaling the exchange to disconnect the call.

Calls to parties beyond the local exchange are carried over "trunk" lines which establish connections between exchanges. In modern telephone networks, fiber-optic cable and digital technology are often employed in such connections. Satellite technology may be used for communication over very long distances.

In most landline telephones, the transmitter and receiver (microphone and speaker) are located in the handset, although in a speakerphone these components may be located in the base or in a separate enclosure. Powered by the line, the microphone (A2) produces a modulated electrical current which varies its frequency and amplitude in response to the sound waves arriving at its diaphragm. The resulting current is transmitted along the telephone line to the local exchange then on to the other phone (via the local exchange or via a larger network), where it passes through the coil of the receiver (A3). The varying current in the coil produces a corresponding movement of the receiver's diaphragm, reproducing the original sound waves present at the transmitter.

Along with the microphone and speaker, additional circuitry is incorporated to prevent the incoming speaker signal and the outgoing microphone signal from interfering with each other. This is accomplished through a hybrid coil (A3). The incoming audio signal passes through a resistor (A8) and the primary winding of the coil (A3) which passes it to the speaker (A1). Since the current path A8 - A3 has a far lower impedance than the microphone (A2), virtually all of the incoming signal passes through it and bypasses the microphone.

At the same time the DC voltage across the line causes a DC current which is split between the resistor-coil (A8-A3) branch and the microphone-coil (A2-A3) branch. The DC current through the resistor-coil branch has no effect on the incoming audio signal. But the DC current passing through the microphone is turned into AC current (in response to voice sounds) which then passes through only the upper branch of the coil's (A3) primary winding, which has far fewer turns than the lower primary winding. This causes a small portion of the microphone output to be fed back to the speaker, while the rest of the AC current goes out through the phone line.

Early Commercial Instruments

Early telephones were technically diverse. Some used a liquid transmitter, some had a metal diaphragm that induced current in an electromagnet wound around a permanent magnet, and some were "dynamic" - their diaphragm vibrated a coil of wire in the field of a permanent magnet or the coil vibrated the diaphragm. The sound-powered dynamic kind survived in small numbers through the 20th century in military and maritime applications, where its ability to create its own electrical power was crucial. Most, however, used the Edison/Berliner carbon transmitter, which was much louder than the other kinds, even though it required an induction coil which was an impedance matching transformer to make it compatible with the impedance of the line. The Edison patents kept the Bell monopoly viable into the 20th century, by which time the network was more important than the instrument.

Early telephones were locally powered, using either a dynamic transmitter or by the powering of a transmitter with a local battery. One of the jobs of outside plant personnel was to visit each telephone periodically to inspect the battery. During the 20th century, "common battery" operation came to dominate, powered by "talk battery" from the telephone exchange over the same wires that carried the voice signals.

Early telephones used a single wire for the subscriber's line, with ground return used to complete the circuit (as used in telegraphs). The earliest dynamic telephones also had only one port opening for sound, with the user alternately listening and speaking (or rather, shouting) into the same hole. Sometimes the instruments were operated in pairs at each end, making conversation more convenient but also more expensive.

At first, the benefits of a telephone exchange were not exploited. Instead telephones were leased in pairs to a subscriber, who had to arrange for a telegraph contractor to construct a line between them, for example between a home and a shop. Users who wanted the ability to speak to several different locations would need to obtain and set up three or four pairs of telephones. Western Union, already using telegraph exchanges, quickly extended the principle to its telephones in New York City and San Francisco, and Bell was not slow in appreciating the potential.

Signalling began in an appropriately primitive manner. The user alerted the other end, or the exchange operator, by whistling into the transmitter. Exchange operation soon resulted in telephones being equipped with a bell in a ringer box, first operated over a second wire, and later over the same wire, but with a condenser (capacitor) in series with the bell coil to allow the AC ringer signal through while still blocking DC (keeping the phone "on hook"). Telephones connected to the earliest Strowger automatic exchanges had seven wires, one for the knife switch, one for each telegraph key, one for the bell, one for the push-button and two for speaking. Large wall telephones in the early 20th century usually incorporated the bell, and separate bell boxes for desk phones dwindled away in the middle of the century.

Rural and other telephones that were not on a common battery exchange had a magneto or hand-cranked generator to produce a high voltage alternating signal to ring the bells of other telephones on the line and to alert the operator. Some local farming communities that were not connected to the main networks set up barbed wire telephone lines that exploited the existing system of field fences to transmit the signal.

In the 1890s a new smaller style of telephone was introduced, packaged in three parts. The transmitter stood on a stand, known as a "candlestick" for its shape. When not in use, the receiver hung on a hook with a switch in it, known as a "switchhook." Previous telephones required the user to operate a separate switch to connect either the voice or the bell. With the new kind, the user was less likely to leave the phone "off the hook". In phones connected to magneto exchanges, the bell, induction coil, battery and magneto were in a separate bell box or "ringer box". In phones connected to common battery exchanges, the ringer box was installed under a desk, or other out of the way place, since it did not need a battery or magneto.

Cradle designs were also used at this time, having a handle with the receiver and transmitter attached, now called a handset, separate from the cradle base that housed the magneto crank and other parts. They were larger than the "candlestick" and more popular.

Disadvantages of single wire operation such as crosstalk and hum from nearby AC power wires had already led to the use of twisted pairs and, for long distance telephones, four-wire circuits. Users at the beginning of the 20th century did not place long distance calls from their own telephones but made an appointment to use a special sound proofed long distance telephone booth furnished with the latest technology.

What turned out to be the most popular and longest lasting physical style of telephone was introduced in the early 20th century, including Bell's Model 102. A carbon granule transmitter and electromagnetic receiver were united in a single molded plastic handle, which when not in use sat in a cradle in the base unit. The circuit diagram of the Model 102 shows the direct connection of the receiver to the line, while the transmitter was induction coupled, with energy supplied by a local battery. The coupling transformer, battery, and ringer were in a separate enclosure. The dial switch in the base interrupted the line current by repeatedly but very briefly disconnecting the line 1–10 times for each digit, and the hook switch (in the center of the circuit diagram) disconnected the line and the transmitter battery while the handset was on the cradle.

After the 1930s, the base also enclosed the bell and induction coil, obviating the old separate ringer box. Power was supplied to each subscriber line by central office batteries instead of a local battery, which required periodic service. For the next half century, the network behind the telephone became progressively larger and much more efficient, but after the telephone dial was added the instrument itself changed little until American Telephone & Telegraph Company (AT&T) introduced touch-tone dialing in the 1960s.

Digital Telephony

The Public Switched Telephone Network (PSTN) has gradually evolved towards digital telephony which has improved the capacity and quality of the network. End-to-end analog telephone networks were first modified in the early 1960s by upgrading transmission networks with T1 carrier systems, designed to support the basic 3 kHz voice channel by sampling the bandwidth-limited analog voice signal and encoding using PCM. While digitization allows wideband voice on the same channel, the improved quality of a wider analog voice channel did not find a large market in the PSTN.

Later transmission methods such as SONET and fiber optic transmission further advanced digital transmission. Although analog carrier systems existed that multiplexed multiple analog voice channels onto a single transmission medium, digital transmission allowed lower cost and more channels multiplexed on the transmission medium. Today the end instrument often remains analog but the analog signals are typically converted to digital signals at the (serving area interface (SAI), central office (CO), or other aggregation point. Digital loop carriers (DLC) place the digital network ever closer to the customer premises, relegating the analog local loop to legacy status.

IP Telephony

Internet Protocol (IP) telephony (also known as Voice over Internet Protocol, VoIP), is a disruptive technology that is rapidly gaining ground against traditional telephone network technologies. As of January 2005, up to 10% of telephone subscribers in Japan and South Korea have switched to this digital telephone service. A January 2005 Newsweek article suggested that Internet telephony may be "the next big thing." As of 2006 many VoIP companies offer service to consumers and businesses.

IP telephony uses an Internet connection and hardware IP Phones or softphones installed on personal computers to transmit conversations encoded as data packets. In addition to replacing POTS (plain old telephone service), IP telephony services are also competing with mobile phone services by offering free or lower cost connections via WiFi hotspots. VoIP is also used on private networks which may or may not have a connection to the global telephone network.

IP telephones have two notable disadvantages compared to traditional telephones. Unless the IP telephone's components are backed up with an uninterruptible power supply or other emergency power source, the phone will cease to function during a power outage as can occur during an emergency or disaster, exactly when the phone is most needed. Traditional phones connected to the older PSTN network do not experience that problem since they are powered by the telephone company's battery supply, which will continue to function even if there's a prolonged power black-out. A second distinct problem for an IP phone is the lack of a 'fixed address' which can impact the provision of emergency services such as police, fire or ambulance, should someone call for them. Unless the registered user updates the IP phone's physical address location after moving to a new residence, emergency services can be, and have been, dispatched to the wrong location.

References

Baker, Burton H. (2000), *The Gray Matter: The Forgotten Story of the Telephone*, Telepress, St. Joseph, MI.

Bruce, Robert V. (1990), *Alexander Graham Bell and the Conquest of Solitude*, Cornell University Press, Ithaca.

Coe, Lewis (1995), *The Telephone and Its Several Inventors: A History*, McFarland, North Carolina.

Huurdeman, Anton A. (2003), *The Worldwide History of Telecommunications*, IEEE Press and J. Wiley & Sons.

John, Richard R. (2010) *Network Nation: Inventing American Telecommunications*, Harvard University Press.

Wheen, Andrew (2011), *DOT-DASH TO DOT.COM: How Modern Telecommunications Evolved from the Telegraph to the Internet*, Springer.

3

Radio

Radio is the wireless transmission of signals through free space by electromagnetic radiation of a frequency significantly below that of visible light, in the radio frequency range, from about 30 kHz to 300 GHz. These waves are called radio waves. Electromagnetic radiation travels by means of oscillating electromagnetic fields that pass through the air and the vacuum of space.

Information, such as sound, is carried by systematically changing (modulating) some property of the radiated waves, such as their amplitude, frequency, phase, or pulse width. When radio waves strike an electrical conductor, the oscillating fields induce an alternating current in the conductor. The information in the waves can be extracted and transformed back into its original form.

Processes of Radio systems

Radio systems used for communications will have the following elements. With more than 100 years of development, each process is implemented by a wide range of methods, specialized for different communications purposes.

Transmitter and Modulation

Each system contains a transmitter. This consists of a source of electrical energy, producing alternating current of a desired frequency of oscillation. The transmitter contains a system to modulate (change) some property of the energy produced to impress a signal on it. This modulation might be as simple as turning the energy on and off, or altering more subtle properties such as amplitude, frequency, phase, or combinations of these properties. The transmitter sends the modulated electrical energy to a tuned resonant antenna; this structure converts the rapidly changing alternating current into an electromagnetic wave that can move through free space (sometimes with a particular polarization).

Amplitude modulation of a carrier wave works by varying the strength of the transmitted signal in proportion to the information being sent. For example, changes in the signal strength can be used to reflect the sounds to be reproduced by a speaker, or to specify the light intensity of television pixels. It was the method used for the first audio radio transmissions, and remains in use today. "AM" is often used to refer to the mediumwave broadcast band.

Frequency modulation varies the frequency of the carrier. The instantaneous frequency of the carrier is directly proportional to the instantaneous value of the input signal. Digital data can be sent by shifting the carrier's frequency among a set of discrete values, a technique known as frequency-shift keying.

FM is commonly used at VHF radio frequencies for high-fidelity broadcasts of music and speech. Normal (analog) TV sound is also broadcast using FM. Angle modulation alters the instantaneous phase of a carrier wave to transmit a signal. It is another term for Phase modulation.

Antenna

An antenna (or aerial) is an electrical device which converts electric currents into radio waves, and vice versa. It is usually used with a radio transmitter or radio receiver. In transmission, a radio transmitter applies an oscillating radio frequency electric current to the antenna's terminals, and the antenna radiates the energy from the current as electromagnetic waves (radio waves). In reception, an antenna intercepts some of the power of an electromagnetic wave in order to produce a tiny voltage at its terminals, that is applied to a receiver to be amplified. An antenna can be used for both transmitting and receiving.

Propagation

Once generated, electromagnetic waves travel through space either directly, or have their path altered by reflection, refraction or diffraction. The intensity of the waves diminishes due to geometric dispersion (the inverse-square law); some energy may also be absorbed by the intervening medium in some cases. Noise will generally alter the desired signal; this electromagnetic interference comes from natural sources, as well as from artificial sources such as other transmitters and accidental radiators. Noise is also produced at every step due to the inherent properties of the devices used. If the magnitude of the noise is large enough, the desired signal will no longer be discernible; this is the fundamental limit to the range of radio communications.

Resonance

Electrical resonance of tuned circuits in radios allow individual stations to be selected. A resonant circuit will respond strongly to a particular frequency, and much less so to differing frequencies. This allows the radio receiver to discriminate between multiple signals differing in frequency.

Receiver and Demodulation

The electromagnetic wave is intercepted by a tuned receiving antenna; this structure captures some of the energy of the wave and returns it to the form of oscillating electrical currents. At the receiver, these currents are demodulated, which is conversion to a usable signal form by a detector sub-system. The receiver is "tuned" to respond preferentially to the desired signals, and reject undesired signals.

Early radio systems relied entirely on the energy collected by an antenna to produce signals for the operator. Radio became more useful after the invention of electronic devices such as the vacuum tube and later the transistor, which made it possible to amplify weak signals. Today radio systems are used for applications from walkie-talkie children's toys to the control of space vehicles, as well as for broadcasting, and many other applications.

A radio receiver receives its input from an antenna, uses electronic filters to separate a wanted radio signal from all other signals picked up by this antenna, amplifies it to a level suitable for further processing, and finally converts through demodulation and decoding the signal into a form usable for the consumer, such as sound, pictures, digital data, measurement values, navigational positions, etc.

Radio Band

Radio frequencies occupy the range from a few hertz to 300 GHz, although commercially important uses of radio use only a small part of this spectrum. Other types of electromagnetic radiation, with frequencies above the RF range, are infrared, visible light, ultraviolet, X-rays and gamma rays. Since the energy of an individual photon of radio frequency is too low to remove an electron from an atom, radio waves are classified as non-ionizing radiation.

Communication Systems

A radio communication system sends signals by radio. Types of radio communication systems deployed depend on technology, standards, regulations, radio spectrum allocation, user requirements, service positioning, and investment.

The radio equipment involved in communication systems includes a transmitter and a receiver, each having an antenna and appropriate terminal equipment such as a microphone at the transmitter and a loudspeaker at the receiver in the case of a voice-communication system.

The power consumed in a transmitting station varies depending on the distance of communication and the transmission conditions. The power received at the receiving station is usually only a tiny fraction of the transmitter's output, since communication depends on receiving the information, not the energy, that was transmitted.

Classical radio communications systems use frequency-division multiplexing (FDM) as a strategy to split up and share the available radio-frequency bandwidth for use by different parties communications concurrently. Modern radio communication systems include those that divide up a radio-frequency band by time-division multiplexing (TDM) and code-division multiplexing (CDM) as alternatives to the classical FDM strategy. These systems offer different tradeoffs in supporting multiple users, beyond the FDM strategy that was ideal for broadcast radio but less so for applications such as mobile telephony.

A radio communication system may send information only one way. For example, in broadcasting a single transmitter sends signals to many receivers. Two stations may take turns sending and receiving, using a single radio frequency; this is called "simplex." By using two radio frequencies, two stations may continuously and concurrently send and receive signals - this is called "duplex" operation.

Development of Radio Technology

The meaning and usage of the word "radio" has developed in parallel with developments within the field of communications and can be seen to have three distinct phases: electromagnetic waves and experimentation; wireless communication and technical development; and radio broadcasting and commercialization. Many individuals—inventors, engineers, developers, businessmen - contributed to produce the modern idea of radio and thus the origins and 'invention' are multiple and controversial. Early radio designs could not transmit sound or speech and were called the "wireless telegraph."

Development from a laboratory demonstration to a commercial entity spanned several decades and required the efforts of many practitioners. In 1878, David E. Hughes noticed that sparks could be heard in a telephone receiver when experimenting with his carbon microphone. He developed this carbon-based detector further and eventually could detect signals over a few hundred yards. He demonstrated his discovery to the Royal Society in 1880, but was told it was merely induction, and therefore abandoned further research.

Experiments were undertaken by Thomas Edison and his employees of Menlo Park. Edison applied in 1885 to the U.S. Patent Office for a patent on an electrostatic coupling system between elevated terminals. The patent was granted as U.S. Patent 465,971 on December 29, 1891. The Marconi Company would later purchase rights to the Edison patent to protect them legally from lawsuits.

In 1893, in St. Louis, Missouri, Nikola Tesla made devices for his experiments with electricity. Addressing the Franklin Institute in Philadelphia and the National Electric Light Association, he described and demonstrated the principles of his wireless work. The descriptions contained all the elements that were later incorporated into radio systems before the development of the vacuum tube. He initially experimented with magnetic receivers, unlike the coherers (detecting devices consisting of tubes filled with iron filings which had been invented by Temistocle Calzecchi-Onesti at Fermo in Italy in 1884) used by Guglielmo Marconi and other early experimenters.

A demonstration of wireless telegraphy took place in the lecture theater of the Oxford University Museum of Natural History on August 14, 1894, carried out by Professor Oliver Lodge and Alexander Muirhead. During the demonstration a radio signal was sent from the neighboring Clarendon laboratory building, and received by apparatus in the lecture theater.

In November 1894 public demonstration at Town Hall of Kolkata, Jagadish Chandra Bose ignited gunpowder and rang a bell at a distance using millimetre range wavelength microwaves. Bose wrote in a Bengali essay, Adrisya Alok (Invisible Light), "The invisible light can easily pass through brick walls, buildings etc. Therefore, messages can be transmitted by means of it without the mediation of wires." Bose's first scientific paper, "On polarisation of electric rays by double-refracting crystals" was communicated to the Asiatic Society of Bengal in May 1895. His second paper was communicated to the Royal Society of London by Lord Rayleigh in October 1895. In December 1895, the London journal the Electrician (Vol. 36) published Bose's paper, "On a new electro-polariscope". At that time, the word 'coherer', coined by Lodge, was used in the English-speaking world for Hertzian wave receivers or detectors. The Electrician readily commented on Bose's coherer. (December 1895). The Englishman (18 January 1896) quoted from the Electrician and commented as follows:"Should Professor Bose succeed in perfecting and patenting his 'Coherer', we may in time see the whole system of coast lighting throughout the navigable world revolutionised by a Bengali scientist working single handed in our Presidency College Laboratory." Bose planned to "perfect his coherer" but never thought of patenting it.

In 1895 Alexander Stepanovich Popov built his first radio receiver, which contained a coherer. Further refined as a lightning detector, it was presented to the Russian Physical and Chemical Society on May 7, 1895. A depiction of Popov's lightning detector was printed in the Journal of the Russian Physical and Chemical Society the same year. Until recently, mistakenly believed that it was the first description, but in fact the first description of the device gave Dmitry Aleksandrovich Lachinov in July 1895 in the 2nd edition of his course "Fundamentals of Meteorology and climatology" — the first in Russia. Popov's receiver was created on the improved basis of Lodge's receiver, and originally intended for reproduction of its experiments.

Marconi was the first scientist to achieve successful radio transmission. In 1895, Marconi built a wireless system capable of transmitting signals at long distances (1.5 mi./ 2.4 km). In radio transmission technology, early public experimenters had made short distance broadcasts. Marconi achieved long range signalling due to a wireless transmitting apparatus and a radio receiver claimed by him. From Marconi's experiments, the phenomenon that transmission range is proportional to the square of antenna height is known as "Marconi's law."

Marconi's experimental apparatus proved to be the first engineering complete, commercially successful radio transmission system. According to the Proceedings of the United States Naval Institute in 1899, the Marconi instruments had a "[...] coherer, principle of which was discovered some twenty years ago, [and was] the only electrical instrument or device contained in the apparatus that is at all new."

In 1896, Marconi was awarded British patent 12039, Improvements in transmitting electrical impulses and signals and in apparatus there-for, for radio. In 1897, he established a radio station on the Isle of Wight, England. Marconi opened his "wireless" factory in the former silk-works at Hall Street, Chelmsford, England in 1898, employing around 60 people. Shortly after the 1900s, Marconi held the patent rights for radio.

In 1900, Brazilian priest Roberto Landell de Moura transmitted the human voice by wireless. According the newspaper Jornal do Comercio (June 10, 1900), he conducted his first public experiment on June 3, 1900, in front of journalists and the General Consul of Great Britain, C.P. Lupton, in São Paulo, Brazil, for a distance of approximately 8 km. The points of transmission and reception were Alto de Santana and Paulista Avenue.

One year after that experiment, he received his first patent from the Brazilian government. It was described as "equipment for the purpose of phonetic transmissions through space, land and water elements at a distance with or without the use of wires." Four months later, knowing that his invention had real value, he left Brazil for the United States of America with the intent of patenting the machine at the US Patent Office in Washington, DC.

Having few resources, he had to rely on friends to push his project. In spite of great difficulty, three patents were awarded: "The Wave Transmitter" (October 11, 1904) which is the precursor of today's radio transceiver; "The

Wireless Telephone" and the "Wireless Telegraph," both dated November 22, 1904

In June 1912 after the RMS Titanic disaster, due to increased production Marconi opened the world's first purpose-built radio factory at New Street Works, also in Chelmsford, England.

The next advancement was the vacuum tube detector, invented by Westinghouse engineers. On Christmas Eve 1906, Reginald Fessenden used a synchronous rotary-spark transmitter for the first radio program broadcast, from Ocean Bluff-Brant Rock, Massachusetts. Ships at sea heard a broadcast that included Fessenden playing O Holy Night on the violin and reading a passage from the Bible.

This was, for all intents and purposes, the first transmission of what is now known as amplitude modulation or AM radio. The first radio news program was broadcast August 31, 1920 by station 8MK in Detroit, Michigan, which survives today as all-news format station WWJ under ownership of the CBS network. The first college radio station began broadcasting on October 14, 1920 from Union College, Schenectady, New York under the personal call letters of Wendell King, an African-American student at the school.

That month 2ADD (renamed WRUC in 1947), aired what is believed to be the first public entertainment broadcast in the United States, a series of Thursday night concerts initially heard within a 100-mile (160 km) radius and later for a 1,000-mile (1,600 km) radius. In November 1920, it aired the first broadcast of a sporting event. At 9 pm on August 27, 1920, Sociedad Radio Argentina aired a live performance of Richard Wagner's opera Parsifal from the Coliseo Theater in downtown Buenos Aires. Only about twenty homes in the city had receivers to tune in this radio program. Meanwhile, regular entertainment broadcasts commenced in 1922 from the Marconi Research Centre at Writtle, England.

Sports broadcasting began at this time as well, including the college football on radio broadcast of a 1921 West Virginia vs. Pittsburgh football game.

In 1943, the United States Supreme Court invalidated one of the Marconi patents, number 763,772 (1904), on the basis it had been anticipated by Tesla, Lodge, and others. After years of patent battles by Marconi's company, the United States Supreme Court, in the 1943 case of Marconi

Wireless Telegraph co. of America v. United States, 320 U.S. 1 (1943), said that "it is now held that in the important advance upon his basic patent Marconi did nothing that had not already been seen and disclosed."

Although Marconi claimed that he had no knowledge of prior art regarding adjustable "four-circuit" transformer configuration for radio transmission and reception, the Supreme Court considered his claim false. In addition to that ruling from the Supreme Court, the United States Court of Claims invalidated the fundamental 1935 Marconi patent. The 1943 decision didn't overturn Marconi's original patents, or his reputation as the first person to develop practical radiotelegraphic communication. It just said that the adoption of adjustable transformers in the transmitting and receiving circuits, which was an improvement of the initial invention, was anticipated by patents issued to Oliver Lodge and John Stone Stone.

In contrast, related developments in the United Kingdom saw the High Court of Justice uphold Marconi's British Patent, issued on April 26, 1900. This patent disclosed a four-circuit system, which was strikingly similar to a four-circuit system disclosed in U.S. patent #645,576 that was issued earlier to Tesla on March 20, 1900. It must be emphasized that Tesla's patent was not meant to be used in a radio transmission apparatus and it didn't exhibit any presence of a variable inductance for varying the tuning frequency of the four circuits. This is not surprising since Tesla had only a barely understanding of electromagnetic radio physic and at least through 1919, he didn't believe that the radio signals predicted by Maxwell and experimentally shown by Hertz really existed. On the matter of invention, it is held that Marconi knowingly and unknowingly used the scientific and experimental work of others who were devising their own radio tuning apparatus' around the same time, such as the work of American electrical engineer John Stone Stone who was issued several U.S. patents between 1904 and 1908. However, what made Marconi more successful than any other was his ability to commercialize radio and its associated equipment into a global business.

One of the first developments in the early 20th century was that aircraft used commercial AM radio stations for navigation. This continued until the early 1960s when VOR systems became widespread. In the early 1930s, single sideband and frequency modulation were invented by amateur radio operators. By the end of the decade, they were established commercial modes. Radio was used to transmit pictures visible as television as early as the 1920s. Commercial television transmissions started in North America and Europe in the 1940s.

In 1954, the Regency company introduced a pocket transistor radio, the TR-1, powered by a "standard 22.5 V Battery." In 1955, the newly formed Sony company introduced its first transistorized radio. It was small enough to fit in a vest pocket, powered by a small battery. It was durable, because it had no vacuum tubes to burn out. Over the next 20 years, transistors replaced tubes almost completely except for high-power transmitters.

By 1963, color television was being broadcast commercially (though not all broadcasts or programs were in color), and the first (radio) communication satellite, Telstar, was launched. In the late 1960s, the U.S. long-distance telephone network began to convert to a digital network, employing digital radios for many of its links. In the 1970s, LORAN became the premier radio navigation system.

Soon, the U.S. Navy experimented with satellite navigation, culminating in the launch of the Global Positioning System (GPS) constellation in 1987. In the early 1990s, amateur radio experimenters began to use personal computers with audio cards to process radio signals. In 1994, the U.S. Army and DARPA launched an aggressive, successful project to construct a software-defined radio that can be programmed to be virtually any radio by changing its software program. Digital transmissions began to be applied to broadcasting in the late 1990s.

Uses of Radio

Early uses were maritime, for sending telegraphic messages using Morse code between ships and land. The earliest users included the Japanese Navy scouting the Russian fleet during the Battle of Tsushima in 1905. One of the most memorable uses of marine telegraphy was during the sinking of the RMS Titanic in 1912, including communications between operators on the sinking ship and nearby vessels, and communications to shore stations listing the survivors.

Radio was used to pass on orders and communications between armies and navies on both sides in World War I; Germany used radio communications for diplomatic messages once it discovered that its submarine cables had been tapped by the British. The United States passed on President Woodrow Wilson's Fourteen Points to Germany via radio during the war. Broadcasting began from San Jose, California in 1909, and became feasible in the 1920s, with the widespread introduction of radio receivers, particularly in Europe and the United States. Besides broadcasting, point-to-point broadcasting, including telephone messages and relays of radio programs, became widespread in the 1920s and 1930s. Another use of radio in the pre-war years was the development of detection and locating of aircraft and ships by the use of radar).

Today, radio takes many forms, including wireless networks and mobile communications of all types, as well as radio broadcasting. Before the advent of television, commercial radio broadcasts included not only news and music, but dramas, comedies, variety shows, and many other forms of entertainment (the era from the late 1920s to the mid-1950s is commonly called radio's "Golden Age"). Radio was unique among methods of dramatic presentation in that it used only sound.

Audio

AM radio uses amplitude modulation, in which the amplitude of the transmitted signal is made proportional to the sound amplitude captured (transduced) by the microphone, while the transmitted frequency remains unchanged. Transmissions are affected by static and interference because lightning and other sources of radio emissions on the same frequency add their amplitudes to the original transmitted amplitude.

In the early part of the 20th century, American AM radio stations broadcast with powers as high as 500 kW, and some could be heard worldwide; these stations' transmitters were commandeered for military use by the US Government during World War II. Currently, the maximum broadcast power for a civilian AM radio station in the United States and Canada is 50 kW, and the majority of stations that emit signals this powerful were grandfathered in.

In 1986 KTNN received the last granted 50,000 watt license. These 50 kW stations are generally called "clear channel" stations (not to be confused with Clear Channel Communications), because within North America each of these stations has exclusive use of its broadcast frequency throughout part or all of the broadcast day.

FM broadcast radio sends music and voice with higher fidelity than AM radio. In frequency modulation, amplitude variation at the microphone causes the transmitter frequency to fluctuate. Because the audio signal modulates the frequency and not the amplitude, an FM signal is not subject to static and interference in the same way as AM signals. Due to its need for a wider bandwidth, FM is transmitted in the Very High Frequency (VHF, 30 MHz to 300 MHz) radio spectrum.

VHF radio waves act more like light, traveling in straight lines; hence the reception range is generally limited to about 50–200 miles. During unusual upper atmospheric conditions, FM signals are occasionally reflected back towards the Earth by the ionosphere, resulting in long distance FM reception. FM receivers are subject to the capture effect, which causes the radio to only receive the strongest signal when multiple signals appear on the same frequency. FM receivers are relatively immune to lightning and spark interference.

High power is useful in penetrating buildings, diffracting around hills, and refracting in the dense atmosphere near the horizon for some distance beyond the horizon. Consequently, 100,000 watt FM stations can regularly be heard up to 100 miles (160 km) away, and farther (e.g., 150 miles, 240 km) if there are no competing signals.

A few old, "grandfathered" stations do not conform to these power rules. WBCT-FM (93.7) in Grand Rapids, Michigan, US, runs 320,000 watts ERP, and can increase to 500,000 watts ERP by the terms of its original license. Such a huge power level does not usually help to increase range as much as one might expect, because VHF frequencies travel in nearly straight lines over the horizon and off into space. Nevertheless, when there were fewer FM stations competing, this station could be heard near Bloomington, Illinois, US, almost 300 miles (500 km) away.

FM subcarrier services are secondary signals transmitted in a "piggyback" fashion along with the main program. Special receivers are required to utilize these services. Analog channels may contain alternative programming, such as reading services for the blind, background music or stereo sound signals. In some extremely crowded metropolitan areas, the sub-channel program might be an alternate foreign-language radio program for various ethnic groups. Sub-carriers can also transmit digital data, such as station identification, the current song's name, web addresses, or stock quotes. In some countries, FM radios automatically re-tune themselves to the same channel in a different district by using sub-bands.

Aviation voice radios use VHF AM. AM is used so that multiple stations on the same channel can be received. (Use of FM would result in stronger stations blocking out reception of weaker stations due to FM's capture effect). Aircraft fly high enough that their transmitters can be received hundreds of miles (or kilometres) away, even though they are using VHF.

Marine voice radios can use single sideband voice (SSB) in the shortwave High Frequency (HF—3 MHz to 30 MHz) radio spectrum for very long ranges or narrowband FM in the VHF spectrum for much shorter ranges. Narrowband FM sacrifices fidelity to make more channels available within the radio spectrum, by using a smaller range of radio frequencies, usually with five kHz of deviation, versus the 75 kHz used by commercial FM broadcasts, and 25 kHz used for TV sound.

Government, police, fire and commercial voice services also use narrowband FM on special frequencies. Early police radios used AM receivers to receive one-way dispatches.

Civil and military HF (high frequency) voice services use shortwave radio to contact ships at sea, aircraft and isolated settlements. Most use single sideband voice (SSB), which uses less bandwidth than AM. On an AM radio SSB sounds like ducks quacking, or the adults in a Charlie Brown cartoon. Viewed as a graph of frequency versus power, an AM signal shows power where the frequencies of the voice add and subtract with the main radio frequency. SSB cuts the bandwidth in half by suppressing the carrier and one of the sidebands. This also makes the transmitter about three times more powerful, because it doesn't need to transmit the unused carrier and sideband.

TETRA, Terrestrial Trunked Radio is a digital cell phone system for military, police and ambulances. Commercial services such as XM, WorldSpace and Sirius offer encrypted digital Satellite radio.

Telephony

Mobile phones transmit to a local cell site (transmitter/receiver) that ultimately connects to the public switched telephone network (PSTN) through an optic fiber or microwave radio and other network elements. When the mobile phone nears the edge of the cell site's radio coverage area, the central computer switches the phone to a new cell. Cell phones originally used FM, but now most use various digital modulation schemes. Recent developments in Sweden (such as DROPme) allow for the instant downloading of digital material from a radio broadcast (such as a song) to a mobile phone.

Satellite phones use satellites rather than cell towers to communicate.

Video

Television sends the picture as AM and the sound as AM or FM, with the sound carrier a fixed frequency (4.5 MHz in the NTSC system) away from the video carrier. Analog television also uses a vestigial sideband on the video carrier to reduce the bandwidth required.

Digital television uses 8VSB modulation in North America (under the ATSC digital television standard), and COFDM modulation elsewhere in the world (using the DVB-T standard). A Reed–Solomon error correction code adds redundant correction codes and allows reliable reception during moderate data loss. Although many current and future codecs can be sent in the MPEG transport stream container format, as of 2006 most systems use a standard-definition format almost identical to DVD: MPEG-2 video in Anamorphic widescreen and MPEG layer 2 (MP2) audio. High-definition television is possible simply by using a higher-resolution picture, but H.264/AVC is being considered as a replacement video codec in some regions for its improved compression. With the compression and improved modulation involved, a single "channel" can contain a high-definition program and several standard-definition programs.

Navigation

All satellite navigation systems use satellites with precision clocks. The satellite transmits its position, and the time of the transmission. The receiver listens to four satellites, and can figure its position as being on a line that is tangent to a spherical shell around each satellite, determined by the time-of-flight of the radio signals from the satellite. A computer in the receiver does the math.

Radio direction-finding is the oldest form of radio navigation. Before 1960 navigators used movable loop antennas to locate commercial AM stations near cities. In some cases they used marine radiolocation beacons, which share a range of frequencies just above AM radio with amateur radio operators. LORAN systems also used time-of-flight radio signals, but from radio stations on the ground.

VOR (Very High Frequency Omnidirectional Range), systems (used by aircraft), have an antenna array that transmits two signals simultaneously. A directional signal rotates like a lighthouse at a fixed rate. When the directional signal is facing north, an omnidirectional signal pulses. By measuring the difference in phase of these two signals, an aircraft can determine its bearing or radial from the station, thus establishing a line of position. An aircraft can get readings from two VORs and locate its position at the intersection of the two radials, known as a "fix."

When the VOR station is collocated with DME (Distance Measuring Equipment), the aircraft can determine its bearing and range from the station, thus providing a fix from only one ground station. Such stations are called VOR/DMEs. The military operates a similar system of navaids, called TACANs, which are often built into VOR stations. Such stations are called VORTACs. Because TACANs include distance measuring equipment, VOR/DME and VORTAC stations are identical in navigation potential to civil aircraft.

Radar

Radar (Radio Detection And Ranging) detects objects at a distance by bouncing radio waves off them. The delay caused by the echo measures the distance. The direction of the beam determines the direction of the reflection. The polarization and frequency of the return can sense the type of surface. Navigational radars scan a wide area two to four times per minute. They use very short waves that reflect from earth and stone. They are common on commercial ships and long-distance commercial aircraft.

General purpose radars generally use navigational radar frequencies, but modulate and polarize the pulse so the receiver can determine the type of surface of the reflector. The best general-purpose radars distinguish the rain of heavy storms, as well as land and vehicles. Some can superimpose sonar data and map data from GPS position.

Search radars scan a wide area with pulses of short radio waves. They usually scan the area two to four times a minute. Sometimes search radars use the Doppler effect to separate moving vehicles from clutter. Targeting radars use the same principle as search radar but scan a much smaller area far more often, usually several times a second or more. Weather radars resemble search radars, but use radio waves with circular polarization and a wavelength to reflect from water droplets. Some weather radar use the Doppler effect to measure wind speeds.

Data (digital radio)

Most new radio systems are digital. The oldest form of digital broadcast was spark gap telegraphy, used by pioneers such as Marconi. By pressing the key, the operator could send messages in Morse code by energizing a rotating commutating spark gap. The rotating commutator produced a tone in the receiver, where a simple spark gap would produce a hiss, indistinguishable from static. Spark-gap transmitters are now illegal, because their transmissions span several hundred megahertz. This is very wasteful of both radio frequencies and power.

The next advance was continuous wave telegraphy, or CW (Continuous Wave), in which a pure radio frequency, produced by a vacuum tube electronic oscillator was switched on and off by a key. A receiver with a local oscillator would "heterodyne" with the pure radio frequency, creating a whistle-like audio tone. CW uses less than 100 Hz of bandwidth. CW is still used, these days primarily by amateur radio operators (hams). Strictly, on-off keying of a carrier should be known as "Interrupted Continuous Wave" or ICW or on-off keying (OOK).

Radioteletype equipment usually operates on short-wave (HF) and is much loved by the military because they create written information without a skilled operator. They send a bit as one of two tones using frequency-shift keying. Groups of five or seven bits become a character printed by a teleprinter. From about 1925 to 1975, radioteletype was how most commercial messages were sent to less developed countries. These are still used by the military and weather services.

Aircraft use a 1200 Baud radioteletype service over VHF to send their ID, altitude and position, and get gate and connecting-flight data. Microwave dishes on satellites, telephone exchanges and TV stations usually use quadrature amplitude modulation (QAM). QAM sends data by changing both the phase and the amplitude of the radio signal. Engineers like QAM because it packs the most bits into a radio signal when given an exclusive (non-shared) fixed narrowband frequency range. Usually the bits are sent in "frames" that repeat. A special bit pattern is used to locate the beginning of a frame.

Communication systems that limit themselves to a fixed narrowband frequency range are vulnerable to jamming. A variety of jamming-resistant spread spectrum techniques were initially developed for military use, most famously for Global Positioning System satellite transmissions. Commercial use of spread spectrum began in the 1980s. Bluetooth, most cell phones, and the 802.11b version of Wi-Fi each use various forms of spread spectrum.

Systems that need reliability, or that share their frequency with other services, may use "coded orthogonal frequency-division multiplexing" or COFDM. COFDM breaks a digital signal into as many as several hundred slower subchannels. The digital signal is often sent as QAM on the subchannels. Modern COFDM systems use a small computer to make and decode the signal with digital signal processing, which is more flexible and far less expensive than older systems that implemented separate electronic channels.

COFDM resists fading and ghosting because the narrow-channel QAM signals can be sent slowly. An adaptive system, or one that sends error-correction codes can also resist interference, because most interference can affect only a few of the QAM channels. COFDM is used for Wi-Fi, some cell phones, Digital Radio Mondiale, Eureka 147, and many other local area network, digital TV and radio standards.

Heating

Radio-frequency energy generated for heating of objects is generally not intended to radiate outside of the generating equipment, to prevent interference with other radio signals. Microwave ovens use intense radio waves to heat food. Diathermy equipment is used in surgery for sealing of blood vessels. Induction furnaces are used for melting metal for casting, and induction hobs for cooking.

Amateur Radio Service

Amateur radio, also known as "ham radio," is a hobby in which enthusiasts are licensed to communicate on a number of bands in the radio frequency spectrum non-commercially and for their own enjoyment. They may also provide emergency and public service assistance. This has been very beneficial in emergencies, saving lives in many instances.

Radio amateurs use a variety of modes, including nostalgic ones like Morse code and experimental ones like Low-Frequency Experimental Radio.

Several forms of radio were pioneered by radio amateurs and later became commercially important, including FM, single-sideband (SSB), AM, digital packet radio and satellite repeaters. Some amateur frequencies may be disrupted illegally by power-line internet service.

Unlicensed Radio Services

Unlicensed, government-authorized personal radio services such as Citizens' band radio in Australia, the US, and Europe, and Family Radio Service and Multi-Use Radio Service in North America exist to provide simple, (usually) short range communication for individuals and small groups, without the overhead of licensing. Similar services exist in other parts of the world. These radio services involve the use of handheld units.

Free radio stations, sometimes called pirate radio or "clandestine" stations, are unauthorized, unlicensed, illegal broadcasting stations. These are often low power transmitters operated on sporadic schedules by hobbyists, community activists, or political and cultural dissidents. Some pirate stations operating offshore in parts of Europe and the United Kingdom more closely resembled legal stations, maintaining regular schedules, using high power, and selling commercial advertising time.

References

Asa Briggs. (1961). *The History of Broadcasting in the United Kingdom* (Oxford University Press.

Christopher H. Sterling with Michael C. Keith (ed.). (2004). *Encyclopedia of Radio.* New York; London: Fitzroy Dearborn, 2004 (three vols.)

Henry Ewbank and Sherman P. Lawton. (1952). *Broadcasting: Radio and Television* (Harper & Brothers.

Llewellyn White. (1947). *The American Radio* (University of Chicago Press, 1947).

Marc Fisher. (2007). *Something In The Air: Radio, Rock, and the Revolution That Shaped A Generation* (Random House, 2007).

W. Rupert Maclaurin. (1949). *Invention and Innovation in the Radio Industry.* The Macmillan Company.

4

Television

Television (TV) is a telecommunication medium for transmitting and receiving moving images that can be monochrome (black-and-white) or colored, with or without accompanying sound. "Television" may also refer specifically to a television set, television programming, or television transmission.

Commercially available since the late 1920s, the television set has become commonplace in homes, businesses and institutions, particularly as a vehicle for advertising, a source of entertainment, and news. Since the 1950s, television has been the main medium for molding public opinion. Since the 1970s the availability of video cassettes, laserdiscs, DVDs and now Blu-ray Discs, have resulted in the television set frequently being used for viewing recorded as well as broadcast material. In recent years Internet television has seen the rise of television available via the Internet, e.g. iPlayer and Hulu.

Although other forms such as closed-circuit television (CCTV) are in use, the most common usage of the medium is for broadcast television, which was modeled on the existing radio broadcasting systems developed in the 1920s, and uses high-powered radio-frequency transmitters to broadcast the television signal to individual TV receivers.

The broadcast television system is typically disseminated via radio transmissions on designated channels in the 54–890 MHz frequency band. Signals are now often transmitted with stereo or surround sound in many countries. Until the 2000s broadcast TV programs were generally transmitted as an analog television signal, but during the decade several countries went almost exclusively digital.

A standard television set comprises multiple internal electronic circuits, including those for receiving and decoding broadcast signals. A visual display device which lacks a tuner is properly called a video monitor, rather than a television. A television system may use different technical standards such as digital television (DTV) and high-definition television (HDTV). Television systems are also used for surveillance, industrial process control, and guiding of weapons, in places where direct observation is difficult or dangerous. Some studies have found a link between infancy exposure to television and ADHD.

History of Television

In its early stages of development, television employed a combination of optical, mechanical and electronic technologies to capture, transmit and display a visual image. By the late 1920s, however, those employing only optical and electronic technologies were being explored. All modern television systems relied on the latter, although the knowledge gained from the work on electromechanical systems was crucial in the development of fully electronic television.

The first images transmitted electrically were sent by early mechanical fax machines, including the pantelegraph, developed in the late nineteenth century. The concept of electrically powered transmission of television images in motion was first sketched in 1878 as the telephonoscope, shortly after the invention of the telephone. At the time, it was imagined by early science fiction authors, that someday that light could be transmitted over copper wires, as sounds were.

The idea of using scanning to transmit images was put to actual practical use in 1881 in the pantelegraph, through the use of a pendulum-based scanning mechanism. From this period forward, scanning in one form or another has been used in nearly every image transmission technology to date, including television. This is the concept of "rasterization", the process of converting a visual image into a stream of electrical pulses.

In 1884 Paul Gottlieb Nipkow, a 23-year-old university student in Germany, patented the first electromechanical television system which employed a scanning disk, a spinning disk with a series of holes spiraling toward the center, for rasterization. The holes were spaced at equal angular intervals such that in a single rotation the disk would allow light to pass through each hole and onto a light-sensitive selenium sensor which produced the electrical pulses. As an image was focused on the rotating disk, each hole captured a horizontal "slice" of the whole image.

Nipkow's design would not be practical until advances in amplifier tube technology became available. Later designs would use a rotating mirror-drum scanner to capture the image and a cathode ray tube (CRT) as a display device, but moving images were still not possible, due to the poor sensitivity of the selenium sensors. In 1907 Russian scientist Boris Rosing became the first inventor to use a CRT in the receiver of an experimental television system. He used mirror-drum scanning to transmit simple geometric shapes to the CRT.

Using a Nipkow disk, Scottish inventor John Logie Baird succeeded in demonstrating the transmission of moving silhouette images in London in 1925, and of moving, monochromatic images in 1926. Baird's scanning disk produced an image of 30 lines resolution, just enough to discern a human face, from a double spiral of Photographic lenses. This demonstration by Baird is generally agreed to be the world's first true demonstration of television, albeit a mechanical form of television no longer in use. Remarkably, in 1927 Baird also invented the world's first video recording system, "Phonovision": by modulating the output signal of his TV camera down to the audio range, he was able to capture the signal on a 10-inch wax audio disc using conventional audio recording technology. A handful of Baird's 'Phonovision' recordings survive and these were finally decoded and rendered into viewable images in the 1990s using modern digital signal-processing technology.

In 1926, Hungarian engineer Kálmán Tihanyi designed a television system utilizing fully electronic scanning and display elements, and employing the principle of "charge storage" within the scanning (or "camera") tube.

On December 25, 1926, Kenjiro Takayanagi demonstrated a television system with a 40-line resolution that employed a CRT display at Hamamatsu Industrial High School in Japan. This was the first working example of a fully electronic television receiver. Takayanagi did not apply for a patent.

By 1927, Russian inventor Léon Theremin developed a mirror-drum-based television system which used interlacing to achieve an image resolution of 100 lines.

In 1927, Philo Farnsworth made the world's first working television system with electronic scanning of both the pickup and display devices, which he first demonstrated to the press on 1 September 1928.

WRGB claims to be the world's oldest television station, tracing its roots to an experimental station founded on January 13, 1928, broadcasting from the General Electric factory in Schenectady, NY, under the call letters W2XB. It was popularly known as "WGY Television" after its sister radio station. Later in 1928, General Electric started a second facility, this one in New York City, which had the call letters W2XBS, and which today is known as WNBC. The two stations were experimental in nature and had no regular programming, as receivers were operated by engineers within the company. The image of a Felix the Cat doll, rotating on a turntable, was broadcast for 2 hours every day for several years, as new technology was being tested by the engineers.

In 1936 the Olympic Games in Berlin were carried by cable to television stations in Berlin and Leipzig where the public could view the games live.

In 1935 the German firm of Fernseh A.G. and the United States firm Farnsworth Television owned by Philo Farnsworth signed an agreement to exchange their television patents and technology to speed development of television transmitters and stations in their respective countries.

On 2 November 1936 the BBC began transmitting the world's first public regular high-definition service from the Victorian Alexandra Palace in north London. It therefore claims to be the birthplace of television broadcasting as we know it today.

In 1936, Kálmán Tihanyi described the principle of plasma display, the first flat panel display system.

Mexican inventor Guillermo González Camarena also played an important role in early television. His experiments with television (known as telectroescopía at first) began in 1931 and led to a patent for the "trichromatic field sequential system" color television in 1940,.

Although television became more familiar in the United States with the general public at the 1939 World's Fair, the outbreak of World War II prevented it from being manufactured on a large scale until after the end of the war. True regular commercial television network programming did not begin in the U.S. until 1948. During that year, legendary conductor Arturo

Toscanini made his first of ten TV appearances conducting the NBC Symphony Orchestra, and Texaco Star Theater, starring comedian Milton Berle, became television's first gigantic hit show. Since the 1950s, television has been the main medium for molding public opinion.

Amateur television (ham TV or ATV) was developed for non-commercial experimentation, pleasure and public service events by amateur radio operators. Ham TV stations were on the air in many cities before commercial TV stations came on the air.

In 2012, it was reported that television was growing into a larger component of major media companies' revenues than film.

Geographical Usage

The geographical usage of television varies around the world with a number of different transmission standards in use and differing approaches by government in relation to ownership and programme content.

African Networks and Stations

Despite being the most economically advanced country on the continent, South Africa did not introduce TV until 1976, owing to opposition from the apartheid regime. Nigeria was one of the first countries in Africa to introduce television, in 1959, followed by Zimbabwe (then Rhodesia) in 1961, while Zanzibar was the first in Africa to introduce colour television, in 1973. (Tanzania itself did not introduce television until 1994). The main satellite TV providers are the South African Multichoice DStv service, and the predominantly French language Canal Horizons, owned by France's Canal Plus.

Asian Networks and Stations

In Asia, television has traditionally been state-controlled, although the number of private stations is increasing, as is competition from satellite and cable television. Japan's NHK is a non-commercial network similar to the BBC, funded by a television license fee, and has more editorial independence over news and current affairs than broadcasters like India's state-run Doordarshan or China's China Central Television (CCTV). In Malaysia, television was dominated by Radio Televisyen Malaysia (RTM), a government-owned agency, from 1963 until 1984. From 1984, however, private television stations started emerging, and as of March 2009, there are

4 private stations and 2 government-owned ones in the country. Free-to-air television in Singapore is currently monopolised by MediaCorp, with 8 channels broadcast there.

From 2000 onwards, India also encouraged new private stations. Star TV, which is based in Hong Kong, has expanded to other areas in Asia recently. The number of private broadcasters are indeed increasing in some countries (2004) for example: Indonesia's 10 private national stations compared to only 1 in 1989.

Middle East Networks and Stations

Similarly in the Middle East, television has been heavily state-controlled, with considerable censorship of both news coverage and entertainment, particularly that imported from the West. This control of the medium has been eroded by the increasing availability of satellite TV, and the number of satellite channels in Arabic is second only to the number of satellite channels in English, the best known of which being the Qatar-based news service Al Jazeera.

Australasian Networks and Stations

Australian television began in 1956, just in time for the Melbourne Olympics. Australia has three nationwide metropolitan commercial networks (Seven, Nine and Ten) as well as the ABC (Australian Broadcasting Corporation), a government owned, commercial free network; and SBS (Special Broadcasting Service) a commercial-supported, multi-lingual, government-owned station. The Australian Broadcasting Authority has also issued licenses to community groups to establish "community television stations" in most capital cities on the UHF Ch 31 frequency (Channel 31). In regional and rural areas, numerous commercial stations are affiliated with one of the three metropolitan networks, and carry programming generally indistinguishable from their city cousins.

New Zealand Networks and Stations

Through a Crown Entity named Television New Zealand (TVNZ), the New Zealand government owns two television networks TV ONE and TV2. Although both networks are required to screen advertisements to pay for their operation, the One network receives additional funding to provide local content under a government broadcasting charter. A purely commercial network, TV3 is owned by CanWest, a Canadian media company, and also operate a music channel, C4. Another network called Prime Television is a subsidiary of pay television company, SKY Network Television, and carries programming from a number of sources including Australia's Nine Network. SKY Network Television operates a UHF terrestrial and digital satellite TV service. The New Zealand government also funds the Maori Television Service with the aim of putting Maori language and culture on New Zealand television screens. This service is delivered via Sky's UHF and satellite services. Additionally there are a range of low-power UHF regional television channels operating independently throughout the country.

European Networks and Stations

In much of Europe, television broadcasting has historically been state dominated, rather than commercially organised, although commercial stations have grown in number recently.

In most countries, the public broadcasters were the only television services available until the 1980s. These were usually funded by the state or a television license, but many countries have eventually adopted advertising in the public channels.

The United Kingdom was an early adopter of private television, launching the ITV network in 1955. Italy followed in the 1970s. Most countries got commercial broadcasters in the 1980s and 1990s, either by allowing private broadcasters to broadcast terrestrially or from broadcasters located in other countries. Some countries made room for private television by closing down or selling one of the state channels.

Most countries had two to six national broadcasters in the days of analogue television. Digital television has however allowed the number of terrestrial channels to multiply. Cable and satellite are also contributing to the increased number of channels, with hundreds of channels available to those willing to pay for it.

The largest commercial European broadcaster is the Luxembourg-based RTL Group. Other media groups controlling European television broadcasters are ProSiebenSat.1 Media, News Corporation, Central European Media Enterprises and Modern Times Group.

As Europe is a linguistical and culturally varied continent, the dominating broadcasters are either national or are operating in countries that share a language. Pan-European broadcasters exist, but they tend to adapt their content for different markets by providing different audio streams or completely separate channels with the same name. Channels available to all of Europe include Euronews and Eurosport.

Latin American Networks and Stations

Television has reached a great expansion in all the Latin American scope. Currently, there exist more than 1,500 television stations in all Latin America, according to the number of apparatuses by homes (more than 60 million), of more than two hundred million people. Because of the financial and political troubles that occurred between the mid-1970s and the early 1990s, television networks in some countries of this region had a development more irregular than the North American and European networks. In countries like Mexico or Brazil, one or two networks claim almost all the audience. In other countries like Colombia or Chile, television broadcasting has historically been public-broadcast dominated until the 1990s. In countries like Nicaragua or Peru, television had a troubled history. The largest commercial television groups are Mexico-based Televisa, Brazil-based Globo and Canada-based Canwest Latin American Group.

North American Networks and Stations

In Canada, there are a number of national networks, including three main networks for English Canada. One, CBC Television, is owned by the Canadian Broadcasting Corporation, a government-funded Crown corporation. The other two, CTV and Global, are privately run. The private networks usually use most of their primetime hours to rebroadcast U.S. shows, while the CBC airs more Canadian programming. Private systems — essentially mini-networks whose stations have a somewhat enhanced local focus and which do not reach all of Canada — include Citytv, E! and A-Channel.

In French Canada, particularly Quebec, the main networks are the CBC-owned Télévision de Radio-Canada, and private networks TVA and TQS. These networks tend to air substantially more domestic programming in primetime than their English counterparts. There are also the Aboriginal Peoples Television Network, multiethnic broadcaster Omni Television, provincial educational networks, and a limited number of niche-interest or independent stations. Radio-Canada broadcasts across Canada, while TVA and TQS only broadcast terrestrial signals in Quebec and APTN only broadcasts terrestrially in the territories. TVA and APTN, however, are available on cable in all Canadian markets. TQS does not have national cable carriage rights, although it is available in some markets outside of Quebec with larger francophone communities.

Additional premium television or specialty channels are also available in both languages through cable and satellite television. Notable examples include CBC Newsworld, TSN, MuchMusic, Showcase, and The Movie Network.

The Canadian Radio-television and Telecommunications Commission (CRTC) requires all television services in Canada to broadcast a minimum percentage of Canadian content, both during the day and during primetime.

United States Networks and Stations

In the U.S., the three traditional commercial television networks (ABC, CBS, and NBC) provide prime-time programs for their affiliate stations to air from 8pm–11pm Monday-Saturday and 7pm–11pm on Sunday. (7pm to 10pm, 6pm to 10pm respectively in the Central and Mountain time zones). Most stations procure other programming, often syndicated, off prime time. The FOX Network does not provide programming for the last hour of prime time; as a result, many FOX affiliates air a local news program at that time. Three newer broadcasting networks, The CW, ION Television, and MyNetworkTV also do not provide the same amount of network programming as so-called traditional networks. Sinclair Broadcast Group operates the largest network of local television stations, reaching about 24% of U.S. households. Trinity Broadcast Network, or TBN, runs the world's largest Christian television network, and owns twenty-three U.S. full-power television stations as well as 252 low-power stations serving smaller cities and rural areas. PBS is the U.S.'s public broadcaster.

Over the past thirty years, cable and satellite television have come to provide most homes with dozens or even hundreds of television services. Cable television was originally created to allow residents of weak-signal areas to benefit from a large, well-located common antenna. In the 1970s, Premium Services such as HBO, Showtime, and The Movie Channel used satellites to deliver movies to cable head-ends, who would re-distribute it to customers for an added charge. During the same period, it has seen the emergence of numerous specialty cable networks, such as CBN (now ABC

Family), CNN, ESPN (sports), Lifetime (women's programming), The Learning Channel, MTV, Nickelodeon (children's shows), VH-1, The Weather Channel, and others. The advent of digital compression technology in the 1990s, along with the rapidly growing popularity of direct-to-home satellite television allowed for content providers to pack more channels into a single satellite slot, and a number of new networks, especially those fulfilling certain niches, aimed at digital cable and satellite systems were established.

Content of TV Programs

A television program, also called television show, is a segment of content intended for broadcast on television. It may be a one-time production or part of a periodically recurring series. A single program in a series is called an episode.

A television series that is intended to comprise a limited number of episodes is usually called a miniseries or serial. Series without a fixed length are usually divided into seasons or series, yearly or biannual installments of new episodes. While there is no defined length, US industry practice tends to favor longer seasons than those of some other countries.

A one-time broadcast may be called a "special", or particularly in the UK a "special episode". A television movie ("made-for-TV movie" or television film), is a film that is initially broadcast on television rather than released in cinemas or direct-to-video, although many successful TV movies are later released on DVD.

A program can be either recorded—as on video tape or other various electronic media forms—or considered live television.

Television programming may be fictional (as in comedies and dramas), or non-fictional (as in documentary, news, and reality television). It may be topical (as in the case of a local newscast and some made-for-television movies), or historical (as in the case of many documentaries and fictional series). They could be primarily instructional or educational, or entertaining as is the case in situation comedy and game shows.

A drama program usually features a set of actors in a somewhat familiar setting. The program follows their lives and their adventures. With the exception of soap operas, many shows especially before the 1980s, remained static without story arcs, the main characters and the premise changed little.

If some change happened to the characters lives during the episode, it was usually undone by the end. (Because of this, the episodes could be broadcast in any order.) Since the 1980s, there are many series that feature progressive change to the plot, the characters, or both.

Common television program periods include regular broadcasts (like news), series (usually seasonal and ongoing with a duration of only a few episodes to many seasons), or miniseries, which is an extended film, usually with a small predetermined number of episodes and a set plot and timeline. Miniseries usually range from about 3 to 10 hours in length. In the UK, the term "miniseries" is only usually used in reference to imported programmes, and such short-run series are usually called "serials".

Until recently, all scripted shows began with a title sequence showing opening credits at the bottom lower third of the screen during the beginning, and included closing credits at the end of the show. Beginning in the 1990s, some shows began with a "cold open", followed by a title sequence and a commercial break. Many serial-type shows begin with a "Previously on…" (such as the series 24) introduction before the new episode. And, to save time, some shows omit the title sequence altogether, folding the names normally featured there into the opening credits.

While series appearing on networks are usually commissioned by those networks, their producers earn greater revenue when the program is sold into syndication. With the rise of the DVD home video format, box sets containing entire seasons or the complete run of a program have become a significant revenue source as well. Many of the prime-time comedy shows and Saturday morning cartoons were digitally remastered for U.S. television around mid-May 2008, as there are more original and reissued DVD sets of television programs containing either entire seasons or complete series to come. Typically, a DVD of a series or TV movie may contain extended or additional scenes not shown during the broadcast, scenes not allowed for broadcast, or additional background information/documentaries.

In 2012, it was reported that television was growing into a larger component of major media companies' revenues than film. Some also noted the increase in quality of some television programs. In 2012, Academy-Award winning film director Steven Soderbergh, commenting on ambiguity and complexity of character and narrative, stated: "I think those qualities are now being seen on television and that people who want to see stories that have those kinds of qualities are watching television."

FUNDING

Around the globe, broadcast television is financed by either government, advertising, licensing (a form of tax), subscription or any combination of these. To protect revenues, subscription TV channels are usually encrypted to ensure that only subscription payers receive the decryption codes to see the signal. Unencrypted channels are known as free to air or FTA.

In 2009 the global TV market represented 1,217.2 million TV households with at least one television, and total revenues of 268.9 billion EUR (declining 1.2% compared to 2008). North America had the biggest TV revenue market share with 39%, followed by Europe (31%), Asia-Pacific (21%), Latin America (8%) and Africa and the Middle East (2%).

Globally, the different TV revenue sources divide into 45 to 50% TV advertising revenues, 40 to 45% subscription fees and 10% public funding.

Advertising

Television's broad reach makes it a powerful and attractive medium for advertisers. Many television networks and stations sell blocks of broadcast time to advertisers ("sponsors") in order to fund their programming.

Since inception in the U.S. in 1941, television commercials have become one of the most effective, persuasive, and popular methods of selling products of many sorts, especially consumer goods. During the 1940s and into the 1950s, programs were hosted by single advertisers. This, in turn, gave great creative license to the advertisers over the content of the show. Perhaps due to the quiz show scandals in the 1950s, networks shifted to the magazine concept introducing advertising breaks with multiple advertisers.

U.S. advertising rates are determined primarily by Nielsen ratings. The time of the day and popularity of the channel determine how much a television commercial can cost. For example, the highly popular American Idol can cost approximately $750,000 for a 30-second block of commercial time; while the same amount of time for the World Cup and the Super Bowl can cost several million dollars. Conversely, lesser-viewed time slots, such as early mornings and weekday afternoons, are often sold in bulk to producers of infomercials which is less expensive.

In recent years, the paid program or infomercial has become common, usually in lengths of 30 minutes or one hour. Some drug companies and other businesses have even created "news" items for broadcast, known in the industry as video news releases, paying program directors to use them.

Some TV programs also weave advertisements into their shows, a practice begun in film and known as product placement. For example, a character could be drinking a certain kind of soda, going to a particular chain restaurant, or driving a certain make of car. (This is sometimes very subtle, where shows have vehicles provided by manufacturers for low cost, rather than wrangling them.) Sometimes a specific brand or trade mark, or music from a certain artist or group, is used. (This excludes guest appearances by artists, who perform on the show.)

The TV regulator oversees TV advertising in the United Kingdom. Its restrictions have applied since the early days of commercially funded TV. Despite this, an early TV mogul, Roy Thomson, likened the broadcasting licence as being a "licence to print money". Restrictions mean that the big three national commercial TV channels: ITV, Channel 4, and Five can show an average of only seven minutes of advertising per hour (eight minutes in the peak period). Other broadcasters must average no more than nine minutes (twelve in the peak). This means that many imported TV shows from the US have unnatural breaks where the UK company has edited out the breaks intended for US advertising. Advertisements must not be inserted in the course of certain specific proscribed types of programs which last less than half an hour in scheduled duration; this list includes any news or current affairs program, documentaries, and programs for children. Nor may advertisements be carried in a program designed and broadcast for reception in schools or in any religious broadcasting service or other devotional program, or during a formal Royal ceremony or occasion. There also must be clear demarcations in time between the programs and the advertisements.

The BBC, being strictly non-commercial is not allowed to show advertisements on television in the UK, although it has many advertising-funded channels abroad. The majority of its budget comes from television license fees and broadcast syndication, the sale of content to other broadcasters.

The Broadcasting Commission of Ireland (BCI) (Irish: Coimisiún Craolacháin na hÉireann) oversees advertising on television and radio within Ireland on both private and state owned broadcasters. Similar to other European countries, advertising is found on both private and state owned broadcasters. There are some restrictions based on advertising, especially in relation to the advertising of alcohol. Such advertisements are prohibited until after 7pm. Broadcasters in Ireland adhere to broadcasting legislation implemented by the Broadcasting Commission of Ireland and the European Union. Sponsorship of current affairs programming is prohibited at all times.

Taxation or license

Television services in some countries may be funded by a television licence or a form of taxation which means advertising plays a lesser role or no role at all. For example, some channels may carry no advertising at all and some very little, including:

- Australia (ABC)
- Japan (NHK)
- Norway (NRK)
- Sweden (SVT)
- United Kingdom (BBC)
- United States (PBS)
- Denmark (DR)

The BBC carries no television advertising on its UK channels and is funded by an annual television license paid by all households owning a television. This television license fee is set by government, but the BBC is not answerable to or controlled by government.

The two main BBC TV channels are watched by almost 90 percent of the population each week and overall have 27 per cent share of total viewing. This in spite of the fact that 85% of homes are multichannel, with 42% of these having access to 200 free to air channels via satellite and another 43% having access to 30 or more channels via Freeview. The licence that funds the seven advertising-free BBC TV channels currently costs £139.50 a year (about US$215) irrespective of the number of TV sets owned. When the same sporting event has been presented on both BBC and commercial channels, the BBC always attracts the lion's share of the audience, indicating viewers prefer to watch TV uninterrupted by advertising.

The Australian Broadcasting Corporation (ABC) carries no advertising (except for internal promotional material) as it is banned under the ABC Act 1983. The ABC receives its funding from the Australian Government every three years. In the 2008/09 Federal Budget the ABC received A$1.13 Billion. The funds assist in providing the ABC's Television, Radio, Online and International outputs. The ABC also receives funds from its many ABC

Shops across Australia. However funded by the Australian Government the editorial independence of the ABC is ensured through law.

In France and Ireland government-funded channels carry advertisements yet those who own television sets have to pay an annual tax.

In Japan, NHK is paid for by license fees. The Broadcast Law which governs NHK's funding stipulates that any television equipped to receive NHK is required to pay. The fee is standardized, with discounts for office workers and students who commute, as well a general discount for residents of Okinawa prefecture.

Subscription

Some TV channels are partly funded from subscriptions therefore the signals are encrypted during broadcast to ensure that only the paying subscribers have access to the decryption codes to watch pay television or specialty channels. Most subscription services are also funded by advertising.

Television Genres

Television genres include a broad range of programming types that entertain, inform, and educate viewers. The most expensive entertainment genres to produce are usually drama and dramatic miniseries. However, other genres, such as historical Western genres, may also have high production costs.

Popular culture entertainment genres include action-oriented shows such as police, crime, detective dramas, horror, or thriller shows. As well, there are also other variants of the drama genre, such as medical dramas and daytime soap operas. Science fiction shows can fall into either the drama or action category, depending on whether they emphasize philosophical questions or high adventure. Comedy is a popular genre which includes situation comedy (sitcom) and animated shows for the adult demographic such as South Park.

The least expensive forms of entertainment programming genres are game shows, talk shows, variety shows, and Reality television. Game shows show contestants answering questions and solving puzzles to win prizes. Talk shows feature interviews with film, television and music celebrities and public figures. Variety shows feature a range of musical performers and other entertainers such as comedians and magicians introduced by a host or Master of Ceremonies. There is some crossover between some talk shows and variety shows, because leading talk shows often feature performances by bands, singers, comedians, and other performers in between the interview segments. Reality TV shows "regular" people (i.e., not actors) who are facing unusual challenges or experiences, ranging from arrest by police officers (COPS) to weight loss (The Biggest Loser). A variant version of reality shows depicts celebrities doing mundane activities such as going about their everyday life (The Osbournes, Snoop Dogg's Father Hood) or doing manual labor (The Simple Life).

Social Aspects of Television

The social aspects of television are influences this medium has had on society since its inception. The belief that this impact has been dramatic has been largely unchallenged in media theory since its inception. However, there is much dispute as to what those effects are, how serious thc ramifications are and if these effects are more or less evolutionary with human communication.

Current research is discovering that individuals suffering from social isolation can employ television to create what is termed a parasocial or faux relationship with characters from their favorite television shows and movies as a way of deflecting feelings of loneliness and social deprivation. Just as an individual would spend time with a real person sharing opinions and thoughts, pseudo-relationships are formed with TV characters by becoming personally invested in their lives as if they were a close friend so that the individual can satiate the human desire to form meaningful relationships and establish themselves in society. Jaye Derrick and Shira Gabriel of the University of Buffalo, and Kurt Hugenberg of Miami University found that when an individual is not able to participate in interactions with real people, they are less likely to indicate feelings of loneliness when watching their favorite TV show.

They refer to this finding as the Social Surrogacy Hypothesis. Furthermore, when an event such as a fight or argument disrupts a personal relationship, watching a favorite TV show was able to create a cushion and prevent the individual from experiencing reduced self-esteem and feelings of inadequacy that can often accompany the perceived threat. By providing a temporary substitute for acceptance and belonging that is experienced through social relationships TV is helping to relieve feelings of depression and loneliness when those relationships are not available. This benefit is considered a positive consequence of watching television as it can counteract the psychological damage that is caused by isolation from social relationships.

Educational Advantages

Several studies have found that educational television has many advantages. The Media Awareness Network, explains in its article, The Good Things about Television, that television can be a very powerful and effective learning tool for children if used wisely. The article states that television can help young people discover where they fit into society, develop closer relationships with peers and family, and teach them to understand complex social aspects of communication. Dimitri Christakis cites studies in which those who watched "Sesame Street" and other educational programs as preschoolers had higher grades, were reading more books, placed more value on achievement and were more creative. Similarly, while those exposed to negative role models suffered, those exposed to positive models behaved better.

Negative Effects

There are many pejorative terms for television, including "boob tube" and "chewing gum for the mind", showing the disdain held by many people for this medium. Newton N. Minow spoke of the "vast wasteland" that was the television programming of the day in his 1961 speech.

Complaints about the social influence of television have been heard from the U.S. justice system as investigators and prosecutors decry what they refer to as "the CSI Syndrome." They complain that, because of the popularity and considerable viewership of CSI and its spin-offs, juries today expect to be "dazzled," and will acquit criminals of charges unless presented with impressive physical evidence, even when motive, testimony, and lack of alibi are presented by the prosecution.

Television has also been credited with changing the norms of social propriety, although the direction and value of this change are disputed. Milton Shulman, writing about television in the 1960s, wrote that "TV cartoons showed cows without udders and not even a pause was pregnant," and noted that on-air vulgarity was highly frowned upon. Shulman suggested that, even by the 1970s, television was shaping the ideas of propriety and appropriateness in the countries the medium blanketed. He asserted that, as a particularly "pervasive and ubiquitous" medium, television could create a comfortable familiarity with and acceptance of language and behavior once deemed socially unacceptable. Television, as well as influencing its viewers, evoked an imitative response from other competing media as they struggle to keep pace and retain viewer- or readership.

According to a study published in 2008, conducted by John Robinson and Steven Martin from the University of Maryland, people who are not satisfied with their lives spend 30% more time watching TV than satisfied people do. The research was conducted with 30,000 people during the period between 1975 and 2006. This contrasted with a previous study, which indicated that watching TV was the happiest time of the day for some people. Based on his study, Robinson commented that the pleasurable effects of television may be likened to an addictive activity, producing "momentary pleasure but long-term misery and regret."

Psychological Effects

There is a theory that when a person plays video games or watches TV, the basal ganglia portion of the brain becomes very active and dopamine is released. Some scientists believe that release of high amounts of dopamine reduces the amount of the neurotransmitter available for control of movement, perception of pain and pleasure and formation of feelings, although this remains a controversial conclusion. A study conducted by Herbert Krugman found that while viewers are watching television the right side of the brain is twice as active as the left which causes a state of hypnosis.

Physical Effects

Studies in both children and adults have found an association between the number of hours of television watched and obesity. A study found that watching television decreases the metabolic rate in children to below that found in children at rest. Author John Steinbeck describes television watchers:

"I have observed the physical symptoms of television-looking on children as well as on adults. The mouth grows slack and the lips hang open; the eyes take on a hypnotized or doped look; the nose runs rather more than usual; the backbone turns to water and the fingers slowly and methodically pick the designs out of brocade furniture. Such is the appearance of semiconsciousness that one wonders how much of the 'message' of television is getting through to the brain."

The American Academy of Pediatrics (AAP) recommends that children under two years of age should not watch any television and children two and older should watch one to two hours at most. Children who watch more than four hours of television a day are more likely to become overweight.

TV watching and other sedentary activities are associated with greater risk of heart attack.

Alleged Dangers

Legislators, scientists and parents are debating the effects of television violence on viewers, particularly youth. Fifty years of research on the impact of television on children's emotional and social development have not ended this debate.

Some scholars have claimed that the evidence clearly supports a causal relationship between media violence and societal violence. However other authors note significant methodological problems with the literature and mismatch between increasing media violence and decreasing crime rates in the United States.

A 2002 article in Scientific American suggested that compulsive television watching, television addiction, was no different from any other addiction, a finding backed up by reports of withdrawal symptoms among families forced by circumstance to cease watching. However this view has not yet received widespread acceptance among all scholars, and "television addiction" is not a diagnoseable condition according to the Diagnostic and Statistical Manual -IV -TR.

A longitudinal study in New Zealand involving 1000 people (from childhood to 26 years of age) demonstrated that "television viewing in childhood and adolescence is associated with poor educational achievement by 12 years of age". The same paper noted that there was a significant negative association between time spent watching television per day as a child and educational attainment by age 26: the more time a child spent watching television at ages 5 to 15, the less likely they were to have a university degree by age 26. However recent research (Schmidt et al., 2009) has indicated that, once other factors are controlled for, television viewing appears to have little to no impact on cognitive performance, contrary to previous thought. However this study was limited to cognitive performance in childhood. Numerous studies have also examined the relationship between TV viewing and school grades.

A study published in the Journal of Sexuality Research and Social Policy concluded that parental television involvement was associated with greater body satisfaction among adolescent girls, less sexual experience amongst both male and female adolescents, and that parental television involvement may influence self-esteem and body image, in part by increasing parent-child closeness. However a more recent article by Christopher Ferguson, Benjamin Winegard, and Bo Winegard cautioned that the literature on media and body dissatisfaction is weaker and less consistent than often claimed and that media effects have been overemphasized. Similarly recent work by Laurence Steinbrerg and Kathryn Monahan has found that, using propensity score matching to control for other variables, television viewing of sexual media had no impact on teen sexual behavior in a longitudinal analysis.

Many studies have found little or no effect of television viewing on viewers. For example a recent long-term outcome study of youth found no long-term relationship between watching violent television and youth violence or bullying

On July 26, 2000 the American Academy of Pediatrics, the American Medical Association, the American Psychological Association, the American Academy of Family Physicians, and the American Academy of Child and Adolescent Psychiatry stated that "prolonged viewing of media violence can lead to emotional desensitization toward violence in real life." However, scholars have since analyzed several statements in this release, both about the number of studies conducted, and a comparison with medical effects, and found many errors.

Propaganda

Television is used to promote commercial, social and political agendas. Use of public service announcements (including those paid for by governing bodies or politicians), news and current affairs, television advertisement, advertorials and talk shows are used to influence public opinion. The Cultivation Hypothesis suggests that some viewers may begin to repeat questionable or even blatantly fictitious information gleaned from the media as if it were factual. Considerable debate remains, however, whether the Cultivation Hypothesis is well supported by scientific literature, however, the effectiveness of television for propaganda (including commercial advertising) is unsurpassed. The US military and State Department often turn to media to broadcast into hostile territory or nation.

Politics

While the effects of television programs depend on what is actually consumed, Neil Postman argues that the dominance of entertaining, but not informative programming, creates a politically ignorant society, undermining democracy: "Americans are the best entertained and quite likely the least-informed people in the Western world." However some broadcasters do offer Americans intelligent political narrative and argument. This offers otherwise ignorant viewers, who may not read about politics elsewhere, the opportunity to access current or historical political views, for example.

Technology Trends

In its infancy, television was a time-dependent, fleeting medium; it acted on the schedule of the institutions that broadcast the television signal or operated the cable. Fans of regular shows planned their schedules so that they could be available to watch their shows at their time of broadcast. The term appointment television was coined by marketers to describe this kind of attachment.

The viewership's dependence on schedule lessened with the invention of programmable video recorders, such as the Videocassette recorder and the Digital video recorder. Consumers could watch programs on their own schedule once they were broadcast and recorded. Television service providers also offer video on demand, a set of programs which could be watched at any time.

Both mobile phone networks and the Internet can give us video streams; video sharing websites have become popular. In addition, the jumps in processing power within smartphone and tablet devices has facilitated uptake of "hybridised" TV viewing, where viewers simultaneously watch programs on TV sets and interact with online social networks via their mobile devices. A 2012 study by Australian media company Yahoo!7 found 36% of Australians will call or text family and friends and 41% will post on Facebook while watching TV. Yahoo!7 has already experienced significant early uptake of its Fango mobile app, which encourages social sharing and discussion of TV programs on Australian free-to-air networks.

Gender and Television

While women, who were "traditionally more isolated than men" were given equal opportunity to consume shows about more "manly" endeavors, men's feminine sides are tapped by the emotional nature of many television programs.

Television played a significant role in the feminist movement. Although most of the women portrayed on television conformed to stereotypes, television also showed the lives of men as well as news and current affairs. These "other lives" portrayed on television left many women unsatisfied with their current socialization. The representation of males and females on the television screen has been a subject of much discussion since the television became commercially available in the late 1930s. In 1964 Betty Friedan claimed that "television has represented the American Woman as a "stupid, unattractive, insecure little household drudge who spends her martyred mindless, boring days dreaming of love—and plotting nasty revenge against her husband." As women started to revolt and protest to become equals in society in the 1960s and 1970s, their portrayal on the television was an issue that they addressed. Journalist Susan Faludi suggested, "The practices and programming of network television in the 1980s were an attempt to get back to those earlier stereotypes of women." Through television, even the most homebound women can experience parts of our culture once considered primarily male, such as sports, war, business, medicine, law, and politics. For the last since at least the 1990s there has been a trend of showing males as insufferable and possibly spineless fools .

From 1930 to 2007 daytime television hasn't changed much. Soap operas and talk shows still dominate the daytime time slot. Prime time television since the 1950s has been aimed at and catered towards males. In 1952, 68% of characters in primetime dramas were male; in 1973, 74% of characters in these shows were male. In 1970 the National Organization for Women (NOW) took action. They formed a task force to study and change the "derogatory stereotypes of women on television." In 1972 they challenged the licences of two network-owned stations on the basis of their sexist programming. In the 1960s the shows I Dream of Jeannie and Bewitched insinuated that the only way that a woman could escape her duties was to use magic. Industry analysis Shari Anne Brill of Carat USA states, "For years, when men were behind the camera, women were really ditsy. Now you have female leads playing superheroes, or super business women." Current network broadcasting features a range of female portrayals. This is evident in a 1999 study by Lauzen and Dozier showing that "43% of all major characters on television are female".

References

Albert Abramson. (2003). *The History of Television, 1942 to 2000*, Jefferson, NC, and London, McFarland.

Jacques Derrida and Bernard Stiegler. (2003). *Echographies of Television*, Polity Press.

Jerry Mander. (1978). *Four Arguments for the Elimination of Television*, Perennial.

Neil Postman. (1985). *Amusing Ourselves to Death: Public Discourse in the Age of Show Business*, New York, Penguin US.

Pierre Bourdieu. (2001). *On Television*, The New Press.

Steven Johnson. (2005). *Everything Bad is Good for You: How Today's Popular Culture Is Actually Making Us Smarter*, New York, Riverhead, Penguin.

Tim Brooks and Earle March. (2002). *The Complete Guide to Prime Time Network and Cable TV Shows*, 8th ed., Ballantine.

5

Computer Networks

Networks are collections of computers, software, and hardware that are all connected to help their users work together. A network connects computers by means of cabling systems, specialized software, and devices that manage data traffic. A network enables users to share files and resources, such as printers, as well as send messages electronically (e-mail) to each other.

Computer networks fall into two main types: client/server networks and peer-to-peer networks. A client/server network uses one or more dedicated machines (the server) to share the files, printers, and applications. A peer-to-peer network allows any user to share files with any other user and doesn't require a central, dedicated server.

The most common networks are Local Area Networks or LANs for short. A LAN connects computers within a single geographical location, such as one office building, office suite, or home. By contrast, Wide Area Networks (WANs) span different cities or even countries, using phone lines or satellite links.

Networks are often categorized in other ways, too. You can refer to a network by what sort of circuit boards the computers use to link to each other – Ethernet and Token-Ring are the most popular choices. You can also refer to a network by how it packages data for transmission across the cable, with terms such as TCP/IP (Transmission Control Protocol/Internet Protocol) and IPX/SPX (Internet Package eXchnage/Sequenced Package eXchange).

History of Computer Networks

Before the advent of computer networks that were based upon some type of telecommunications system, communication between calculation machines and early computers was performed by human users by carrying instructions between them. Many of the social behaviors seen in today's Internet were demonstrably present in the 19th century and arguably in even earlier networks using visual signals.

In September 1940, George Stibitz used a Teletype machine to send instructions for a problem set from his Model at Dartmouth College to his Complex Number Calculator in New York and received results back by the same means. Linking output systems like teletypewriters to computers was an interest at the Advanced Research Projects Agency (ARPA) when, in 1962, J.C.R. Licklider was hired and developed a working group he called the "Intergalactic Computer Network", a precursor to the ARPANET.

Early networks of communicating computers included the military radar system Semi-Automatic Ground Environment (SAGE), started in the late 1950s.

The commercial airline reservation system semi-automatic business research environment (SABRE) went online with two connected mainframes in 1960.

In 1964, researchers at Dartmouth developed the Dartmouth Time Sharing System for distributed users of large computer systems. The same year, at Massachusetts Institute of Technology, a research group supported by General Electric and Bell Labs used a computer to route and manage telephone connections.

Throughout the 1960s Leonard Kleinrock, Paul Baran and Donald Davies independently conceptualized and developed network systems which used packets that could be used in a network between computer systems.

1965 Thomas Marill and Lawrence G. Roberts created the first wide area network (WAN). This was an immediate precursor to the ARPANET, of which Roberts became program manager.

The first widely used telephone switch that used true computer control was introduced by Western Electric in 1965.

In 1969 the University of California at Los Angeles, the Stanford Research Institute, University of California at Santa Barbara, and the

University of Utah were connected as the beginning of the ARPANET network using 50 kbit/s circuits.

Commercial services using X.25 were deployed in 1972, and later used as an underlying infrastructure for expanding TCP/IP networks.

Today, computer networks are the core of modern communication. All modern aspects of the public switched telephone network (PSTN) are computer-controlled, and telephony increasingly runs over the Internet Protocol, although not necessarily the public Internet. The scope of communication has increased significantly in the past decade, and this boom in communications would not have been possible without the progressively advancing computer network. Computer networks, and the technologies needed to connect and communicate through and between them, continue to drive computer hardware, software, and peripherals industries. This expansion is mirrored by growth in the numbers and types of users of networks, from the researcher to the home user.

Properties of Computer Networks

Facilitate communications

Using a network, people can communicate efficiently and easily via email, instant messaging, chat rooms, telephone, video telephone calls, and video conferencing.

Permit sharing of files, data, and other types of information

In a network environment, authorized users may access data and information stored on other computers on the network. The capability of providing access to data and information on shared storage devices is an important feature of many networks.

Share network and computing resources

In a networked environment, each computer on a network may access and use resources provided by devices on the network, such as printing a document on a shared network printer. Distributed computing uses computing resources across a network to accomplish tasks.

May be insecure

A computer network may be used by computer hackers to deploy computer viruses or computer worms on devices connected to the network, or to prevent these devices from normally accessing the network (denial of service).

May interfere with other technologies

Power line communication strongly disturbs certain forms of radio communication, e.g., amateur radio. It may also interfere with last mile access technologies such as ADSL and VDSL.

May be difficult to set up

A complex computer network may be difficult to set up. It may also be very costly to set up an effective computer network in a large organization or company.

Communication Media

Computer networks can be classified according to the hardware and associated software technology that is used to interconnect the individual devices in the network, such as electrical cable (HomePNA, power line communication, G.hn), optical fiber, and radio waves (wireless LAN). In the OSI model, these are located at levels 1 and 2.

A well-known family of communication media is collectively known as Ethernet. It is defined by IEEE 802 and utilizes various standards and media that enable communication between devices. Wireless LAN technology is designed to connect devices without wiring. These devices use radio waves or infrared signals as a transmission medium.

Wired Technologies

The order of the following wired technologies is, roughly, from slowest to fastest transmission speed.

- Twisted pair wire is the most widely used medium for telecommunication. Twisted-pair cabling consist of copper wires that are twisted into pairs. Ordinary telephone wires consist of two insulated copper wires twisted into pairs. Computer networking cabling (wired Ethernet as defined by IEEE 802.3) consists of 4 pairs of copper cabling that can be utilized for both voice and data transmission. The use of two wires twisted together helps to reduce crosstalk and electromagnetic induction. The transmission speed ranges from 2 million bits per second to 10 billion bits per second. Twisted pair cabling comes in two forms: unshielded twisted pair (UTP) and shielded twisted-pair (STP). Each form comes in several category ratings, designed for use in various scenarios.

- Coaxial cable is widely used for cable television systems, office buildings, and other work-sites for local area networks. The cables consist of copper or aluminum wire surrounded by an insulating layer (typically a flexible material with a high dielectric constant), which itself is surrounded by a conductive layer. The insulation helps minimize interference and distortion. Transmission speed ranges from 200 million bits per second to more than 500 million bits per second.
- ITU-T G.hn technology uses existing home wiring (coaxial cable, phone lines and power lines) to create a high-speed (up to 1 Gigabit/s) local area network.
- An optical fiber is a glass fiber. It uses pulses of light to transmit data. Some advantages of optical fibers over metal wires are less transmission loss, immunity from electromagnetic radiation, and very fast transmission speed, up to trillions of bits per second. One can use different colors of lights to increase the number of messages being sent over a fiber optic cable.

Wireless Technologies

- *Terrestrial microwave* – Terrestrial microwave communication uses Earth-based transmitters and receivers resembling satellite dishes. Terrestrial microwaves are in the low-gigahertz range, which limits all communications to line-of-sight. Relay stations are spaced approximately 48 km (30 mi) apart.
- *Communications satellites* – The satellites communicate via microwave radio waves, which are not deflected by the Earth's atmosphere. The satellites are stationed in space, typically in geosynchronous orbit 35,400 km (22,000 mi) above the equator. These Earth-orbiting systems are capable of receiving and relaying voice, data, and TV signals.
- *Cellular and PCS systems use several radio communications technologies.* The systems divide the region covered into multiple geographic areas. Each area has a low-power transmitter or radio relay antenna device to relay calls from one area to the next area.
- *Radio and spread spectrum technologies* – Wireless local area network use a high-frequency radio technology similar to digital cellular and a

low-frequency radio technology. Wireless LANs use spread spectrum technology to enable communication between multiple devices in a limited area. IEEE 802.11 defines a common flavor of open-standards wireless radio-wave technology.

- *Infrared communication can transmit signals for small distances,* typically no more than 10 meters. In most cases, line-of-sight propagation is used, which limits the physical positioning of communicating devices.
- *A global area network (GAN)* is a network used for supporting mobile across an arbitrary number of wireless LANs, satellite coverage areas, etc. The key challenge in mobile communications is handing off user communications from one local coverage area to the next. In IEEE Project 802, this involves a succession of terrestrial wireless LANs.

Exotic Technologies

There have been various attempts at transporting data over more or less exotic media:

- IP over Avian Carriers was a humorous April fool's Request for Comments, issued as RFC 1149. It was implemented in real life in 2001.
- Extending the Internet to interplanetary dimensions via radio waves.

Both cases have a large round-trip delay time, which prevents useful communication.

Communications Protocols and Network Programming

A communications protocol is a set of rules for exchanging information over a network. It is typically a protocol stack, which is a "stack" of protocols, in which each protocol uses the protocol below it. An important example of a protocol stack is HTTP running over TCP over IP over IEEE 802.11 (TCP and IP are members of the Internet Protocol Suite, and IEEE 802.11 is a member of the Ethernet protocol suite). This stack is used between the wireless router and the home user's personal computer when the user is surfing the web.

Communication protocols have various properties, such as whether they are connection-oriented or connectionless, whether they use circuit mode or packet switching, or whether they use hierarchical or flat addressing.

There are many communication protocols, a few of which are described below.

Ethernet

Ethernet is a family of computer networking technologies for local area networks (LANs). Ethernet was commercially introduced in 1980 and standardized in 1985 as IEEE 802.3. Ethernet has largely replaced competing wired LAN technologies.

The Ethernet standards comprise several wiring and signaling variants of the OSI physical layer in use with Ethernet. The original 10BASE5 Ethernet used coaxial cable as a shared medium. Later the coaxial cables were replaced by twisted pair and fiber optic links in conjunction with hubs or switches. Data rates were periodically increased from the original 10 megabits per second, to 100 gigabits per second.

Systems communicating over Ethernet divide a stream of data into shorter pieces called frames. Each frame contains source and destination addresses and error-checking data so that damaged data can be detected and re-transmitted. As per the OSI model Ethernet provides services up to and including the data link layer.

Since its commercial release, Ethernet has retained a good degree of compatibility. Features such as the 48-bit MAC address and Ethernet frame format have influenced other networking protocols.

Ethernet was developed at Xerox PARC between 1973 and 1974. It was inspired by ALOHAnet, which Robert Metcalfe had studied as part of his PhD dissertation. The idea was first documented in a memo that Metcalfe wrote on May 22, 1973. In 1975, Xerox filed a patent application listing Metcalfe, David Boggs, Chuck Thacker and Butler Lampson as inventors. In 1976, after the system was deployed at PARC, Metcalfe and Boggs published a seminal paper.

Metcalfe left Xerox in June 1979 to form 3Com. He convinced Digital Equipment Corporation (DEC), Intel, and Xerox to work together to promote Ethernet as a standard. The so-called "DIX" standard, for "Digital/Intel/ Xerox" specified 10 Mbit/s Ethernet, with 48-bit destination and source addresses and a global 16-bit Ethertype-type field. It was published on September 30, 1980 as "The Ethernet, A Local Area Network. Data Link Layer and Physical Layer Specifications". Version 2 was published in

November, 1982 and defines what has become known as Ethernet II. Formal standardization efforts proceeded at the same time.

Ethernet initially competed with two largely proprietary systems, Token Ring and Token Bus. Because Ethernet was able to adapt to market realities and shift to inexpensive and ubiquitous twisted pair wiring, these proprietary protocols soon found themselves competing in a market inundated by Ethernet products and by the end of the 1980s, Ethernet was clearly the dominant network technology. In the process, 3Com became a major company. 3Com shipped its first 10 Mbit/s Ethernet 3C100 transceiver in March 1981, and that year started selling adapters for PDP-11s and VAXes, as well as Multibus-based Intel and Sun Microsystems computers.:9 This was followed quickly by DEC's Unibus to Ethernet adapter, which DEC sold and used internally to build its own corporate network, which reached over 10,000 nodes by 1986, making it one of the largest computer networks in the world at that time. An Ethernet adapter card for the IBM PC was released in 1982 and by 1985, 3Com had sold 100,000.

Since then Ethernet technology has evolved to meet new bandwidth and market requirements. In addition to computers, Ethernet is now used to interconnect appliances and other personal devices. It is used in industrial applications and is quickly replacing legacy data transmission systems in the world's telecommunications networks. By 2010, the market for Ethernet equipment amounted to over $16 billion per year.

Standardization

In February 1980, the Institute of Electrical and Electronics Engineers (IEEE) started project 802 to standardize local area networks (LAN). The "DIX-group" with Gary Robinson (DEC), Phil Arst (Intel), and Bob Printis (Xerox) submitted the so-called "Blue Book" CSMA/CD specification as a candidate for the LAN specification. In addition to CSMA/CD, Token Ring (supported by IBM) and Token Bus (selected and henceforward supported by General Motors) were also considered as candidates for a LAN standard. Competing proposals and broad interest in the initiative led to strong disagreement over which technology to standardize. In December 1980, the group was split into three subgroups, and standardization proceeded separately for each proposal.

Delays in the standards process put at risk the market introduction of the Xerox Star workstation and 3Com's Ethernet LAN products. With such business implications in mind, David Liddle (General Manager, Xerox Office Systems) and Metcalfe (3Com) strongly supported a proposal of Fritz Röscheisen (Siemens Private Networks) for an alliance in the emerging office communication market, including Siemens' support for the international standardization of Ethernet (April 10, 1981). Ingrid Fromm, Siemens' representative to IEEE 802, quickly achieved broader support for Ethernet beyond IEEE by the establishment of a competing Task Group "Local Networks" within the European standards body ECMA TC24. As early as March 1982 ECMA TC24 with its corporate members reached agreement on a standard for CSMA/CD based on the IEEE 802 draft.:8 Because the DIX proposal was most technically complete and because of the speedy action taken by ECMA which decisively contributed to the conciliation of opinions within IEEE, the IEEE 802.3 CSMA/CD standard was approved in December 1982. IEEE published the 802.3 standard as a draft in 1983 and as a standard in 1985.

Approval of Ethernet on the international level was achieved by a similar, cross-partisan action with Fromm as liaison officer working to integrate International Electrotechnical Commission, TC83 and International Organization for Standardization (ISO) TC97SC6, and the ISO/IEEE 802/3 standard was approved in 1984.

Evolution

Ethernet evolved to include higher bandwidth, improved media access control methods, and different physical media. The coaxial cable was replaced with point-to-point links connected by Ethernet repeaters or switches to reduce installation costs, increase reliability, and improve management and troubleshooting. Many variants of Ethernet remain in common use.

Ethernet stations communicate by sending each other data packets: blocks of data individually sent and delivered. As with other IEEE 802 LANs, each Ethernet station is given a 48-bit MAC address. The MAC addresses are used to specify both the destination and the source of each data packet. Ethernet establishes link level connections, which can be defined using both the destination and source addresses. On reception of a transmission, the receiver uses the destination address to determine whether the transmission is relevant to the station or should be ignored. Network interfaces normally do not accept packets addressed to other Ethernet stations. Adapters come programmed with a globally unique address. An Ethertype field in each frame is used by the operating system on the receiving station to select the appropriate protocol module (i.e. the Internet protocol module). Ethernet frames are said to be self-identifying, because of the frame type. Self-identifying frames make it possible to intermix multiple protocols on the same physical network and allow a single computer to use multiple protocols together. Despite the evolution of Ethernet technology, all generations of Ethernet (excluding early experimental versions) use the same frame formats (and hence the same interface for higher layers), and can be readily interconnected through bridging.

Due to the ubiquity of Ethernet, the ever-decreasing cost of the hardware needed to support it, and the reduced panel space needed by twisted pair Ethernet, most manufacturers now build Ethernet interfaces directly into PC motherboards, eliminating the need for installation of a separate network card.

Shared media

Ethernet was originally based on the idea of computers communicating over a shared coaxial cable acting as a broadcast transmission medium. The methods used were similar to those used in radio systems, with the common cable providing the communication channel likened to the Luminiferous aether in 19th century physics, and it was from this reference that the name "Ethernet" was derived.

Original Ethernet's shared coaxial cable (the shared medium) traversed a building or campus to every attached machine. A scheme known as carrier sense multiple access with collision detection (CSMA/CD) governed the way the computers shared the channel. This scheme was simpler than the competing token ring or token bus technologies. Computers were connected to an Attachment Unit Interface (AUI) transceiver, which was in turn connected to the cable (later with thin Ethernet the transceiver was integrated into the network adapter). While a simple passive wire was highly reliable for small networks, it was not reliable for large extended networks, where damage to the wire in a single place, or a single bad connector, could make the whole Ethernet segment unusable.

Through the first half of the 1980s, Ethernet's 10BASE5 implementation used a coaxial cable 0.375 inches (9.5 mm) in diameter, later called "thick Ethernet" or "thicknet". Its successor, 10BASE2, called "thin Ethernet" or "thinnet", used a cable similar to cable television cable of the era. The emphasis was on making installation of the cable easier and less costly.

Since all communications happen on the same wire, any information sent by one computer is received by all, even if that information is intended for just one destination. The network interface card interrupts the CPU only when applicable packets are received: The card ignores information not addressed to it. Use of a single cable also means that the bandwidth is shared, such that, for example, available bandwidth to each device is halved when two stations are simultaneously active.

Collisions corrupt transmitted data and require stations to retransmit. The lost data and retransmissions reduce throughput. In the worst case where multiple active hosts connected with maximum allowed cable length attempt to transmit many short frames, excessive collisions can reduce throughput dramatically. However, a Xerox report in 1980 studied performance of an existing Ethernet installation under both normal and artificially generated heavy load. The report claims that 98% throughput on the LAN was observed. This is in contrast with token passing LANs (token ring, token bus), all of which suffer throughput degradation as each new node comes into the LAN, due to token waits. This report was controversial, as modeling showed that collision-based networks became unstable under loads as low as 40% of nominal capacity. Many early researchers failed to understand the subtleties of the CSMA/CD protocol and how important it was to get the details right, and were really modeling somewhat different networks (usually not as good as real Ethernet).

Repeaters and hubs

For signal degradation and timing reasons, coaxial Ethernet segments had a restricted size. Somewhat larger networks could be built by using an Ethernet repeater. Early repeaters had only two ports, allowing, at most, a doubling of network size. Once repeaters with more than two ports became available, it was possible to wire the network in a star topology. Early experiments with star topologies (called "Fibernet") using optical fiber were published by 1978.

Shared cable Ethernet was always hard to install in offices because its bus topology was in conflict with the star topology cable plans designed into buildings for telephony. Modifying Ethernet to conform to twisted pair telephone wiring already installed in commercial buildings provided another opportunity to lower costs, expand the installed base, and leverage building design, and, thus, twisted-pair Ethernet was the next logical development in the mid-1980s.

Ethernet on unshielded twisted-pair cables (UTP) began with StarLAN at 1 Mbit/s in the mid-1980s. In 1987 SynOptics introduced the first twisted-pair Ethernet at 10 Mbit/s in a star-wired cabling topology with a central hub, later called LattisNet. These evolved into 10BASE-T, which was designed for point-to-point links only, and all termination was built into the device. This changed repeaters from a specialist device used at the center of large networks to a device that every twisted pair-based network with more than two machines had to use. The tree structure that resulted from this made Ethernet networks easier to maintain by preventing most faults with one peer or its associated cable from affecting other devices on the network.

Despite the physical star topology and the presence of separate transmit and receive channels in the twisted pair and fiber media, repeater based Ethernet networks still use half-duplex and CSMA/CD, with only minimal activity by the repeater, primarily the Collision Enforcement signal, in dealing with packet collisions. Every packet is sent to every port on the repeater, so bandwidth and security problems are not addressed. The total throughput of the repeater is limited to that of a single link, and all links must operate at the same speed.

Bridging and switching

While repeaters could isolate some aspects of Ethernet segments, such as cable breakages, they still forwarded all traffic to all Ethernet devices. This created practical limits on how many machines could communicate on an Ethernet network. The entire network was one collision domain, and all hosts had to be able to detect collisions anywhere on the network. This limited the number of repeaters between the farthest nodes. Segments joined by repeaters had to all operate at the same speed, making phased-in upgrades impossible.

To alleviate these problems, bridging was created to communicate at the data link layer while isolating the physical layer. With bridging, only well-formed Ethernet packets are forwarded from one Ethernet segment to another; collisions and packet errors are isolated. Prior to learning of network devices on the different segments, Ethernet bridges (and switches) work somewhat like Ethernet repeaters, passing all traffic between segments. After the bridge learns the addresses associated with each port, it forwards network traffic only to the necessary segments, improving overall performance. Broadcast traffic is still forwarded to all network segments. Bridges also overcame the limits on total segments between two hosts and allowed the mixing of speeds, both of which are critical to deployment of Fast Ethernet.

In 1989, the networking company Kalpana introduced their EtherSwitch, the first Ethernet switch. This worked somewhat differently from an Ethernet bridge, where only the header of the incoming packet would be examined before it was either dropped or forwarded to another segment. This greatly reduced the forwarding latency and the processing load on the network device. One drawback of this cut-through switching method was that packets that had been corrupted would still be propagated through the network, so a jabbering station could continue to disrupt the entire network. The eventual remedy for this was a return to the original store and forward approach of bridging, where the packet would be read into a buffer on the switch in its entirety, verified against its checksum and then forwarded, but using more powerful application-specific integrated circuits. Hence, the bridging is then done in hardware, allowing packets to be forwarded at full wire speed.

When a twisted pair or fiber link segment is used and neither end is connected to a repeater, full-duplex Ethernet becomes possible over that segment. In full-duplex mode, both devices can transmit and receive to and from each other at the same time, and there is no collision domain. This doubles the aggregate bandwidth of the link and is sometimes advertised as double the link speed (e.g., 200 Mbit/s). The elimination of the collision domain for these connections also means that all the link's bandwidth can be used by the two devices on that segment and that segment length is not limited by the need for correct collision detection.

Since packets are typically delivered only to the port they are intended for, traffic on a switched Ethernet is less public than on shared-medium Ethernet. Despite this, switched Ethernet should still be regarded as an insecure network technology, because it is easy to subvert switched Ethernet systems by means such as ARP spoofing and MAC flooding.

The bandwidth advantages, the slightly better isolation of devices from each other, the ability to easily mix different speeds of devices and the elimination of the chaining limits inherent in non-switched Ethernet have made switched Ethernet the dominant network technology.

Advanced networking

Simple switched Ethernet networks, while a great improvement over repeater-based Ethernet, suffer from single points of failure, attacks that trick switches or hosts into sending data to a machine even if it is not intended for it, scalability and security issues with regard to broadcast radiation and multicast traffic, and bandwidth choke points where a lot of traffic is forced down a single link.

Advanced networking features in switches and routers combat these issues through means including spanning-tree protocol to maintain the active links of the network as a tree while allowing physical loops for redundancy, port security and protection features such as MAC lock down and broadcast radiation filtering, virtual LANs to keep different classes of users separate while using the same physical infrastructure, multilayer switching to route between different classes and link aggregation to add bandwidth to overloaded links and to provide some measure of redundancy.

IEEE 802.1aq (shortest path bridging) includes the use of the link-state routing protocol IS-IS to allow larger networks with shortest path routes between devices. In 2012 it was stated by David Allan and Nigel Bragg, in 802.1aq Shortest Path Bridging Design and Evolution: The Architect's Perspective that shortest path bridging is one of the most significant enhancements in Ethernet's history.

Varieties of Ethernet

The Ethernet physical layer evolved over a considerable time span and encompasses coaxial, twisted pair and fiber optic physical media interfaces and speeds from 10 Mbit to 100 Gbit. The most common forms used are 10BASE-T, 100BASE-TX, and 1000BASE-T. All three utilize twisted pair cables and 8P8C modular connectors. They run at 10 Mbit/s, 100 Mbit/s, and 1 Gbit/s, respectively. Fiber optic variants of Ethernet offer high performance, electrical isolation and distance (tens of kilometers with some versions). In general, network protocol stack software will work similarly on all varieties.

Internet Protocol Suite

The Internet protocol suite is the set of communications protocols used for the Internet and similar networks, and generally the most popular protocol stack for wide area networks. It is commonly known as TCP/IP, because of its most important protocols: Transmission Control Protocol (TCP) and Internet Protocol (IP), which were the first networking protocols defined in this standard. It is occasionally known as the DoD model due to the foundational influence of the ARPANET in the 1970s (operated by DARPA, an agency of the United States Department of Defense).

TCP/IP provides end-to-end connectivity specifying how data should be formatted, addressed, transmitted, routed and received at the destination. It has four abstraction layers, each with its own protocols. From lowest to highest, the layers are:

- The link layer (commonly Ethernet) contains communication technologies for a local network.
- The internet layer (IP) connects local networks, thus establishing internetworking.
- The transport layer (TCP) handles host-to-host communication.
- The application layer (for example HTTP) contains all protocols for specific data communications services on a process-to-process level (for example how a web browser communicates with a web server).
- The TCP/IP model and related protocols are maintained by the Internet Engineering Task Force (IETF).

Early research

The Internet protocol suite resulted from research and development conducted by the Defense Advanced Research Projects Agency (DARPA) in the early 1970s. After initiating the pioneering ARPANET in 1969, DARPA started work on a number of other data transmission technologies. In 1972, Robert E. Kahn joined the DARPA Information Processing Technology Office, where he worked on both satellite packet networks and ground-based radio packet networks, and recognized the value of being able to communicate across both. In the spring of 1973, Vinton Cerf, the developer of the existing ARPANET Network Control Program (NCP) protocol, joined Kahn to work on open-architecture interconnection models with the goal of designing the next protocol generation for the ARPANET.

By the summer of 1973, Kahn and Cerf had worked out a fundamental reformulation, where the differences between network protocols were hidden by using a common internetwork protocol, and, instead of the network being responsible for reliability, as in the ARPANET, the hosts became responsible. Cerf credits Hubert Zimmerman and Louis Pouzin, designer of the CYCLADES network, with important influences on this design.

The network's design included the recognition it should provide only the functions of efficiently transmitting and routing traffic between end nodes and that all other intelligence should be located at the edge of the network, in the end nodes. Using a simple design, it became possible to connect almost any network to the ARPANET, irrespective of their local characteristics, thereby solving Kahn's initial problem. One popular expression is that TCP/IP, the eventual product of Cerf and Kahn's work, will run over "two tin cans and a string." As a joke, the IP over Avian Carriers formal protocol specification was created and successfully tested.

A computer called a router is provided with an interface to each network. It forwards packets back and forth between them. Originally a router was called gateway, but the term was changed to avoid confusion with other types of gateways.

Specification

From 1973 to 1974, Cerf's networking research group at Stanford worked out details of the idea, resulting in the first TCP specification. A significant technical influence was the early networking work at Xerox PARC, which produced the PARC Universal Packet protocol suite, much of which existed around that time.

DARPA then contracted with BBN Technologies, Stanford University, and the University College London to develop operational versions of the protocol on different hardware platforms. Four versions were developed: TCP v1, TCP v2, TCP v3 and IP v3, and TCP/IP v4. The last protocol is still in use today.

In 1975, a two-network TCP/IP communications test was performed between Stanford and University College London (UCL). In November, 1977, a three-network TCP/IP test was conducted between sites in the US, the UK, and Norway. Several other TCP/IP prototypes were developed at multiple research centers between 1978 and 1983. The migration of the ARPANET to TCP/IP was officially completed on flag day January 1, 1983, when the new protocols were permanently activated.

Adoption

In March 1982, the US Department of Defense declared TCP/IP as the standard for all military computer networking. In 1985, the Internet Architecture Board held a three-day workshop on TCP/IP for the computer industry, attended by 250 vendor representatives, promoting the protocol and leading to its increasing commercial use.

In 1985, the first Interop conference was held, focusing on network interoperability via further adoption of TCP/IP. It was founded by Dan Lynch, an early Internet activist. From the beginning, it was attended by large corporations, such as IBM and DEC. Interoperability conferences have been held every year since then. Every year from 1985 through 1993, the number of attendees tripled.

IBM, ATT and DEC were the first major corporations to adopt TCP/IP, despite having competing internal protocols (SNA, XNS, etc.). In IBM, from 1984, Barry Appelman's group did TCP/IP development. (Appelman later moved to AOL to be the head of all its development efforts.) They navigated the corporate politics to get a stream of TCP/IP products for various IBM systems, including MVS, VM, and OS/2. At the same time, several smaller companies began offering TCP/IP stacks for DOS and MS Windows, such as the company FTP Software, and the Wollongong Group. The first VM/CMS TCP/IP stack came from the University of Wisconsin.

Back then, most of these TCP/IP stacks were written single-handedly by a few talented programmers. For example, John Romkey of FTP Software was the author of the MIT PC/IP package. John Romkey's PC/IP implementation was the first IBM PC TCP/IP stack. Jay Elinsky and Oleg Vishnepolsky of IBM Research wrote TCP/IP stacks for VM/CMS and OS/2, respectively.

The spread of TCP/IP was fueled further in June 1989, when AT&T agreed to put into the public domain the TCP/IP code developed for UNIX. Various vendors, including IBM, included this code in their own TCP/IP stacks. Many companies sold TCP/IP stacks for Windows until Microsoft released its own TCP/IP stack in Windows 95. This event was a little late in the evolution of the Internet, but it cemented TCP/IP's dominance over other protocols, which eventually disappeared. These protocols included IBM's SNA, OSI, Microsoft's native NetBIOS, and Xerox' XNS.

Key architectural principles

An early architectural document, RFC 1122, emphasizes architectural principles over layering.

- End-to-end principle: This principle has evolved over time. Its original expression put the maintenance of state and overall intelligence at the edges, and assumed the Internet that connected the edges retained no state and concentrated on speed and simplicity. Real-world needs for firewalls, network address translators, web content caches and the like have forced changes in this principle.
- Robustness Principle: "In general, an implementation must be conservative in its sending behavior, and liberal in its receiving behavior. That is, it must be careful to send well-formed datagrams, but must accept any datagram that it can interpret (e.g., not object to technical errors where the meaning is still clear)." "The second part of the principle is almost as important: software on other hosts may contain deficiencies that make it unwise to exploit legal but obscure protocol features."

Layers in the Internet protocol suite

The Internet protocol suite uses encapsulation to provide abstraction of protocols and services. Encapsulation is usually aligned with the division of the protocol suite into layers of general functionality. In general, an application (the highest level of the model) uses a set of protocols to send its data down the layers, being further encapsulated at each level.

The "layers" of the protocol suite near the top are logically closer to the user application, while those near the bottom are logically closer to the physical transmission of the data. Viewing layers as providing or consuming a service is a method of abstraction to isolate upper layer protocols from the nitty-gritty detail of transmitting bits over, for example, Ethernet and collision detection, while the lower layers avoid having to know the details of each and every application and its protocol.

Even when the layers are examined, the assorted architectural documents—there is no single architectural model such as ISO 7498, the Open Systems Interconnection (OSI) model—have fewer and less rigidly defined layers than the OSI model, and thus provide an easier fit for real-world protocols. In point of fact, one frequently referenced document, RFC 1958, does not contain a stack of layers. The lack of emphasis on layering is a strong difference between the IETF and OSI approaches. It only refers to the existence of the "internetworking layer" and generally to "upper layers"; this document was intended as a 1996 "snapshot" of the architecture: "The Internet and its architecture have grown in evolutionary fashion from modest beginnings, rather than from a Grand Plan. While this process of evolution is one of the main reasons for the technology's success, it nevertheless seems useful to record a snapshot of the current principles of the Internet architecture."

RFC 1122, entitled Host Requirements, is structured in paragraphs referring to layers, but the document refers to many other architectural principles not emphasizing layering. It loosely defines a four-layer model, with the layers having names, not numbers, as follows:

- *Application layer (process-to-process)*: This is the scope within which applications create user data and communicate this data to other processes or applications on another or the same host. The communications partners are often called peers. This is where the "higher level" protocols such as SMTP, FTP, SSH, HTTP, etc. operate.
- *Transport layer (host-to-host)*: The transport layer constitutes the networking regime between two network hosts, either on the local network or on remote networks separated by routers. The transport layer provides a uniform networking interface that hides the actual topology (layout) of the underlying network connections. This is where flow-control, error-correction, and connection protocols exist, such as TCP. This layer deals with opening and maintaining connections between Internet hosts.
- *Internet layer (internetworking)*: The internet layer has the task of exchanging datagrams across network boundaries. It is therefore also referred to as the layer that establishes internetworking, indeed, it defines and establishes the Internet. This layer defines the addressing and routing structures used for the TCP/IP protocol suite. The primary protocol in this scope is the Internet Protocol, which defines IP addresses. Its function in routing is to transport datagrams to the next IP router that has the connectivity to a network closer to the final data destination.
- *Link layer*: This layer defines the networking methods within the scope of the local network link on which hosts communicate without

intervening routers. This layer describes the protocols used to describe the local network topology and the interfaces needed to effect transmission of Internet layer datagrams to next-neighbor hosts. (cf. the OSI data link layer).

The Internet protocol suite and the layered protocol stack design were in use before the OSI model was established. Since then, the TCP/IP model has been compared with the OSI model in books and classrooms, which often results in confusion because the two models use different assumptions, including about the relative importance of strict layering.

This abstraction also allows upper layers to provide services that the lower layers cannot, or choose not, to provide. Again, the original OSI model was extended to include connectionless services (OSIRM CL). For example, IP is not designed to be reliable and is a best effort delivery protocol. This means that all transport layer implementations must choose whether or not to provide reliability and to what degree. UDP provides data integrity (via a checksum) but does not guarantee delivery; TCP provides both data integrity and delivery guarantee (by retransmitting until the receiver acknowledges the reception of the packet).

This model lacks the formalism of the OSI model and associated documents, but the IETF does not use a formal model and does not consider this a limitation, as in the comment by David D. Clark, "We reject: kings, presidents and voting. We believe in: rough consensus and running code." Criticisms of this model, which have been made with respect to the OSI model, often do not consider ISO's later extensions to that model.

For multiaccess links with their own addressing systems (e.g. Ethernet) an address mapping protocol is needed. Such protocols can be considered to be below IP but above the existing link system. While the IETF does not use the terminology, this is a subnetwork dependent convergence facility according to an extension to the OSI model, the internal organization of the network layer (IONL).

ICMP & IGMP operate on top of IP but do not transport data like UDP or TCP. Again, this functionality exists as layer management extensions to the OSI model, in its Management Framework (OSIRM MF)

The SSL/TLS library operates above the transport layer (uses TCP) but below application protocols. Again, there was no intention, on the part of the designers of these protocols, to comply with OSI architecture.

The link is treated like a black box here. This is fine for discussing IP (since the whole point of IP is it will run over virtually anything). The IETF explicitly does not intend to discuss transmission systems, which is a less academic but practical alternative to the OSI model.

The following is a description of each layer in the TCP/IP networking model starting from the lowest level.

Link layer

The link layer is the networking scope of the local network connection to which a host is attached. This regime is called the link in Internet literature. This is the lowest component layer of the Internet protocols, as TCP/IP is designed to be hardware independent. As a result TCP/IP is able to be implemented on top of virtually any hardware networking technology.

The link layer is used to move packets between the Internet layer interfaces of two different hosts on the same link. The processes of transmitting and receiving packets on a given link can be controlled both in the software device driver for the network card, as well as on firmware or specialized chipsets. These will perform data link functions such as adding a packet header to prepare it for transmission, then actually transmit the frame over a physical medium. The TCP/IP model includes specifications of translating the network addressing methods used in the Internet Protocol to data link addressing, such as Media Access Control (MAC), however all other aspects below that level are implicitly assumed to exist in the link layer, but are not explicitly defined.

This is also the layer where packets may be selected to be sent over a virtual private network or other networking tunnel. In this scenario, the link layer data may be considered application data which traverses another instantiation of the IP stack for transmission or reception over another IP connection. Such a connection, or virtual link, may be established with a transport protocol or even an application scope protocol that serves as a tunnel in the link layer of the protocol stack. Thus, the TCP/IP model does not dictate a strict hierarchical encapsulation sequence.

Internet layer

The internet layer has the responsibility of sending packets across potentially multiple networks. Internetworking requires sending data from the source network to the destination network. This process is called routing.

In the Internet protocol suite, the Internet Protocol performs two basic functions:

- Host addressing and identification: This is accomplished with a hierarchical addressing system.
- Packet routing: This is the basic task of sending packets of data (datagrams) from source to destination by sending them to the next network node (router) closer to the final destination.

The internet layer is not only agnostic of application data structures at the transport layer, but it also does not distinguish between operation of the various transport layer protocols. So, IP can carry data for a variety of different upper layer protocols. These protocols are each identified by a unique protocol number: for example, Internet Control Message Protocol (ICMP) and Internet Group Management Protocol (IGMP) are protocols 1 and 2, respectively.

Some of the protocols carried by IP, such as ICMP (used to transmit diagnostic information about IP transmission) and IGMP (used to manage IP Multicast data) are layered on top of IP but perform internetworking functions. This illustrates the differences in the architecture of the TCP/IP stack of the Internet and the OSI model.

The internet layer only provides an unreliable datagram transmission facility between hosts located on potentially different IP networks by forwarding the transport layer datagrams to an appropriate next-hop router for further relaying to its destination. With this functionality, the internet layer makes possible internetworking, the interworking of different IP networks, and it essentially establishes the Internet. The Internet Protocol is the principal component of the internet layer, and it defines two addressing systems to identify network hosts computers, and to locate them on the network. The original address system of the ARPANET and its successor, the Internet, is Internet Protocol version 4 (IPv4). It uses a 32-bit IP address and is therefore capable of identifying approximately four billion hosts. This limitation was eliminated by the standardization of Internet Protocol version 6 (IPv6) in 1998, and beginning production implementations in approximately 2006.

Transport layer

The transport layer establishes host-to-host connectivity, meaning it handles the details of data transmission that are independent of the structure of user data and the logistics of exchanging information for any particular specific purpose. Its responsibility includes end-to-end message transfer independent of the underlying network, along with error control, segmentation, flow control, congestion control, and application addressing (port numbers). End to end message transmission or connecting applications at the transport layer can be categorized as either connection-oriented, implemented in TCP, or connectionless, implemented in UDP.

The transport layer can be thought of as a transport mechanism, e.g., a vehicle with the responsibility to make sure that its contents (passengers/ goods) reach their destination safely and soundly, unless another protocol layer is responsible for safe delivery. The layer simply establishes a basic data channel that an application uses in its task-specific data exchange.

For this purpose the layer establishes the concept of the port, a numbered logical construct allocated specifically for each of the communication channels an application needs. For many types of services, these port numbers have been standardized so that client computers may address specific services of a server computer without the involvement of service announcements or directory services.

Since IP provides only a best effort delivery, the transport layer is the first layer of the TCP/IP stack to offer reliability. IP can run over a reliable data link protocol such as the High-Level Data Link Control (HDLC).

For example, the TCP is a connection-oriented protocol that addresses numerous reliability issues to provide a reliable byte stream:

- data arrives in-order
- data has minimal error (i.e. correctness)
- duplicate data is discarded
- lost/discarded packets are resent
- includes traffic congestion control

The newer Stream Control Transmission Protocol (SCTP) is also a reliable, connection-oriented transport mechanism. It is message-stream-oriented — not byte-stream-oriented like TCP — and provides multiple streams multiplexed over a single connection. It also provides multi-homing support, in which a connection end can be represented by multiple IP addresses (representing multiple physical interfaces), such that if one fails, the connection is not interrupted. It was developed initially for telephony applications (to transport SS7 over IP), but can also be used for other applications.

User Datagram Protocol is a connectionless datagram protocol. Like IP, it is a best effort, "unreliable" protocol. Reliability is addressed through error detection using a weak checksum algorithm. UDP is typically used for applications such as streaming media (audio, video, Voice over IP etc.) where on-time arrival is more important than reliability, or for simple query/ response applications like DNS lookups, where the overhead of setting up a reliable connection is disproportionately large. Real-time Transport Protocol (RTP) is a datagram protocol that is designed for real-time data such as streaming audio and video.

The applications at any given network address are distinguished by their TCP or UDP port. By convention certain well known ports are associated with specific applications.

Application layer

The application layer contains the higher-level protocols used by most applications for network communication. Examples of application layer protocols include the File Transfer Protocol (FTP) and the Simple Mail Transfer Protocol (SMTP). Data coded according to application layer protocols are then encapsulated into one or (occasionally) more transport layer protocols (such as TCP or UDP), which in turn use lower layer protocols to effect actual data transfer.

Since the IP stack defines no layers between the application and transport layers, the application layer must include any protocols that act like the OSI's presentation and session layer protocols. This is usually done through libraries.

Application layer protocols generally treat the transport layer (and lower) protocols as black boxes which provide a stable network connection across which to communicate, although the applications are usually aware of key qualities of the transport layer connection such as the end point IP addresses and port numbers. As noted above, layers are not necessarily clearly defined in the Internet protocol suite. Application layer protocols are most often associated with client–server applications, and the commoner servers have specific ports assigned to them by the IANA: HTTP has port 80; Telnet has port 23; etc. Clients, on the other hand, tend to use ephemeral ports, i.e. port numbers assigned at random from a range set aside for the purpose.

Transport and lower level layers are largely unconcerned with the specifics of application layer protocols. Routers and switches do not typically "look inside" the encapsulated traffic to see what kind of application protocol it represents, rather they just provide a conduit for it. However, some firewall and bandwidth throttling applications do try to determine what's inside, as with the Resource Reservation Protocol (RSVP). It's also sometimes necessary for Network Address Translation (NAT) facilities to take account of the needs of particular application layer protocols.

OSI and TCP/IP layering differences

The three top layers in the OSI model—the application layer, the presentation layer and the session layer—are not distinguished separately in the TCP/IP model where it is just the application layer. While some pure OSI protocol applications, such as X.400, also combined them, there is no requirement that a TCP/IP protocol stack must impose monolithic architecture above the transport layer. For example, the NFS application protocol runs over the eXternal Data Representation (XDR) presentation protocol, which, in turn, runs over a protocol called Remote Procedure Call (RPC). RPC provides reliable record transmission, so it can run safely over the best-effort UDP transport.

Different authors have interpreted the RFCs differently, about whether the link layer (and the TCP/IP model) covers OSI model layer 1 (physical layer) issues, or if a hardware layer is assumed below the link layer.

Several authors have attempted to incorporate the OSI model's layers 1 and 2 into the TCP/IP model, since these are commonly referred to in modern standards (for example, by IEEE and ITU). This often results in a model with five layers, where the link layer or network access layer is split into the OSI model's layers 1 and 2.

The session layer roughly corresponds to the Telnet virtual terminal functionality, which is part of text based protocols such as the HTTP and SMTP TCP/IP model application layer protocols. It also corresponds to TCP and UDP port numbering, which is considered as part of the transport layer in the TCP/IP model. Some functions that would have been performed by an OSI presentation layer are realized at the Internet application layer using the MIME standard, which is used in application layer protocols such as HTTP and SMTP.

The IETF protocol development effort is not concerned with strict layering. Some of its protocols may not fit cleanly into the OSI model, although RFCs sometimes refer to it and often use the old OSI layer numbers. The IETF has repeatedly stated that Internet protocol and architecture development is not intended to be OSI-compliant. RFC 3439, addressing Internet architecture, contains a section entitled: "Layering Considered Harmful".

Conflicts are apparent also in the original OSI model, ISO 7498, when not considering the annexes to this model (e.g., ISO 7498/4 Management Framework), or the ISO 8648 Internal Organization of the Network layer (IONL). When the IONL and Management Framework documents are considered, the ICMP and IGMP are neatly defined as layer management protocols for the network layer. In like manner, the IONL provides a structure for "subnetwork dependent convergence facilities" such as ARP and RARP.

IETF protocols can be encapsulated recursively, as demonstrated by tunneling protocols such as Generic Routing Encapsulation (GRE). GRE uses the same mechanism that OSI uses for tunneling at the network layer.

Implementations

No specific hardware or software implementation is required by the protocols or the layered model, so there are many. Most computer operating systems in use today, including all consumer-targeted systems, include a TCP/IP implementation.

A minimally acceptable implementation includes the following protocols, listed from most essential to least essential: IP, ARP, ICMP, UDP, TCP and sometimes IGMP. In principle, it is possible to support only one transport protocol, such as UDP, but this is rarely done, because it limits usage of the whole implementation. IPv6, beyond its own version of ARP (NDP), ICMP (ICMPv6) and IGMP (IGMPv6), has some additional required functions, and often is accompanied by an integrated IPSec security layer. Other protocols could be easily added later (possibly being implemented entirely in userspace), such as DNS for resolving domain names to IP addresses, or DHCP for automatically configuring network interfaces.

Normally, application programmers are concerned only with interfaces in the application layer and often also in the transport layer, while the layers below are services provided by the TCP/IP stack in the operating system.

Most IP implementations are accessible to programmers through sockets and APIs.

Unique implementations include Lightweight TCP/IP, an open source stack designed for embedded systems, and KA9Q NOS, a stack and associated protocols for amateur packet radio systems and personal computers connected via serial lines.

Microcontroller firmware in the network adapter typically handles link issues, supported by driver software in the operational system. Non-programmable analog and digital electronics are normally in charge of the physical components below the link layer, typically using an application-specific integrated circuit (ASIC) chipset for each network interface or other physical standard. High-performance routers are to a large extent based on fast non-programmable digital electronics, carrying out link level switching.

Synchronous Optical Networking

Synchronous Optical Networking (SONET) and Synchronous Digital Hierarchy (SDH) are standardized protocols that transfer multiple digital bit streams over optical fiber using lasers or highly coherent light from light-emitting diodes (LEDs). At low transmission rates data can also be transferred via an electrical interface. The method was developed to replace the Plesiochronous Digital Hierarchy (PDH) system for transporting large amounts of telephone calls and data traffic over the same fiber without synchronization problems. SONET generic criteria are detailed in Telcordia Technologies Generic Requirements document GR-253-CORE. Generic criteria applicable to SONET and other transmission systems (e.g., asynchronous fiber optic systems or digital radio systems) are found in Telcordia GR-499-CORE.

SONET and SDH, which are essentially the same, were originally designed to transport circuit mode communications (e.g., DS1, DS3) from a variety of different sources, but they were primarily designed to support real-time, uncompressed, circuit-switched voice encoded in PCM format. The primary difficulty in doing this prior to SONET/SDH was that the synchronization sources of these various circuits were different. This meant that each circuit was actually operating at a slightly different rate and with different phase. SONET/SDH allowed for the simultaneous transport of many different circuits of differing origin within a single framing protocol. SONET/SDH is not itself a communications protocol per se, but a transport protocol.

Due to SONET/SDH's essential protocol neutrality and transport-oriented features, SONET/SDH was the obvious choice for transporting the fixed length Asynchronous Transfer Mode (ATM) frames also known as cells. It quickly evolved mapping structures and concatenated payload containers to transport ATM connections. In other words, for ATM (and eventually other protocols such as Ethernet), the internal complex structure previously used to transport circuit-oriented connections was removed and replaced with a large and concatenated frame (such as STS-3c) into which ATM cells, IP packets, or Ethernet frames are placed.

Both SDH and SONET are widely used today: SONET in the United States and Canada, and SDH in the rest of the world. Although the SONET standards were developed before SDH, it is considered a variation of SDH because of SDH's greater worldwide market penetration.

The SDH standard was originally defined by the European Telecommunications Standards Institute (ETSI), and is formalized as International Telecommunication Union (ITU) standards G.707, G.783, G.784, and G.803. The SONET standard was defined by Telcordia and American National Standards Institute (ANSI) standard T1.105.

Difference from PDH

SDH differs from Plesiochronous Digital Hierarchy (PDH) in that the exact rates that are used to transport the data on SONET/SDH are tightly synchronized across the entire network, using atomic clocks. This synchronization system allows entire inter-country networks to operate synchronously, greatly reducing the amount of buffering required between elements in the network.

Both SONET and SDH can be used to encapsulate earlier digital transmission standards, such as the PDH standard, or they can be used to directly support either Asynchronous Transfer Mode (ATM) or so-called packet over SONET/SDH (POS) networking. Therefore, it is inaccurate to think of SDH or SONET as communications protocols in and of themselves; they are generic, all-purpose transport containers for moving both voice and data. The basic format of a SONET/SDH signal allows it to carry many different services in its virtual container (VC), because it is bandwidth-flexible.

Protocol overview

SONET and SDH often use different terms to describe identical features or functions. This can cause confusion and exaggerate their differences. With a few exceptions, SDH can be thought of as a superset of SONET.

SONET is a set of transport containers that allow for delivery of a variety of protocols, including traditional telephony, ATM, Ethernet, and TCP/IP traffic. SONET therefore isn't in itself a native communications protocol per se and should not be confused as being necessarily 'connection-oriented' in the way that term is usually used. Indeed, the 'connectionless' HTTP traffic that is used to populate this very page is without a doubt transported within SONET frames.

The protocol is a heavily multiplexed structure, with the header interleaved between the data in a complex way. This permits the encapsulated data to have its own frame rate and be able to "float around" relative to the SDH/SONET frame structure and rate. This interleaving permits a very low latency for the encapsulated data. Data passing through equipment can be delayed by at most 32 microseconds (μs), compared to a frame rate of 125 μs; many competing protocols buffer the data during such transits for at least one frame or packet before sending it on. Extra padding is allowed for the multiplexed data to move within the overall framing, as the data is clocked at a different rate than the frame rate. The protocol is made more complex by the decision to permit this padding at most levels of the multiplexing structure, but it improves all-around performance.

The basic unit of transmission

The basic unit of framing in SDH is a STM-1 (Synchronous Transport Module, level 1), which operates at 155.520 megabits per second (Mbit/s). SONET refers to this basic unit as an STS-3c (Synchronous Transport Signal 3, concatenated) or OC-3c, depending on whether the signal is carried electrically (STS) or optically (OC), but its high-level functionality, frame size, and bit-rate are the same as STM-1.

SONET offers an additional basic unit of transmission, the STS-1 (Synchronous Transport Signal 1) or OC-1, operating at 51.84 Mbit/s—exactly one third of an STM-1/STS-3c/OC-3c carrier. This speed is dictated by the bandwidth requirements for PCM-encoded telephonic voice signals: at this rate, an STS-1/OC-1 circuit can carry the bandwidth equivalent of a standard DS-3 channel, which can carry 672 64-kbit/s voice channels. In SONET, the STS-3c/OC-3c signal is composed of three multiplexed STS-1 signals; the STS-3c/OC-3c may be carried on an OC-3 signal. Some manufacturers also support the SDH equivalent of the STS-1/OC-1, known as STM-0.

Framing

In packet-oriented data transmission, such as Ethernet, a packet frame usually consists of a header and a payload. The header is transmitted first, followed by the payload (and possibly a trailer, such as a CRC). In synchronous optical networking, this is modified slightly. The header is termed the overhead, and instead of being transmitted before the payload, is interleaved with it during transmission. Part of the overhead is transmitted, then part of the payload, then the next part of the overhead, then the next part of the payload, until the entire frame has been transmitted.

In the case of an STS-1, the frame is 810 octets in size, while the STM-1/STS-3c frame is 2,430 octets in size. For STS-1, the frame is transmitted as three octets of overhead, followed by 87 octets of payload. This is repeated nine times, until 810 octets have been transmitted, taking 125 μs. In the case of an STS-3c/STM-1, which operates three times faster than an STS-1, nine octets of overhead are transmitted, followed by 261 octets of payload. This is also repeated nine times until 2,430 octets have been transmitted, also taking 125 μs. For both SONET and SDH, this is often represented by displaying the frame graphically: as a block of 90 columns and nine rows for STS-1, and 270 columns and nine rows for STM1/STS-3c. This representation aligns all the overhead columns, so the overhead appears as a contiguous block, as does the payload.

The internal structure of the overhead and payload within the frame differs slightly between SONET and SDH, and different terms are used in the standards to describe these structures. Their standards are extremely similar in implementation, making it easy to interoperate between SDH and SONET at any given bandwidth.

In practice, the terms STS-1 and OC-1 are sometimes used interchangeably, though the OC designation refers to the signal in its optical form. It is therefore incorrect to say that an OC-3 contains 3 OC-1s: an OC-3 can be said to contain 3 STS-1s.

SDH frame

The STM-1 (Synchronous Transport Module, level 1) frame is the basic transmission format for SDH—the first level of the synchronous digital hierarchy. The STM-1 frame is transmitted in exactly 125 μs, therefore, there are 8,000 frames per second on a 155.52 Mbit/s OC-3 fiber-optic circuit The STM-1 frame consists of overhead and pointers plus information payload. The first nine columns of each frame make up the Section Overhead and Administrative Unit Pointers, and the last 261 columns make up the Information Payload. The pointers (H1, H2, H3 bytes) identify administrative units (AU) within the information payload. Thus, an OC-3 circuit can carry 150.336 Mbit/s of payload, after accounting for the overhead.

Carried within the information payload, which has its own frame structure of nine rows and 261 columns, are administrative units identified by pointers. Also within the administrative unit are one or more virtual containers (VCs). VCs contain path overhead and VC payload. The first column is for path overhead; it is followed by the payload container, which can itself carry other containers. Administrative units can have any phase alignment within the STM frame, and this alignment is indicated by the pointer in row four.

The section overhead (SOH) of a STM-1 signal is divided into two parts: the regenerator section overhead (RSOH) and the multiplex section overhead (MSOH). The overheads contain information from the transmission system itself, which is used for a wide range of management functions, such as monitoring transmission quality, detecting failures, managing alarms, data communication channels, service channels, etc.

For STS-1, the payload is referred to as the synchronous payload envelope (SPE), which in turn has 18 stuffing bytes, leading to the STS-1 payload capacity of 756 bytes.

The STS-1 payload is designed to carry a full PDH DS3 frame. When the DS3 enters a SONET network, path overhead is added, and that SONET network element (NE) is said to be a path generator and terminator. The SONET NE is line terminating if it processes the line overhead. Note that wherever the line or path is terminated, the section is terminated also. SONET regenerators terminate the section, but not the paths or line.

An STS-1 payload can also be subdivided into seven virtual tributary groups (VTGs). Each VTG can then be subdivided into four VT1.5 signals, each of which can carry a PDH DS1 signal. A VTG may instead be subdivided into three VT2 signals, each of which can carry a PDH E1 signal. The SDH equivalent of a VTG is a TUG-2; VT1.5 is equivalent to VC-11, and VT2 is equivalent to VC-12.

Three STS-1 signals may be multiplexed by time-division multiplexing to form the next level of the SONET hierarchy, the OC-3 (STS-3), running at 155.52 Mbit/s. The signal is multiplexed by interleaving the bytes of the three STS-1 frames to form the STS-3 frame, containing 2,430 bytes and transmitted in 125 μs.

Higher-speed circuits are formed by successively aggregating multiples of slower circuits, their speed always being immediately apparent from their designation. For example, four STS-3 or AU4 signals can be aggregated to form a 622.08 Mbit/s signal designated OC-12 or STM-4.

The highest rate commonly deployed is the OC-768 or STM-256 circuit, which operates at rate of just under 38.5 Gbit/s. Where fiber exhaustion is a concern, multiple SONET signals can be transported over multiple wavelengths on a single fiber pair by means of wavelength-division multiplexing, including dense wavelength-division multiplexing (DWDM) and coarse wavelength-division multiplexing (CWDM). DWDM circuits are the basis for all modern submarine communications cable systems and other long-haul circuits.

Asynchronous Transfer Mode

Asynchronous Transfer Mode (ATM) is, according to the ATM Forum, "a telecommunications concept defined by ANSI and ITU (formerly CCITT) standards for carriage of a complete range of user traffic, including voice, data, and video signals," and is designed to unify telecommunication and computer networks. It uses asynchronous time-division multiplexing, and it encodes data into small, fixed-sized cells. This differs from approaches such as the Internet Protocol or Ethernet that use variable sized packets or frames. ATM provides data link layer services that run over a wide range of OSI physical Layer links. ATM has functional similarity with both circuit switched networking and small packet switched networking. It was designed for a network that must handle both traditional high-throughput data traffic (e.g., file transfers), and real-time, low-latency content such as voice and video. ATM uses a connection-oriented model in which a virtual circuit must be established between two endpoints before the actual data exchange begins. ATM is a core protocol used over the SONET/SDH backbone of the public switched telephone network (PSTN) and Integrated Services Digital Network (ISDN), but its use is declining in favour of All IP.

ATM was developed to meet the needs of the Broadband Integrated Services Digital Network, as defined in the late 1980s.

Why cells?

Consider a speech signal reduced to packets, and forced to share a link with bursty data traffic (traffic with some large data packets). No matter how small the speech packets could be made, they would always encounter full-size data packets, and under normal queuing conditions, might experience maximum queuing delays. That is why all packets, or "cells," should have the same small size. In addition, the fixed cell structure means that ATM can be readily switched by hardware without the inherent delays introduced by software switched and routed frames.

Thus, the designers of ATM utilized small data cells to reduce jitter (delay variance, in this case) in the multiplexing of data streams. Reduction of jitter (and also end-to-end round-trip delays) is particularly important when carrying voice traffic, because the conversion of digitized voice into an analogue audio signal is an inherently real-time process, and to do a good job, the decoder (codec) that does this needs an evenly spaced (in time) stream of data items. If the next data item is not available when it is needed, the codec has no choice but to produce silence or guess — and if the data is late, it is useless, because the time period when it should have been converted to a signal has already passed.

At the time of the design of ATM, 155 Mbit/s Synchronous Digital Hierarchy (SDH) with 135 Mbit/s payload was considered a fast optical network link, and many Plesiochronous Digital Hierarchy (PDH) links in the digital network were considerably slower, ranging from 1.544 to 45 Mbit/s in the USA, and 2 to 34 Mbit/s in Europe.

At this rate, a typical full-length 1500 byte (12000-bit) data packet would take 77.42 µs to transmit. In a lower-speed link, such as a 1.544 Mbit/s T1 line, a 1500 byte packet would take up to 7.8 milliseconds.

A queuing delay induced by several such data packets might exceed the figure of 7.8 ms several times over, in addition to any packet generation delay in the shorter speech packet. This was clearly unacceptable for speech traffic, which needs to have low jitter in the data stream being fed into the codec if it is to produce good-quality sound. A packet voice system can produce this low jitter in a number of ways:

- Have a playback buffer between the network and the codec, one large enough to tide the codec over almost all the jitter in the data. This allows smoothing out the jitter, but the delay introduced by passage through the buffer would require echo cancellers even in local networks; this was considered too expensive at the time. Also, it would have increased the delay across the channel, and conversation is difficult over high-delay channels.
- Build a system that can inherently provide low jitter (and minimal overall delay) to traffic that needs it.
- Operate on a 1:1 user basis (i.e., a dedicated pipe).

The design of ATM aimed for a low-jitter network interface. However, "cells" were introduced into the design to provide short queuing delays while continuing to support datagram traffic. ATM broke up all packets, data, and voice streams into 48-byte chunks, adding a 5-byte routing header to each one so that they could be reassembled later. The choice of 48 bytes was political rather than technical. When the CCITT (now ITU-T) was standardizing ATM, parties from the United States wanted a 64-byte payload because this was felt to be a good compromise in larger payloads optimized for data transmission and shorter payloads optimized for real-time applications like voice; parties from Europe wanted 32-byte payloads because the small size (and therefore short transmission times) simplify voice applications with respect to echo cancellation. Most of the European parties eventually came around to the arguments made by the Americans, but France and a few others held out for a shorter cell length. With 32 bytes, France would have been able to implement an ATM-based voice network with calls from one end of France to the other requiring no echo cancellation. 48 bytes (plus 5 header bytes = 53) was chosen as a compromise between the two sides. 5-byte headers were chosen because it was thought that 10% of the payload was the maximum price to pay for routing information. ATM multiplexed these 53-byte cells instead of packets which reduced worst-case cell contention jitter by a factor of almost 30, reducing the need for echo cancellers.

Cells in practice

ATM supports different types of services via ATM adaptation layers (AAL). Standardized AALs include AAL1, AAL2, and AAL5, and the rarely used AAL3 and AAL4. AAL1 is used for constant bit rate (CBR) services and circuit emulation. Synchronization is also maintained at AAL1. AAL2 through AAL4 are used for variable bit rate (VBR) services, and AAL5 for data. Which AAL is in use for a given cell is not encoded in the cell. Instead, it is negotiated by or configured at the endpoints on a per-virtual-connection basis.

Following the initial design of ATM, networks have become much faster. A 1500 byte (12000-bit) full-size Ethernet frame takes only 1.2 μs to transmit on a 10 Gbit/s network, reducing the need for small cells to reduce jitter due to contention. Some consider that this makes a case for replacing ATM with Ethernet in the network backbone. However, it should be noted that the increased link speeds by themselves do not alleviate jitter due to queuing. Additionally, the hardware for implementing the service adaptation for IP packets is expensive at very high speeds. Specifically, at speeds of OC-3 and above, the cost of segmentation and reassembly (SAR) hardware makes ATM less competitive for IP than Packet Over SONET (POS); because of its fixed 48-byte cell payload, ATM is not suitable as a data link layer directly underlying IP (without the need for SAR at the data link level) since the OSI layer on which IP operates must provide a maximum transmission unit (MTU) of at least 576 bytes. SAR performance limits mean that the fastest IP router ATM interfaces are STM16 - STM64 which actually compares, while as of 2004 POS can operate at OC-192 (STM64) with higher speeds expected in the future.

On slower or congested links (622 Mbit/s and below), ATM does make sense, and for this reason most asymmetric digital subscriber line (ADSL) systems use ATM as an intermediate layer between the physical link layer and a Layer 2 protocol like PPP or Ethernet.

At these lower speeds, ATM provides a useful ability to carry multiple logical circuits on a single physical or virtual medium, although other techniques exist, such as Multi-link PPP and Ethernet VLANs, which are optional in VDSL implementations. DSL can be used as an access method for an ATM network, allowing a DSL termination point in a telephone central office to connect to many internet service providers across a wide-area ATM network. In the United States, at least, this has allowed DSL providers to provide DSL access to the customers of many internet service providers. Since one DSL termination point can support multiple ISPs, the economic feasibility of DSL is substantially improved.

Why virtual circuits?

ATM operates as a channel-based transport layer, using virtual circuits (VCs). This is encompassed in the concept of the Virtual Paths (VP) and Virtual Channels. Every ATM cell has an 8- or 12-bit Virtual Path Identifier (VPI) and 16-bit Virtual Channel Identifier (VCI) pair defined in its header. Together, these identify the virtual circuit used by the connection. The length of the VPI varies according to whether the cell is sent on the user-network interface (on the edge of the network), or if it is sent on the network-network interface (inside the network).

As these cells traverse an ATM network, switching takes place by changing the VPI/VCI values (label swapping). Although the VPI/VCI values are not necessarily consistent from one end of the connection to the other, the concept of a circuit is consistent (unlike IP, where any given packet could get to its destination by a different route than the others).

Using cells and virtual circuits for traffic engineering

Another key ATM concept involves the traffic contract. When an ATM circuit is set up each switch on the circuit is informed of the traffic class of the connection.

ATM traffic contracts form part of the mechanism by which "quality of service" (QoS) is ensured. There are four basic types (and several variants) which each have a set of parameters describing the connection.

- CBR - Constant bit rate: a Peak Cell Rate (PCR) is specified, which is constant.
- VBR - Variable bit rate: an average or Sustainable Cell Rate (SCR) is specified, which can peak at a certain level, a PCR, for a maximum interval before being problematic.
- ABR - Available bit rate: a minimum guaranteed rate is specified.
- UBR - Unspecified bit rate: traffic is allocated to all remaining transmission capacity.
- VBR has real-time and non-real-time variants, and serves for "bursty" traffic. Non-real-time is sometimes abbreviated to vbr-nrt.

Most traffic classes also introduce the concept of Cell Delay Variation Tolerance (CDVT), which defines the "clumping" of cells in time.

Traffic policing

To maintain network performance, networks may apply traffic policing to virtual circuits to limit them to their traffic contracts at the entry points to the network, i.e. the User–network interfaces (UNIs) and Network-to-network interfaces (NNIs): Usage/Network Parameter Control (UPC and NPC). The reference model given by the ITU-T and ATM Forum for UPC and NPC is the Generic Cell Rate Algorithm (GCRA), which is a version of the leaky bucket algorithm. CBR traffic will normally be policed to a PCR and CDVt alone, whereas VBR traffic will normally be policed using a dual leaky bucket controller to a PCR and CDVt and an SCR and Maximum Burst Size (MBS). The MBS will normally be the packet (SAR-SDU) size for the VBR VC in cells.

If the traffic on a virtual circuit is exceeding its traffic contract, as determined by the GCRA, the network can either drop the cells or mark the Cell Loss Priority (CLP) bit (to identify a cell as potentially redundant). Basic policing works on a cell by cell basis, but this is sub-optimal for encapsulated packet traffic (as discarding a single cell will invalidate the whole packet). As a result, schemes such as Partial Packet Discard (PPD) and Early Packet Discard (EPD) have been created that will discard a whole series of cells until the next packet starts. This reduces the number of useless cells in the network, saving bandwidth for full packets. EPD and PPD work with AAL5 connections as they use the end of packet marker: the ATM User-to-ATM User (AUU) Indication bit in the Payload Type field of the header, which is set in the last cell of a SAR-SDU.

Traffic shaping

Traffic shaping usually takes place in the Network Interface Card (NIC) in user equipment, and attempts to ensure that the cell flow on a VC will meet its traffic contract, i.e. cells will not be dropped or reduced in priority at the UNI. Since the reference model given for traffic policing in the network is the GCRA, this algorithm is normally used for shaping as well, and single and dual leaky bucket implementations may be used as appropriate.

Types of virtual circuits and paths

ATM can build virtual circuits and virtual paths either statically or dynamically. Static circuits (permanent virtual circuits or PVCs) or paths (permanent virtual paths or PVPs) require that the circuit is composed of a series of segments, one for each pair of interfaces through which it passes.

PVPs and PVCs, though conceptually simple, require significant effort in large networks. They also do not support the re-routing of service in the event of a failure. Dynamically built PVPs (soft PVPs or SPVPs) and PVCs (soft PVCs or SPVCs), in contrast, are built by specifying the characteristics of the circuit (the service "contract") and the two end points.

Finally, ATM networks create and remove switched virtual circuits (SVCs) on demand when requested by an end piece of equipment. One application for SVCs is to carry individual telephone calls when a network of telephone switches are inter-connected using ATM. SVCs were also used in attempts to replace local area networks with ATM.

Virtual circuit routing

Most ATM networks supporting SPVPs, SPVCs, and SVCs use the Private Network Node Interface or Private Network-to-Network Interface (PNNI) protocol. PNNI uses the same shortest-path-first algorithm used by OSPF and IS-IS to route IP packets to share topology information between switches and select a route through a network. PNNI also includes a very powerful summarization mechanism to allow construction of very large networks, as well as a call admission control (CAC) algorithm which determines the availability of sufficient bandwidth on a proposed route through a network in order to satisfy the service requirements of a VC or VP.

Computer Network Programming

Computer network programming involves writing computer programs that enable processes to communicate with each other across a computer network.

Client–server model

Interprocess communication, even if it is bidirectional, cannot be implemented in a perfectly symmetric way: to establish a communication channel between two processes, one process must take the initiative, while the other is waiting for it. Therefore, network programming unavoidably assumes a client–server model: The process initiating the communication is a client, and the process waiting for the communication to be initiated is a server. The client and server processes together form a distributed system. In a peer-to-peer communication, the program can act both as a client and a server.

Network socket

The endpoint in an interprocess communication is called a socket, or a network socket for disambiguation. Since most communication between computers is based on the Internet Protocol, an almost equivalent term is Internet socket. The data transmission between two sockets is organised by communications protocols, usually implemented in the operating system of the participating computers. Application programs write to and read from these sockets. Therefore, network programming is essentially socket programming.

Types of Networks

Networks are often classified by their physical or organizational extent or their purpose. Usage, trust level, and access rights differ between these types of networks.

Personal Area Network

A personal area network (PAN) is a computer network used for communication among computerized devices, including telephones and personal digital assistants. PANs can be used for communication among the personal devices themselves (intrapersonal communication), or for connecting to a higher level network and the Internet (an uplink). A wireless personal area network (WPAN) is a PAN carried over wireless network technologies such as IrDA, Bluetooth, Wireless USB, Z-Wave, ZigBee, or even Body Area Network. The reach of a WPAN varies from a few centimeters to a few meters. A PAN may also be carried over wired computer buses such as USB and FireWire.

Wireless Personal Area Network

A wireless personal area network (WPAN) is a personal area network — a network for interconnecting devices centered around an individual person's workspace — in which the connections are wireless. Wireless PAN is based on the standard IEEE 802.15. The two kinds of wireless technologies used for WPAN are Bluetooth and Infrared Data Association.

A WPAN could serve to interconnect all the ordinary computing and communicating devices that many people have on their desk or carry with them today; or it could serve a more specialized purpose such as allowing the surgeon and other team members to communicate during an operation.

A key concept in WPAN technology is known as "plugging in". In the ideal scenario, when any two WPAN-equipped devices come into close proximity (within several meters of each other) or within a few kilometers of a central server, they can communicate as if connected by a cable. Another important feature is the ability of each device to lock out other devices selectively, preventing needless interference or unauthorized access to information.

The technology for WPANs is in its infancy and is undergoing rapid development. Proposed operating frequencies are around 2.4 GHz in digital modes. The objective is to facilitate seamless operation among home or business devices and systems. Every device in a WPAN will be able to plug in to any other device in the same WPAN, provided they are within physical range of one another. In addition, WPANs worldwide will be interconnected. Thus, for example, an archeologist on site in Greece might use a PDA to directly access databases at the University of Minnesota in Minneapolis, and to transmit findings to that database.

Bluetooth

Bluetooth uses short-range radio waves over distances up to approximately 10 metres. For example, Bluetooth devices such as a keyboards, pointing devices, audio head sets, printers may connect to personal digital assistants (PDAs), cell phones, or computers wirelessly.

A Bluetooth PAN is also called a piconet (combination of the prefix "pico," meaning very small or one trillionth, and network), and is composed of up to 8 active devices in a master-slave relationship (a very large number of devices can be connected in "parked" mode). The first Bluetooth device in the piconet is the master, and all other devices are slaves that communicate with the master. A piconet typically has a range of 10 metres (33 ft), although ranges of up to 100 metres (330 ft) can be reached under ideal circumstances.

Recent innovations in Bluetooth antennas have allowed these devices to greatly exceed the range for which they were originally designed. At DEF CON 12, a group of hackers known as "Flexilis" successfully connected two Bluetooth devices more than half a mile (800 m) away. They used an antenna with a scope and Yagi antenna, all attached to a rifle stock. A cable attached the antenna to a Bluetooth card in a computer. They later named the antenna "The BlueSniper."

Infrared Data Association

Infrared Data Association (IrDA) uses infrared light, which has a frequency below the human eye's sensitivity. Infrared in general is used, for instance, in TV remotes. Typical WPAN devices that use IrDA include printers, keyboards, and other serial data interfaces.

WiFi

WiFi uses radio waves for connection over distances up to around 91 metres, usually in a local area network (LAN) environment. Wifi can be used to connect local area networks, to connect cellphones to the Internet to download music and other multimedia, to allow PC multimedia content to be stream to the TV (Wireless Multimedia Adapter), and to connect video game consoles to their networks (Nintendo WiFi Connection).

Body Area Network

Body Area Networks is the IEEE 802.15.6 standard based on transmission via the capacitive near field of human skin allowing near field communication of devices worn by and near the wearer. Skinplex implementation can detect and communicate up to 1 metre (3 ft 3 in) from a human body. It is already used for access control for door locks and jamming protection in convertible car roofs.

Local Area Network

A local area network (LAN) is a computer network that interconnects computers in a limited area such as a home, school, computer laboratory, or office building using network media. The defining characteristics of LANs, in contrast to wide area networks (WANs), include their usually higher data-transfer rates, smaller geographic area, and lack of a need for leased telecommunication lines.

ARCNET, Token Ring and other technology standards have been used in the past, but Ethernet over twisted pair cabling, and Wi-Fi are the two most common technologies currently used to build LANs.

The increasing demand and use of computers in universities and research labs in the late 1960s generated the need to provide high-speed interconnections between computer systems. A 1970 report from the Lawrence Radiation Laboratory detailing the growth of their "Octopus" network gave a good indication of the situation.

Cambridge Ring was developed at Cambridge University in 1974 but was never developed into a successful commercial product.

Ethernet was developed at Xerox PARC in 1973–1975, and filed as U.S. Patent 4,063,220. In 1976, after the system was deployed at PARC, Metcalfe and Boggs published a seminal paper, "Ethernet: Distributed Packet-Switching For Local Computer Networks."

ARCNET was developed by Datapoint Corporation in 1976 and announced in 1977. It had the first commercial installation in December 1977 at Chase Manhattan Bank in New York.

Standards evolution

The development and proliferation of personal computers using the CP/M operating system in the late 1970s, and later DOS-based systems starting in 1981, meant that many sites grew to dozens or even hundreds of computers. The initial driving force for networking was generally to share storage and printers, which were both expensive at the time. There was much enthusiasm for the concept and for several years, from about 1983 onward, computer industry pundits would regularly declare the coming year to be "the year of the LAN".

In practice, the concept was marred by proliferation of incompatible physical layer and network protocol implementations, and a plethora of methods of sharing resources. Typically, each vendor would have its own type of network card, cabling, protocol, and network operating system. A solution appeared with the advent of Novell NetWare which provided even-handed support for dozens of competing card/cable types, and a much more sophisticated operating system than most of its competitors. Netware dominated the personal computer LAN business from early after its introduction in 1983 until the mid 1990s when Microsoft introduced Windows NT Advanced Server and Windows for Workgroups.

Of the competitors to NetWare, only Banyan Vines had comparable technical strengths, but Banyan never gained a secure base. Microsoft and 3Com worked together to create a simple network operating system which formed the base of 3Com's 3+Share, Microsoft's LAN Manager and IBM's LAN Server - but none of these were particularly successful.

During the same period, Unix computer workstations from vendors such as Sun Microsystems, Hewlett-Packard, Silicon Graphics, Intergraph, NeXT and Apollo were using TCP/IP based networking. Although this market segment is now much reduced, the technologies developed in this area continue to be influential on the Internet and in both Linux and Apple Mac OS X networking—and the TCP/IP protocol has now almost completely replaced IPX, AppleTalk, NBF, and other protocols used by the early PC LANs.

Cabling

Early LAN cabling had always been based on various grades of coaxial cable. However shielded twisted pair was used in IBM's Token Ring implementation, and in 1984 StarLAN showed the potential of simple unshielded twisted pair by using Cat3—the same simple cable used for telephone systems. This led to the development of 10Base-T (and its successors) and structured cabling which is still the basis of most commercial LANs today. In addition, fiber-optic cabling is increasingly used in commercial applications.

As cabling is not always possible, wireless Wi-Fi is now very common in residential premises - and elsewhere where support for mobile laptops and smartphones is important.

Technical aspects

Network topology describes the layout pattern of interconnections between devices and network segments. Switched Ethernet has been for some time the most common Data Link Layer and Physical Layer implementation for local area networks. At the higher layers, the Internet Protocol (TCP/IP) has become the standard. Smaller LANs generally consist of one or more switches linked to each other, often at least one is connected to a router, cable modem, or ADSL modem for Internet access.

Larger LANs are characterized by their use of redundant links with switches using the spanning tree protocol to prevent loops, their ability to manage differing traffic types via quality of service (QoS), and to segregate traffic with VLANs. Larger LANs also contain a wide variety of network devices such as switches, firewalls, routers, load balancers, and sensors.

LANs may have connections with other LANs via leased lines, leased services, or by tunneling across the Internet using virtual private network technologies. Depending on how the connections are established and secured in a LAN, and the distance involved, a LAN may also be classified as a metropolitan area network (MAN) or a wide area network (WAN).

Home Area Network

A home network or home area network (HAN) is a residential local area network (LAN) for communication between digital devices typically deployed in the home, usually a small number of personal computers and accessories, such as printers and mobile computing devices. An important function is the sharing of Internet access, often a broadband service provisioned by fiber-to-the-home or via Cable Internet access, Digital Subscriber Line (DSL) or mobile broadband by Internet service providers (ISPs). If an ISP only provides one IP address, a router including network address translation (NAT), proxy server software and typically a network firewall, allows several computers to share the external IP address. The router function may be assumed by a PC with several network interfaces, but a dedicated router device is more common, often including a wireless accesspoint, providing WiFi access.

Home group

A home group is a feature that allows shared disk access, shared printer access and shared scanner access among all computers and users (typically all family members) in a home, in a similar fashion as in a small office workgroup, e.g., by means of distributed peer-to-peer networking (without a central server). Additionally, a home server may be added for increased functionality.

A Windows HomeGroup is a new feature in Microsoft Windows 7 that simplifies file sharing. All users (typically all family members), except guest accounts, may access any shared library on any computer that is connected to the home group. Passwords are not required from the family members during logon. Instead, secure file sharing is possible by means of a temporary password that is used when adding a computer to the HomeGroup.

Physical transmission media

Home networks may use wired or wireless technologies. Wired systems typically use shielded or unshielded twisted pair cabling, such as any of the Category 3 (CAT3) through Category 6 (CAT6) classes, but may also be implemented with coaxial cable, or over the existing electrical power wiring within homes.

Wireless radio

One of the most common ways of creating a home network is by using wireless radio signal technology; the 802.11 network as certified by the IEEE. Most products that are wireless-capable operate at a frequency of 2.4 GHz under 802.11b and 802.11g or 5 GHz under 802.11a. Some home networking devices operate in both radio-band signals and fall within the standard 802.11n.

A wireless network can be used for communication between many electronic devices, to connect to the Internet or to wired networks that use Ethernet technology. Wi-Fi is a marketing and compliance certification for IEEE 802.11 technologies. The WiFi Alliance has tested compliant products certifies them for interoperability.

Existing home wiring

As an alternative to wireless networking, the existing home wiring (coax in North America, telephone wiring in multi dwelling units (MDU) and power-line in Europe and USA) can be used as a network medium. With the installation of a home networking device, the network can be accessed by simply plugging the Computer into a wall socket.

Power lines

The ITU-T G.hn and IEEE Powerline standard, which provide high-speed (up to 1 Gbit/s) local area networking over existing home wiring, are examples of home networking technology designed specifically for IPTV delivery. Recently, the IEEE passed proposal P1901 which grounded a standard within the Market for wireline products produced and sold by companies that are part of the HomePlug Alliance. The IEEE is continuously working to push for P1901 to be completely recognized worldwide as the sole standard for all future products that are produced for Home Networking.

Storage Area Network

A Storage Area Network (SAN) is a dedicated network that provides access to consolidated, block level data storage. SANs are primarily used to make storage devices, such as disk arrays, tape libraries, and optical jukeboxes, accessible to servers so that the devices appear like locally attached devices to the operating system. A SAN typically has its own network of storage devices that are generally not accessible through the local area network by other devices. The cost and complexity of SANs dropped in the early 2000s to levels allowing wider adoption across both enterprise and small to medium sized business environments.

A SAN does not provide file abstraction, only block-level operations. However, file systems built on top of SANs do provide file-level access, and are known as SAN filesystems or shared disk file systems.

Storage sharing

Historically, data centers first created "islands" of SCSI disk arrays as direct-attached storage (DAS), each dedicated to an application, and visible as a number of "virtual hard drives" (i.e. LUNs). Essentially, a SAN consolidates such storage islands together using a high-speed network.

Operating systems maintain their own file systems on their own dedicated, non-shared LUNs, as though they were local to themselves. If multiple systems were simply to attempt to share a LUN, these would interfere with each other and quickly corrupt the data. Any planned sharing of data on different computers within a LUN requires advanced solutions, such as SAN file systems or clustered computing.

Despite such issues, SANs help to increase storage capacity utilization, since multiple servers consolidate their private storage space onto the disk arrays.

Common uses of a SAN include provision of transactionally accessed data that require high-speed block-level access to the hard drives such as email servers, databases, and high usage file servers.

SAN and NAS

Network-attached storage (NAS), in contrast to SAN, uses file-based protocols such as NFS or SMB/CIFS where it is clear that the storage is remote, and computers request a portion of an abstract file rather than a disk block.

SAN-NAS hybrid

Despite the differences between SAN and NAS, it is possible to create solutions that include both technologies.

Benefits

Sharing storage usually simplifies storage administration and adds flexibility since cables and storage devices do not have to be physically moved to shift storage from one server to another.

Other benefits include the ability to allow servers to boot from the SAN itself. This allows for a quick and easy replacement of faulty servers since the SAN can be reconfigured so that a replacement server can use the LUN of the faulty server. While this area of technology is still new many view it as being the future of the enterprise datacenter.

SANs also tend to enable more effective disaster recovery processes. A SAN could span a distant location containing a secondary storage array. This enables storage replication either implemented by disk array controllers, by server software, or by specialized SAN devices. Since IP WANs are often the least costly method of long-distance transport, the Fibre Channel over IP (FCIP) and iSCSI protocols have been developed to allow SAN extension over IP networks. The traditional physical SCSI layer could only support a few meters of distance - not nearly enough to ensure business continuance in a disaster.

The economic consolidation of disk arrays has accelerated the advancement of several features including I/O caching, snapshotting, and volume cloning (Business Continuance Volumes or BCVs).

Types

Most storage networks use the SCSI protocol for communication between servers and disk drive devices. A mapping layer to other protocols is used to form a network:

- ATA over Ethernet (AoE), mapping of ATA over Ethernet
- Fibre Channel Protocol (FCP), the most prominent one, is a mapping of SCSI over Fibre Channel
- Fibre Channel over Ethernet (FCoE)
- ESCON over Fibre Channel (FICON), used by mainframe computers
- HyperSCSI, mapping of SCSI over Ethernet
- iFCP or SANoIP mapping of FCP over IP
- iSCSI, mapping of SCSI over TCP/IP
- iSCSI Extensions for RDMA (iSER), mapping of iSCSI over InfiniBand

Storage networks may also be built using SAS and SATA technologies. SAS evolved from SCSI direct-attached storage. SATA evolved from IDE direct-attached storage. SAS and SATA devices can be networked using SAS Expanders.

SAN infrastructure

SANs often utilize a Fibre Channel fabric topology - an infrastructure specially designed to handle storage communications. It provides faster and more reliable access than higher-level protocols used in NAS. A fabric is similar in concept to a network segment in a local area network. A typical Fibre Channel SAN fabric is made up of a number of Fibre Channel switches.

Today, all major SAN equipment vendors also offer some form of Fibre Channel routing solution, and these bring substantial scalability benefits to the SAN architecture by allowing data to cross between different fabrics without merging them. These offerings use proprietary protocol elements, and the top-level architectures being promoted are radically different. They often enable mapping Fibre Channel traffic over IP or over SONET/SDH.

Compatibility

One of the early problems with Fibre Channel SANs was that the switches and other hardware from different manufacturers were not compatible. Although the basic storage protocols FCP were always quite standard, some of the higher-level functions did not interoperate well. Similarly, many host operating systems would react badly to other operating systems sharing the same fabric. Many solutions were pushed to the market before standards were finalized and vendors have since innovated around the standards.

SANs in media and entertainment

Video editing workgroups require very high data transfer rates and very low latency. Outside of the enterprise market, this is one area that greatly benefits from SANs.

SANs in Media and Entertainment are often referred to as Serverless SANs due to the nature of the configuration which places the video workflow (ingest, editing, playout) clients directly on the SAN rather than attaching to servers. Control of data flow is managed by a distributed file system such as StorNext by Quantum.

Per-node bandwidth usage control, sometimes referred to as Quality of Service (QoS), is especially important in video workgroups as it ensures fair and prioritized bandwidth usage across the network, if there is insufficient open bandwidth available. Active Storage's ActiveSAN, Avid Unity and ISIS, Apple's Xsan and Tiger Technology MetaSAN are specifically designed for video networks and offer this functionality.

Storage virtualization

Storage virtualization is the process of completely abstracting logical storage from physical storage. The physical storage resources are aggregated into storage pools, from which the logical storage is created. It presents to the user a logical space for data storage and transparently handles the process of mapping it to the physical location. This is implemented in modern disk arrays, using vendor proprietary solutions. However, the goal is to virtualize multiple disk arrays from different vendors, scattered over the network, into a single monolithic storage device, which can be managed uniformly.

Campus Area Network

A campus network, campus area network, corporate area network or CAN is a computer network made up of an interconnection of local area networks (LANs) within a limited geographical area. The networking equipments (switches, routers) and transmission media (optical fiber, copper plant, Cat5 cabling etc.) are almost entirely owned by the campus tenant / owner: an enterprise, university, government etc.

University campuses

College or university campus area networks often interconnect a variety of buildings, including administrative buildings, academic buildings, university libraries, campus or student centers, residence halls, gymnasiums, and other outlying structures, like conference centers, technology centers, and training institutes. Early examples include the Stanford University Network at Stanford University, Project Athena at MIT, and the Andrew Project at Carnegie Mellon University.

Corporate campuses

Much like a university campus network, a corporate campus network serves to connect buildings. Examples of such are the networks at Googleplex and Microsoft's campus. Campus networks are normally interconnected with high speed Ethernet links operating over optical fiber such as Gigabit Ethernet and 10 Gigabit Ethernet.

Backbone Network

A backbone network or network backbone is a part of computer network infrastructure that interconnects various pieces of network, providing a path for the exchange of information between different LANs or subnetworks.

A backbone can tie together diverse networks in the same building, in different buildings in a campus environment, or over wide areas. Normally, the backbone's capacity is greater than the networks connected to it.

A large corporation that has many locations may have a backbone network that ties all of the locations together, for example, if a server cluster needs to be accessed by different departments of a company that are located at different geographical locations. The pieces of the network connections (for example: ethernet, wireless) that bring these departments together is often mentioned as network backbone. Network congestion is often taken into consideration while designing backbones. Backbone networks should not be confused with the Internet backbone.

Metropolitan Area Network

A metropolitan area network (MAN) is a computer network that usually spans a city or a large campus. A MAN usually interconnects a number of local area networks (LANs) using a high-capacity backbone technology, such as fiber-optical links, and provides up-link services to wide area networks (or WAN) and the Internet.

The IEEE 802-2002 standard describes a MAN as being:

> A MAN is optimized for a larger geographical area than a LAN, ranging from several blocks of buildings to entire cities. MANs can also depend on communications channels of moderate-to-high data rates. A MAN might be owned and operated by a single organization, but it usually will be used by many individuals and organizations. MANs might also be owned and operated as public utilities. They will often provide means for internetworking of local networks.

Implementation

Some technologies used for this purpose are Asynchronous Transfer Mode (ATM), FDDI, and SMDS. These technologies are in the process of being displaced by Ethernet-based connections (e.g., Metro Ethernet) in most areas. MAN links between local area networks have been built without cables using either microwave, radio, or infra-red laser links. Most companies rent or lease circuits from common carriers because laying long stretches of cable can be expensive.

DQDB, Distributed-queue dual-bus, is the metropolitan area network standard for data communication. It is specified in the IEEE 802.6 standard.

Using DQDB, networks can be up to 20 miles (30 km) long and operate at speeds of 34 to 155 Mbit/s.

Several notable networks started as MANs, such as the Internet peering points MAE-West, MAE-East, and the Sohonet media network.

Wide Area Network

A Wide Area Network (WAN) is a network that covers a broad area (i.e., any telecommunications network that links across metropolitan, regional, or national boundaries) using private or public network transports. Business and government entities utilize WANs to relay data among employees, clients, buyers, and suppliers from various geographical locations. In essence, this mode of telecommunication allows a business to effectively carry out its daily function regardless of location. The Internet can be considered a WAN as well, and is used by businesses, governments, organizations, and individuals for almost any purpose imaginable.

Related terms for other types of networks are personal area networks (PANs), local area networks (LANs), campus area networks (CANs), or metropolitan area networks (MANs) which are usually limited to a room, building, campus or specific metropolitan area (e.g., a city) respectively.

Design options

The textbook definition of a WAN is a computer network spanning regions, countries, or even the world. However, in terms of the application of computer networking protocols and concepts, it may be best to view WANs as computer networking technologies used to transmit data over long distances, and between different LANs, MANs and other localised computer networking architectures. This distinction stems from the fact that common LAN technologies operating at Layer 1/2 (such as the forms of Ethernet or Wifi) are often geared towards physically localised networks, and thus cannot transmit data over tens, hundreds or even thousands of miles or kilometres.

WANs necessarily do not just connect physically disparate LANs. A CAN, for example, may have a localised backbone of a WAN technology, which connects different LANs within a campus. This could be to facilitate higher bandwidth applications, or provide better functionality for users in the CAN.

WANs are used to connect LANs and other types of networks together, so that users and computers in one location can communicate with users and computers in other locations. Many WANs are built for one particular organization and are private. Others, built by Internet service providers, provide connections from an organization's LAN to the Internet. WANs are often built using leased lines. At each end of the leased line, a router connects the LAN on one side with a second router within the LAN on the other. Leased lines can be very expensive. Instead of using leased lines, WANs can also be built using less costly circuit switching or packet switching methods. Network protocols including TCP/IP deliver transport and addressing functions. Protocols including Packet over SONET/SDH, MPLS, ATM and Frame relay are often used by service providers to deliver the links that are used in WANs. X.25 was an important early WAN protocol, and is often considered to be the "grandfather" of Frame Relay as many of the underlying protocols and functions of X.25 are still in use today (with upgrades) by Frame Relay.

Enterprise Private Network

An enterprise private network is a computer network built by a business to interconnect its various company sites (such as production sites, offices and shops) in order to share computer resources.

Beginning with the digitalisation of telecommunication networks, started in the 1970s in the USA by AT&T, and propelled by the growth in computer systems availability and demands, private networks have been built for decades without the need to append the term private to them. The networks were operated over telecommunication networks and, as for voice communications, a certain amount of security and secrecy was expected and delivered.

But with the Internet in the 1990s came a new type of network, virtual private networks, built over this public infrastructure, using encryption to protect the data traffic from eaves-dropping. So the enterprise networks are now commonly referred to enterprise private networks in order to clarify that these are private networks, in contrast to public networks.

Virtual Private Network

A virtual private network (VPN) extends a private network and the resources contained in the network across public networks like the Internet. It enables a host computer to send and receive data across shared or public networks as if it were a private network with all the functionality, security and management policies of the private network. This is done by establishing a virtual point-to-point connection through the use of dedicated connections, encryption, or a combination of the two. The VPN connection across the Internet is technically a wide area network (WAN) link between the sites but appears to the user as a private network link—hence the name "virtual private network".

Types of VPN

Early data networks allowed VPN-style remote connectivity through dial-up modems or through leased line connections utilizing Frame Relay and Asynchronous Transfer Mode (ATM) virtual circuits provisioned through a network owned and operated by telecommunication carriers such as AT&T or Verizon. These networks are not considered true VPNs because they passively secure the data being transmitted by the creation of logical data streams. They have given way to VPNs based on IP and IP/Multi-protocol Label Switching Networks (MPLS) based VPNs due to significant cost-reductions and increased bandwidth provided by new technologies such as Digital Subscriber Line (DSL) and fiber-optic networks.

VPNs can be either remote-access or site-to-site. In a corporate setting, remote-access VPNs allow employees to access their company's intranet from home or while traveling outside the office, and site-to-site VPNs allow employees in geographically separated offices to share one cohesive virtual network. A VPN can also be used to interconnect two similar networks over a dissimilar middle network; for example, two IPv6 networks over an IPv4 network.

VPN systems can be classified by:

- the protocols used to tunnel the traffic
- the tunnel's termination point, i.e., customer edge or network-provider edge
- whether they offer site-to-site or remote-access connectivity
- the levels of security provided
- the OSI layer they present to the connecting network, such as Layer 2 circuits or Layer 3 network connectivity

Security mechanisms

VPNs typically require remote access to be authenticated and make use of encryption techniques to prevent disclosure of private information.

VPNs provide security through tunneling protocols and security procedures such as encryption. Their security model provides:

- Confidentiality such that even if traffic is sniffed, an attacker would only see encrypted data which they cannot understand
- Allowing sender authentication to prevent unauthorized users from accessing the VPN
- Message integrity to detect any instances of transmitted messages having been tampered with

Secure VPN protocols include the following:

- IPSec (Internet Protocol Security) was developed by the Internet Engineering Task Force (IETF), and was initially developed for IPv6, which requires it. This standards-based security protocol is also widely used with IPv4. Layer 2 Tunneling Protocol frequently runs over IPSec. Its design meets most security goals: authentication, integrity, and confidentiality. IPSec functions through encrypting and encapsulating an IP packet inside an IPSec packet. De-encapsulation happens at the end of the tunnel, where the original IP packet is decrypted and forwarded to its intended destination.
- Transport Layer Security (SSL/TLS) can tunnel an entire network's traffic, as it does in the OpenVPN project, or secure an individual connection. A number of vendors provide remote access VPN capabilities through SSL. An SSL VPN can connect from locations where IPsec runs into trouble with Network Address Translation and firewall rules.
- Datagram Transport Layer Security (DTLS), is used in Cisco AnyConnect VPN, to solve the issues SSL/TLS has with tunneling over UDP.
- Microsoft Point-to-Point Encryption (MPPE) works with the Point-to-Point Tunneling Protocol and in several compatible implementations on other platforms.
- Microsoft's Secure Socket Tunneling Protocol (SSTP), introduced in Windows Server 2008 and in Windows Vista Service Pack 1. SSTP tunnels Point-to-Point Protocol (PPP) or Layer 2 Tunneling Protocol traffic through an SSL 3.0 channel.
- MPVPN (Multi Path Virtual Private Network). Ragula Systems Development Company owns the registered trademark "MPVPN".

- Secure Shell (SSH) VPN - OpenSSH offers VPN tunneling (distinct from port forwarding) to secure remote connections to a network or inter-network links. OpenSSH server provides a limited number of concurrent tunnels and the VPN feature itself does not support personal authentication.

VPNs in Mobile Environments

Mobile VPNs are used in a setting where an endpoint of the VPN is not fixed to a single IP address, but instead roams across various networks such as data networks from cellular carriers or between multiple Wi-Fi access points. Mobile VPNs have been widely used in public safety, where they give law enforcement officers access to mission-critical applications, such as computer-assisted dispatch and criminal databases, while they travel between different subnets of a mobile network. They are also used in field service management and by healthcare organizations, among other industries.

Increasingly, mobile VPNs are being adopted by mobile professionals and white-collar workers who need reliable connections. They are used for roaming seamlessly across networks and in and out of wireless-coverage areas without losing application sessions or dropping the secure VPN session. A conventional VPN cannot survive such events because the network tunnel is disrupted, causing applications to disconnect, time out, or fail, or even cause the computing device itself to crash.

Instead of logically tying the endpoint of the network tunnel to the physical IP address, each tunnel is bound to a permanently associated IP address at the device. The mobile VPN software handles the necessary network authentication and maintains the network sessions in a manner transparent to the application and the user. The Host Identity Protocol (HIP), under study by the Internet Engineering Task Force, is designed to support mobility of hosts by separating the role of IP addresses for host identification from their locator functionality in an IP network. With HIP a mobile host maintains its logical connections established via the host identity identifier while associating with different IP addresses when roaming between access networks.

Internetworking

Internetworking (a combination of the words inter ("between") and networking; it is not internet-working or international-network) is the practice of connecting a computer network with other networks through the use of gateways that provide a common method of routing information packets between the networks. The resulting system of interconnected networks is called an internetwork, or simply an internet.

The most notable example of internetworking is the Internet, a network of networks based on many underlying hardware technologies, but unified by an internetworking protocol standard, the Internet Protocol Suite, often also referred to as TCP/IP.

The smallest amount of effort to create an internet (an internetwork, not the Internet), is to have two LAN's of computers connected to each other via a router. Simply using either a switch or a hub to connect two local area networks together doesn't imply internetworking, it just expands the original LAN.

Interconnection of networks

Internetworking started as a way to connect disparate types of networking technology, but it became widespread through the developing need to connect two or more local area networks via some sort of wide area network. The original term for an internetwork was catenet.

The definition of an internetwork today includes the connection of other types of computer networks such as personal area networks. The network elements used to connect individual networks in the ARPANET, the predecessor of the Internet, were originally called gateways, but the term has been deprecated in this context, because of possible confusion with functionally different devices. Today the interconnecting gateways are called Internet routers.

Another type of interconnection of networks often occurs within enterprises at the Link Layer of the networking model, i.e. at the hardware-centric layer below the level of the TCP/IP logical interfaces. Such interconnection is accomplished with network bridges and network switches. This is sometimes incorrectly termed internetworking, but the resulting system is simply a larger, single subnetwork, and no internetworking protocol, such as Internet Protocol, is required to traverse these devices. However, a single computer network may be converted into an internetwork by dividing the network into segments and logically dividing the segment traffic with routers. The Internet Protocol is designed to provide an unreliable (not guaranteed) packet service across the network. The architecture avoids intermediate network elements maintaining any state of the network. Instead, this function is assigned to the endpoints of each communication session. To transfer data reliably, applications must utilize an appropriate Transport Layer protocol, such as Transmission Control Protocol (TCP), which provides a reliable stream. Some applications use a simpler, connection-less transport protocol, User Datagram Protocol (UDP), for tasks which do not require reliable delivery of data or that require real-time service, such as video streaming or voice chat.

Networking models

Two architectural models are commonly used to describe the protocols and methods used in internetworking.

The Open System Interconnection (OSI) reference model was developed under the auspices of the International Organization for Standardization (ISO) and provides a rigorous description for layering protocol functions from the underlying hardware to the software interface concepts in user applications. Internetworking is implemented in the Network Layer (Layer 3) of the model.

The Internet Protocol Suite, also called the TCP/IP model of the Internet was not designed to conform to the OSI model and does not refer to it in any of the normative specifications in Requests for Comment and Internet standards. Despite similar appearance as a layered model, it uses a much less rigorous, loosely defined architecture that concerns itself only with the aspects of logical networking. It does not discuss hardware-specific low-level interfaces, and assumes availability of a Link Layer interface to the local network link to which the host is connected. Internetworking is facilitated by the protocols of its Internet Layer.

Networks: Organizational scope

Networks are typically managed by organizations which own them. According to the owner's point of view, networks are seen as intranets or extranets. A special case of network is the Internet, which has no single owner but a distinct status when seen by an organizational entity – that of permitting virtually unlimited global connectivity for a great multitude of purposes.

Intranets and extranets

Intranets and extranets are parts or extensions of a computer network, usually a LAN.An intranet is a set of networks, using the Internet Protocol and IP-based tools such as web browsers and file transfer applications, that is under the control of a single administrative entity. That administrative entity closes the intranet to all but specific, authorized users. Most commonly, an intranet is the internal network of an organization.

An extranet is a network that is limited in scope to a single organization or entity and also has limited connections to the networks of one or more other usually, but not necessarily, trusted organizations or entities—a company's customers may be given access to some part of its intranet—while at the same time the customers may not be considered trusted from a security standpoint. Technically, an extranet may also be categorized as a CAN, MAN, WAN, or other type of network, although an extranet cannot consist of a single LAN; it must have at least one connection with an external network.

Internet

The Internet is a global system of interconnected governmental, academic, corporate, public, and private computer networks. It is based on the networking technologies of the Internet Protocol Suite. It is the successor of the Advanced Research Projects Agency Network (ARPANET) developed by DARPA of the United States Department of Defense. The Internet is also the communications backbone underlying the World Wide Web (WWW).

Participants in the Internet use a diverse array of methods of several hundred documented, and often standardized, protocols compatible with the Internet Protocol Suite and an addressing system (IP addresses) administered by the Internet Assigned Numbers Authority and address registries. Service providers and large enterprises exchange information about the reachability of their address spaces through the Border Gateway Protocol (BGP), forming a redundant worldwide mesh of transmission paths.

Network Topology

Common Layouts

A network topology is the layout of the interconnections of the nodes of a computer network. Common layouts are:

- A bus network: all nodes are connected to a common medium along this medium. This was the layout used in the original Ethernet, called 10BASE5 and 10BASE2.

- A star network: all nodes are connected to a special central node. This is the typical layout found in a Wireless LAN, where each wireless client connects to the central Wireless access point.
- A ring network: each node is connected to its left and right neighbour node, such that all nodes are connected and that each node can reach each other node by traversing nodes left- or rightwards. The Fiber Distributed Data Interface (FDDI) made use of such a topology.
- A mesh network: each node is connected to an arbitrary number of neighbours in such a way that there is at least one traversal from any node to any other.
- A fully connected network: each node is connected to every other node in the network.

Note that the physical layout of the nodes in a network may not necessarily reflect the network topology. As an example, with FDDI, the network topology is a ring (actually two counter-rotating rings), but the physical topology is a star, because all neighboring connections are routed via a central physical location.

Overlay network

An overlay network is a virtual computer network that is built on top of another network. Nodes in the overlay are connected by virtual or logical links, each of which corresponds to a path, perhaps through many physical links, in the underlying network. The topology of the overlay network may (and often does) differ from that of the underlying one.

For example, many peer-to-peer networks are overlay networks because they are organized as nodes of a virtual system of links run on top of the Internet. The Internet was initially built as an overlay on the telephone network.

The most striking example of an overlay network, however, is the Internet itself: At the IP layer, each node can reach any other by a direct connection to the desired IP address, thereby creating a fully connected network; the underlying network, however, is composed of a mesh-like interconnect of subnetworks of varying topologies (and, in fact, technologies). Address resolution and routing are the means which allows the mapping of the fully connected IP overlay network to the underlying ones.

Overlay networks have been around since the invention of networking when computer systems were connected over telephone lines using modems, before any data network existed.

Another example of an overlay network is a distributed hash table, which maps keys to nodes in the network. In this case, the underlying network is an IP network, and the overlay network is a table (actually a map) indexed by keys.

Overlay networks have also been proposed as a way to improve Internet routing, such as through quality of service guarantees to achieve higher-quality streaming media. Previous proposals such as IntServ, DiffServ, and IP Multicast have not seen wide acceptance largely because they require modification of all routers in the network. On the other hand, an overlay network can be incrementally deployed on end-hosts running the overlay protocol software, without cooperation from Internet service providers. The overlay has no control over how packets are routed in the underlying network between two overlay nodes, but it can control, for example, the sequence of overlay nodes a message traverses before reaching its destination.

For example, Akamai Technologies manages an overlay network that provides reliable, efficient content delivery (a kind of multicast). Academic research includes end system multicast and overcast for multicast; RON (resilient overlay network) for resilient routing; and OverQoS for quality of service guarantees, among others.

Basic Hardware Components

Apart from the physical communications media themselves as described above, networks comprise additional basic hardware building blocks interconnecting their terminals, such as network interface cards (NICs), hubs, bridges, switches, and routers.

Network Interface Cards

A network card, network adapter, or NIC (network interface card) is a piece of computer hardware designed to allow computers to physically access a networking medium. It provides a low-level addressing system through the use of MAC addresses.

Each Ethernet network interface has a unique MAC address which is usually stored in a small memory device on the card, allowing any device to connect to the network without creating an address conflict. Ethernet

MAC addresses are composed of six octets. Uniqueness is maintained by the IEEE, which manages the Ethernet address space by assigning 3-octet prefixes to equipment manufacturers. The list of prefixes is publicly available. Each manufacturer is then obliged to both use only their assigned prefix(es) and to uniquely set the 3-octet suffix of every Ethernet interface they produce.

Repeaters and Hubs

A repeater is an electronic device that receives a signal, cleans it of unnecessary noise, regenerates it, and retransmits it at a higher power level, or to the other side of an obstruction, so that the signal can cover longer distances without degradation. In most twisted pair Ethernet configurations, repeaters are required for cable that runs longer than 100 meters. A repeater with multiple ports is known as a hub. Repeaters work on the Physical Layer of the OSI model. Repeaters require a small amount of time to regenerate the signal. This can cause a propagation delay which can affect network communication when there are several repeaters in a row. Many network architectures limit the number of repeaters that can be used in a row

Bridges

A network bridge connects multiple network segments at the data link layer (layer 2) of the OSI model. Bridges broadcast to all ports except the port on which the broadcast was received. However, bridges do not promiscuously copy traffic to all ports, as hubs do, but learn which MAC addresses are reachable through specific ports. Once the bridge associates a port and an address, it will send traffic for that address to that port only.

Bridges learn the association of ports and addresses by examining the source address of frames that it sees on various ports. Once a frame arrives through a port, its source address is stored and the bridge assumes that MAC address is associated with that port. The first time that a previously unknown destination address is seen, the bridge will forward the frame to all ports other than the one on which the frame arrived.

Bridges come in three basic types:

- Local bridges: Directly connect LANs
- Remote bridges: Can be used to create a wide area network (WAN) link between LANs. Remote bridges, where the connecting link is slower than the end networks, largely have been replaced with routers.

- Wireless bridges: Can be used to join LANs or connect remote stations to LANs.

Switches

A network switch is a device that forwards and filters OSI layer 2 datagrams (chunks of data communication) between ports (connected cables) based on the MAC addresses in the packets. A switch is distinct from a hub in that it only forwards the frames to the ports involved in the communication rather than all ports connected. A switch breaks the collision domain but represents itself as a broadcast domain. Switches make forwarding decisions of frames on the basis of MAC addresses. A switch normally has numerous ports, facilitating a star topology for devices, and cascading additional switches. Some switches are capable of routing based on Layer 3 addressing or additional logical levels; these are called multi-layer switches. The term switch is used loosely in marketing to encompass devices including routers and bridges, as well as devices that may distribute traffic on load or by application content (e.g., a Web URL identifier).

Routers

A router is an internetworking device that forwards packets between networks by processing information found in the datagram or packet (Internet protocol information from Layer 3 of the OSI Model). In many situations, this information is processed in conjunction with the routing table. Routers use routing tables to determine what interface to forward packets (this can include the "null" also known as the "black hole" interface because data can go into it, however, no further processing is done for said data).

Firewalls

A firewall is an important aspect of a network with respect to security. It typically rejects access requests from unsafe sources while allowing actions from recognized ones. The vital role firewalls play in network security grows in parallel with the constant increase in 'cyber' attacks for the purpose of stealing/corrupting data, planting viruses, etc.

Network Performance

Nctwork mperformance refers to the service quality of a telecommunications product as seen by the customer. It should not be seen merely as an attempt to get "more through" the network.

The following list gives examples of Network Performance measures for a circuit-switched network and one type of packet-switched network, viz. ATM:

- Circuit-switched networks: In circuit switched networks, network performance is synonymous with the grade of service. The number of rejected calls is a measure of how well the network is performing under heavy traffic loads. Other types of performance measures can include noise, echo and so on.
- ATM: In an Asynchronous Transfer Mode (ATM) network, performance can be measured by line rate, quality of service (QoS), data throughput, connect time, stability, technology, modulation technique and modem enhancements.

There are many different ways to measure the performance of a network, as each network is different in nature and design. Performance can also be modelled instead of measured; one example of this is using state transition diagrams to model queuing performance in a circuit-switched network. These diagrams allow the network planner to analyze how the network will perform in each state, ensuring that the network will be optimally designed.

8-second rule

A June 2001 Zona Research report entitled "The Need for Speed II" found that the average web user will wait about eight seconds for a page to download, but that current average download time across backbone connection on most web sites is almost ten seconds.

The 8-second rule is an old (by Internet standards) way of determining the adequate response time of a webserver through different bandwidth connections. It specified that if the load-time of a web page exceeds eight seconds, users are unlikely to wait, or "stick around", for its completion. In order to increase the "stickiness" of a website, faster ways to deliver the content to the user needed to be devised. These included stripping away unnecessary HTML code and using fewer images.

It is generally believed that this rule no longer applies, since a much higher percentage of Internet users now have broadband available, making almost every website load up much faster, in some cases in less than a second. However, the rule might not be totally obsolete, as few webpages limit themselves to purely HTML and images nowadays and scripts, Flash and other interactive content take a long time to load even with the best of connections. Anyhow, the rule has remained as a rough unit to measure the performance of a webserver.

Optimized Systems

Web surfing

Users browsing the Internet feel that responses are "instant" when delays are less than 100 ms from click to response. Latency and throughput together affect the perceived speed of a connection. However, the perceived performance of a connection can still vary widely, depending in part on the type of information transmitted and how it is used.In a 2001 study, it was found that a typical web page was 53,400 bytes in size.

Round-trip packet latency over the Internet is fairly low – typically less than a tenth of a second across North America – and an average web page of 30-100 kilobytes would normally transfer fully in 10–30 seconds, over a 56-kbit/s modem, which yields a 3 kbit/s transfer rate. If a user had to wait 10–30 seconds to see anything, after every web-page click, it would be intolerable.

Because latency is so important, the HTTP protocol and HTML markup language were invented to reduce the rendering time of hypertext over the internet. These protocols allow incremental rendering, meaning that page text can begin display after the first packet arrives. HTTP and nearly all browsers support gzip (compressed) transfer encoding, which can typically compress text by 2x. Moreover, HTTP 1.0 and later protocols support a rich set of caching primitives, allowing content to be stored closer to the user, in both browser-caches and ISP proxy-caches, all to reduce latency. And finally, in the early days of HTTP, interlaced photos were transmitted via GIF, which allowed a rough version of an embedded picture to appear when only half the scan lines had arrived. A few years later JPEG was invented, allowing an almost arbitrary tradeoff between latency and image quality. These optimizations of HTTP and HTML, GIF, and JPEG were crucial to reducing latency and improving the perceived performance of the World Wide Web.

Hence, when a user clicks on a web page, there is a delay of 500-550 milliseconds to transfer a 1500-byte packet over a 56 kbit/s modem, before the user can begin to see up to 3,000 bytes (uncompressed) of text. A DSL line with a throughput of 256kbit/s would produce a delay of roughly 60-110 ms, which would be perceived as an "instant" response.

By comparison, to transfer the contents of a DVD over a modem could take a week or more at a 56 kbit/s modem rate. Simply packing the DVD into an envelope and mailing it could be faster.

Online gaming

Some online games utilize the Internet and/or a Local Area Network to coordinate a multiplayer game experience among two or more players, each of whom is running a copy of the game on a local game system (typically a video game console or gaming computer), with messages sent among the multiple game systems (either directly or through a game server reporting the actions of each player so that all the game systems stay synchronized). If the nature of the game is such that the game's local action cannot proceed until it synchronizes with one or more remote game systems, then the latency of the Internet and/or LAN will accordingly delay the responsiveness of a game system. Although such systems may only require very low throughput (e.g. messages of game controller actions may be only a few kilobits per second), the latency of the Internet and/or LAN must be low enough to meet the requirements of the game.

The maximum acceptable latency is game-type dependent. For example, generally, twitch gameplay games such as a first-person shooter like Quake 3 require lower latency for the best experience, while generally, a turn-based game such as chess can tolerate higher latency. But, it entirely depends on the specifics of each game. For example, fast chess is a turn-based game that may have low latency requirements. And, in the case of twitch games, some games can be designed such that only events that impact the outcome of the game are subject to synchronization latency, allowing for fast local response time most of the time.

Cloud gaming is a type of online gaming where the entire game is hosted on a game server in a data center, and the user is only running a thin client locally that forwards game controller upstream to the game server. The game server then renders the next frame of the game video which is compressed using low-latency video compression and is sent downstream and decompressed by the thin client. For the cloud gaming experience to be acceptable, the round-trip latency of all elements of the cloud gaming system (the thin client, the Internet and/or LAN connection the game server, the game execution on the game server, the video and audio compression and decompression, and the display of the video on a display device) must be low enough that the user perception is that the game is running locally. Because of such tight latency requirements, distance considerations of the speed of light through optical fiber come into play, currently limiting the distance between a user and a cloud gaming game server to approximately 1000 miles, according to OnLive, the only company thus far operating a cloud gaming service.

Online game systems utilizing a wireless network may be subject to significant latency, depending on the architecture of the wireless network and local electromagnetic interference impacting that network. Although radio propagation through air is faster than light through optical fiber, wireless systems are often shared among many users and may suffer from latency incurred due to network congestion which can trigger bufferbloat related issues, or due to network protocols that introduce latency. And, in the event of electromagnetic interference, transmitted packets may be lost, requiring a retransmission which also incurs latency.

Network Security

Network security consists of the provisions and policies adopted by a network administrator to prevent and monitor unauthorized access, misuse, modification, or denial of a computer network and network-accessible resources. Network security involves the authorization of access to data in a network, which is controlled by the network administrator. Users choose or are assigned an ID and password or other authenticating information that allows them access to information and programs within their authority. Network security covers a variety of computer networks, both public and private, that are used in everyday jobs conducting transactions and communications among businesses, government agencies and individuals. Networks can be private, such as within a company, and others which might be open to public access. Network security is involved in organizations, enterprises, and other types of institutions. It does as its title explains: It secures the network, as well as protecting and overseeing operations being done. The most common and simple way of protecting a network resource is by assigning it a unique name and a corresponding password.

Network security starts with authenticating the user, commonly with a username and a password. Since this requires just one detail authenticating the user name —i.e. the password, which is something the user 'knows'—this is sometimes termed one-factor authentication. With two-factor authentication, something the user 'has' is also used (e.g. a security token or 'dongle', an ATM card, or a mobile phone); and with three-factor authentication, something the user 'is' is also used (e.g. a fingerprint or retinal scan).

Once authenticated, a firewall enforces access policies such as what services are allowed to be accessed by the network users. Though effective to prevent unauthorized access, this component may fail to check potentially harmful content such as computer worms or Trojans being transmitted over the network. Anti-virus software or an intrusion prevention system (IPS) help detect and inhibit the action of such malware. An anomaly-based intrusion detection system may also monitor the network and traffic for unexpected (i.e. suspicious) content or behavior and other anomalies to protect resources, e.g. from denial of service attacks or an employee accessing files at strange times. Individual events occurring on the network may be logged for audit purposes and for later high-level analysis.

Honeypots, essentially decoy network-accessible resources, may be deployed in a network as surveillance and early-warning tools, as the honeypots are not normally accessed for legitimate purposes. Techniques used by the attackers that attempt to compromise these decoy resources are studied during and after an attack to keep an eye on new exploitation techniques. Such analysis may be used to further tighten security of the actual network being protected by the honeypot.

References

Andrew S. Tanenbaum, (2006). *Computer Networks*, Fourth Edition, Pearson Education.

Cisco Systems, Inc., (2003). *CCNA: network media types.* Retrieved from ciscopress.com

Kurose James F and Keith W. Ross. (2006). *Computer Networking: A Top-Down Approach Featuring the Internet*, Pearson Education.

Wendell Odom,Rus Healy, Denise Donohue. (2010). *CCIE Routing and Switching.* Indianapolis, IN: Cisco Press

William Stallings, (2004). *Computer Networking with Internet Protocols and Technology*, Pearson Education.

6

The Internet

Internet is a short form of the technical term internetwork, the result of interconnecting computer networks with special gateways or routers. Historically the word has been used, uncapitalized, as a verb and adjective since 1883 to refer to interconnected motions. It was also used from 1974 before the Internet, uncapitalized, as a verb meaning to connect together, especially for networks. The Internet is also often referred to as the Net.

The Internet, referring to the specific entire global system of IP networks, is a proper noun and written with an initial capital letter. In the media and common use it is often not capitalized: "the internet". Some guides specify that the word should be capitalized as a noun but not capitalized as an adjective.

The terms Internet and World Wide Web are often used interchangeably in everyday speech; it is common to speak of going on the Internet when invoking a browser to view Web pages. However, the Internet is a particular global computer network connecting millions of computing devices; the World Wide Web is just one of many services running on the Internet. The Web is a collection of interconnected documents (Web pages) and other resources, linked by hyperlinks and URLs. In addition to the Web, a multitude of other services are implemented over the Internet, including e-mail, file transfer, remote computer control, newsgroups, and online games. Web (and other) services can be implemented on any intranet, accessible to network users.

History of the Internet

The history of the Internet began with the development of electronic computers in the 1950s. The public was first introduced to the Internet when a message was sent from computer science Professor Leonard KleinRock's laboratory at University of California, Los Angeles (UCLA), after the second piece of network equipment was installed at Stanford Research Institute (SRI). This connection not only enabled the first transmission to be made, but is also considered to be the first Internet backbone. This began the point-to-point communication between mainframe computers and terminals, expanded to point-to-point connections between computers and then early research into packet switching. Packet switched networks such as ARPANET, Mark I at NPL in the UK, CYCLADES, Merit Network, Tymnet, and Telenet, were developed in the late 1960s and early 1970s using a variety of protocols. The ARPANET in particular led to the development of protocols for internetworking, where multiple separate networks could be joined together into a network of networks.

In 1982 the Internet protocol suite (TCP/IP) was standardized and the concept of a world-wide network of fully interconnected TCP/IP networks called the Internet was introduced. Access to the ARPANET was expanded in 1981 when the National Science Foundation (NSF) developed the Computer Science Network (CSNET) and again in 1986 when NSFNET provided access to supercomputer sites in the United States from research and education organizations. Commercial Internet service providers (ISPs) began to emerge in the late 1980s and 1990s. The ARPANET was decommissioned in 1990. The Internet was commercialized in 1995 when NSFNET was decommissioned, removing the last restrictions on the use of the Internet to carry commercial traffic.

Since the mid-1990s the Internet has had a drastic impact on culture and commerce, including the rise of near-instant communication by electronic mail, instant messaging, Voice over Internet Protocol (VoIP) "phone calls", two-way interactive video calls, and the World Wide Web with its discussion forums, blogs, social networking, and online shopping sites. The research and education community continues to develop and use advanced networks such as NSF's very high speed Backbone Network Service (vBNS), Internet2, and National LambdaRail. Increasing amounts of data are transmitted at higher and higher speeds over fiber optic networks operating at 1-Gbit/s, 10-Gbit/s, or more. The Internet continues to grow, driven by ever greater amounts of online information and knowledge, commerce, entertainment and social networking.

Precursors

The Internet has precursors that date back to the 19th century, especially the telegraph system, more than a century before the digital Internet became widely used in the second half of the 1990s. The concept of data communication – transmitting data between two different places, connected via some kind of electromagnetic medium, such as radio or an electrical wire – predates the introduction of the first computers. Such communication systems were typically limited to point to point communication between two end devices. Telegraph systems and telex machines can be considered early precursors of this kind of communication.

Fundamental theoretical work in data transmission and information theory was developed by Claude Shannon, Harry Nyquist, and Ralph Hartley, during the early 20th century.

Early computers used the technology available at the time to allow communication between the central processing unit and remote terminals. As the technology evolved, new systems were devised to allow communication over longer distances (for terminals) or with higher speed (for interconnection of local devices) that were necessary for the mainframe computer model. Using these technologies it was possible to exchange data (such as files) between remote computers. However, the point to point communication model was limited, as it did not allow for direct communication between any two arbitrary systems; a physical link was necessary. The technology was also deemed as inherently unsafe for strategic and military use, because there were no alternative paths for the communication in case of an enemy attack.

Three Terminals and an ARPA

A fundamental pioneer in the call for a global network, J. C. R. Licklider, articulated the ideas in his January 1960 paper, Man-Computer Symbiosis.

> "A network of such [computers], connected to one another by wide-band communication lines [which provided] the functions of present-day libraries together with anticipated advances in information storage and retrieval and [other] symbiotic functions."—J.C.R. Licklider,

In August 1962, Licklider and Welden Clark published the paper "On-Line Man Computer Communication", which was one of the first descriptions of a networked future.

In October 1962, Licklider was hired by Jack Ruina as Director of the newly established Information Processing Techniques Office (IPTO) within DARPA, with a mandate to interconnect the United States Department of Defense's main computers at Cheyenne Mountain, the Pentagon, and SAC HQ. There he formed an informal group within DARPA to further computer research. He began by writing memos describing a distributed network to the IPTO staff, whom he called "Members and Affiliates of the Intergalactic Computer Network". As part of the information processing office's role, three network terminals had been installed: one for System Development Corporation in Santa Monica, one for Project Genie at the University of California, Berkeley and one for the Compatible Time-Sharing System project at the Massachusetts Institute of Technology (MIT). Licklider's identified need for inter-networking would be made obvious by the apparent waste of resources this caused.

> "For each of these three terminals, I had three different sets of user commands. So if I was talking online with someone at S.D.C. and I wanted to talk to someone I knew at Berkeley or M.I.T. about this, I had to get up from the S.D.C. terminal, go over and log into the other terminal and get in touch with them. [...] I said, it's obvious what to do (But I don't want to do it): If you have these three terminals, there ought to be one terminal that goes anywhere you want to go where you have interactive computing. That idea is the ARPAnet."—Robert W. Taylor, co-writer with Licklider of "The Computer as a Communications Device", in an interview with The New York Times,

Although he left the IPTO in 1964, five years before the ARPANET went live, it was his vision of universal networking that provided the impetus that led his successors such as Lawrence Roberts and Robert Taylor to further the ARPANET development. Licklider later returned to lead the IPTO in 1973 for two years.

Packet Switching

At the tip of the problem lay the issue of connecting separate physical networks to form one logical network. During the 1960s, Paul Baran (RAND Corporation), produced a study of survivable networks for the US military. Information transmitted across Baran's network would be divided into what he called 'message-blocks'. Independently, Donald Davies (National Physical Laboratory, UK), proposed and developed a similar network based on what he called packet-switching, the term that would ultimately be adopted. Leonard Kleinrock (MIT) developed mathematical theory behind this technology. Packet-switching provides better bandwidth utilization and response times than the traditional circuit-switching technology used for telephony, particularly on resource-limited interconnection links.

Packet switching is a rapid store-and-forward networking design that divides messages up into arbitrary packets, with routing decisions made per-packet. Early networks used message switched systems that required rigid routing structures prone to single point of failure. This led Tommy Krash and Paul Baran's U.S. military funded research to focus on using message-blocks to include network redundancy. The widespread urban legend that the Internet was designed to resist nuclear attack likely arose as a result of Baran's earlier work on packet switching, which did focus on redundancy in the face of a nuclear "holocaust."

Networks that Led to the Internet

ARPANET

Promoted to the head of the information processing office at DARPA, Robert Taylor intended to realize Licklider's ideas of an interconnected networking system. Bringing in Larry Roberts from MIT, he initiated a project to build such a network. The first ARPANET link was established between the University of California, Los Angeles (UCLA)and the Stanford Research Institute on 22:30 hours on October 29, 1969.

By December 5, 1969, a 4-node network was connected by adding the University of Utah and the University of California, Santa Barbara. Building on ideas developed in ALOHAnet, the ARPANET grew rapidly. By 1981, the number of hosts had grown to 213, with a new host being added approximately every twenty days.

ARPANET became the technical core of what would become the Internet, and a primary tool in developing the technologies used. ARPANET development was centered around the Request for Comments (RFC) process, still used today for proposing and distributing Internet Protocols and Systems. RFC 1, entitled "Host Software", was written by Steve Crocker from the University of California, Los Angeles, and published on April 7, 1969. These early years were documented in the 1972 film Computer Networks: The Heralds of Resource Sharing.

International collaborations on ARPANET were sparse. For various political reasons, European developers were concerned with developing the X.25 networks. Notable exceptions were the Norwegian Seismic Array (NORSAR) in 1972, followed in 1973 by Sweden with satellite links to the Tanum Earth Station and Peter Kirstein's research group in the UK, initially at the Institute of Computer Science, London University and later at University College London.

NPL

In 1965, Donald Davies of the National Physical Laboratory (United Kingdom) proposed a national data network based on packet-switching. The proposal was not taken up nationally, but by 1970 he had designed and built the Mark I packet-switched network to meet the needs of the multidisciplinary laboratory and prove the technology under operational conditions. By 1976 12 computers and 75 terminal devices were attached and more were added until the network was replaced in 1986.

Merit Network

The Merit Network was formed in 1966 as the Michigan Educational Research Information Triad to explore computer networking between three of Michigan's public universities as a means to help the state's educational and economic development. With initial support from the State of Michigan and the National Science Foundation (NSF), the packet-switched network was first demonstrated in December 1971 when an interactive host to host connection was made between the IBM mainframe computer systems at the University of Michigan in Ann Arbor and Wayne State University in Detroit. In October 1972 connections to the CDC mainframe at Michigan State University in East Lansing completed the triad. Over the next several years in addition to host to host interactive connections the network was enhanced to support terminal to host connections, host to host batch connections (remote job submission, remote printing, batch file transfer), interactive file transfer, gateways to the Tymnet and Telenet public data networks, X.25 host attachments, gateways to X.25 data networks, Ethernet attached hosts, and eventually TCP/IP and additional public universities in Michigan join the network. All of this set the stage for Merit's role in the NSFNET project starting in the mid-1980s.

CYCLADES

The CYCLADES packet switching network was a French research network designed and directed by Louis Pouzin. First demonstrated in 1973, it was developed to explore alternatives to the initial ARPANET design and to support network research generally. It was the first network to make the hosts responsible for the reliable delivery of data, rather than the network itself, using unreliable datagrams and associated end-to-end protocol mechanisms.

X.25 and public data networks

Based on ARPA's research, packet switching network standards were developed by the International Telecommunication Union (ITU) in the form of X.25 and related standards. While using packet switching, X.25 is built on the concept of virtual circuits emulating traditional telephone connections. In 1974, X.25 formed the basis for the SERCnet network between British academic and research sites, which later became JANET. The initial ITU Standard on X.25 was approved in March 1976.

The British Post Office, Western Union International and Tymnet collaborated to create the first international packet switched network, referred to as the International Packet Switched Service (IPSS), in 1978. This network grew from Europe and the US to cover Canada, Hong Kong and Australia by 1981. By the 1990s it provided a worldwide networking infrastructure.

Unlike ARPANET, X.25 was commonly available for business use. Telenet offered its Telemail electronic mail service, which was also targeted to enterprise use rather than the general email system of the ARPANET.

The first public dial-in networks used asynchronous TTY terminal protocols to reach a concentrator operated in the public network. Some networks, such as CompuServe, used X.25 to multiplex the terminal sessions into their packet-switched backbones, while others, such as Tymnet, used proprietary protocols. In 1979, CompuServe became the first service to offer electronic mail capabilities and technical support to personal computer users. The company broke new ground again in 1980 as the first to offer real-time chat with its CB Simulator. Other major dial-in networks were America Online (AOL) and Prodigy that also provided communications, content, and entertainment features. Many bulletin board system (BBS) networks also provided on-line access, such as FidoNet which was popular amongst hobbyist computer users, many of them hackers and amateur radio operators.

UUCP and Usenet

In 1979, two students at Duke University, Tom Truscott and Jim Ellis, came up with the idea of using simple Bourne shell scripts to transfer news and messages on a serial line UUCP connection with nearby University of North Carolina at Chapel Hill. Following public release of the software, the mesh of UUCP hosts forwarding on the Usenet news rapidly expanded. UUCPnet, as it would later be named, also created gateways and links between FidoNet and dial-up BBS hosts. UUCP networks spread quickly due to the lower costs involved, ability to use existing leased lines, X.25 links or even ARPANET connections, and the lack of strict use policies (commercial organizations who might provide bug fixes) compared to later networks like CSnet and Bitnet. All connects were local. By 1981 the number of UUCP hosts had grown to 550, nearly doubling to 940 in 1984. – Sublink Network, operating since 1987 and officially founded in Italy in 1989, based its interconnectivity upon UUCP to redistribute mail and news groups messages throughout its Italian nodes (about 100 at the time) owned both by private individuals and small companies. Sublink Network represented possibly one of the first examples of the internet technology becoming progress through popular diffusion.

Merging the Networks and Creating the Internet

TCP/IP

With so many different network methods, something was needed to unify them. Robert E. Kahn of DARPA and ARPANET recruited Vinton Cerf of Stanford University to work with him on the problem. By 1973, they had worked out a fundamental reformulation, where the differences between network protocols were hidden by using a common internetwork protocol, and instead of the network being responsible for reliability, as in the ARPANET, the hosts became responsible. Cerf credits Hubert Zimmerman, Gerard LeLann and Louis Pouzin (designer of the CYCLADES network) with important work on this design.

The specification of the resulting protocol, RFC 675 – Specification of Internet Transmission Control Program, by Vinton Cerf, Yogen Dalal and Carl Sunshine, Network Working Group, December 1974, contains the first attested use of the term internet, as a shorthand for internetworking; later RFCs repeat this use, so the word started out as an adjective rather than the noun it is today.

With the role of the network reduced to the bare minimum, it became possible to join almost any networks together, no matter what their characteristics were, thereby solving Kahn's initial problem. DARPA agreed to fund development of prototype software, and after several years of work, the first demonstration of a gateway between the Packet Radio network in the SF Bay area and the ARPANET was conducted by the Stanford Research Institute. On November 22, 1977 a three network demonstration was conducted including the ARPANET, the Packet Radio Network and the Atlantic Packet Satellite network.

Stemming from the first specifications of TCP in 1974, TCP/IP emerged in mid-late 1978 in nearly final form. By 1981, the associated standards were published as RFCs 791, 792 and 793 and adopted for use. DARPA sponsored or encouraged the development of TCP/IP implementations for many operating systems and then scheduled a migration of all hosts on all of its packet networks to TCP/IP. On January 1, 1983, known as flag day, TCP/IP protocols became the only approved protocol on the ARPANET, replacing the earlier NCP protocol.

ARPANET to the federal wide area networks: MILNET, NSI, ESNet, CSNET, and NSFNET

After the ARPANET had been up and running for several years, ARPA looked for another agency to hand off the network to; ARPA's primary mission was funding cutting edge research and development, not running a communications utility. Eventually, in July 1975, the network had been turned over to the Defense Communications Agency, also part of the Department of Defense. In 1983, the U.S. military portion of the ARPANET was broken off as a separate network, the MILNET. MILNET subsequently became the unclassified but military-only NIPRNET, in parallel with the SECRET-level SIPRNET and JWICS for TOP SECRET and above. NIPRNET does have controlled security gateways to the public Internet.

The networks based on the ARPANET were government funded and therefore restricted to noncommercial uses such as research; unrelated commercial use was strictly forbidden. This initially restricted connections to military sites and universities. During the 1980s, the connections expanded to more educational institutions, and even to a growing number of companies such as Digital Equipment Corporation and Hewlett-Packard, which were participating in research projects or providing services to those who were.

Several other branches of the U.S. government, the National Aeronautics and Space Agency (NASA), the National Science Foundation (NSF), and the Department of Energy (DOE) became heavily involved in Internet research and started development of a successor to ARPANET. In the mid 1980s, all three of these branches developed the first Wide Area Networks based on TCP/IP. NASA developed the NASA Science Network, NSF developed CSNET and DOE evolved the Energy Sciences Network or ESNet.

NASA developed the TCP/IP based NASA Science Network (NSN) in the mid 1980s, connecting space scientists to data and information stored anywhere in the world. In 1989, the DECnet-based Space Physics Analysis Network (SPAN) and the TCP/IP-based NASA Science Network (NSN) were brought together at NASA Ames Research Center creating the first multiprotocol wide area network called the NASA Science Internet, or NSI. NSI was established to provide a totally integrated communications infrastructure to the NASA scientific community for the advancement of earth, space and life sciences. As a high-speed, multiprotocol, international network, NSI provided connectivity to over 20,000 scientists across all seven continents.

In 1981 NSF supported the development of the Computer Science Network (CSNET). CSNET connected with ARPANET using TCP/IP, and ran TCP/IP over X.25, but it also supported departments without sophisticated network connections, using automated dial-up mail exchange. Its experience with CSNET lead NSF to use TCP/IP when it created NSFNET, a 56 kbit/s backbone established in 1986, that connected the NSF supported supercomputing centers and regional research and education networks in the United States. However, use of NSFNET was not limited to supercomputer users and the 56 kbit/s network quickly became overloaded. NSFNET was upgraded to 1.5 Mbit/s in 1988. The existence of NSFNET and the creation of Federal Internet Exchanges (FIXes) allowed the ARPANET to be decommissioned in 1990. NSFNET was expanded and upgraded to 45 Mbit/s in 1991, and was decommissioned in 1995 when it was replaced by backbones operated by several commercial Internet Service Providers.

Transition towards the Internet

The term "internet" was adopted in the first RFC published on the TCP protocol (RFC 675: Internet Transmission Control Program, December 1974) as an abbreviation of the term internetworking and the two terms were used interchangeably. In general, an internet was any network using TCP/IP. It was around the time when ARPANET was interlinked with NSFNET in the late 1980s, that the term was used as the name of the network, Internet, being a large and global TCP/IP network.

As interest in widespread networking grew and new applications for it were developed, the Internet's technologies spread throughout the rest of the world. The network-agnostic approach in TCP/IP meant that it was easy to use any existing network infrastructure, such as the IPSS X.25 network, to carry Internet traffic. In 1984, University College London replaced its transatlantic satellite links with TCP/IP over IPSS.

Many sites unable to link directly to the Internet started to create simple gateways to allow transfer of e-mail, at that time the most important application. Sites which only had intermittent connections used UUCP or FidoNet and relied on the gateways between these networks and the Internet. Some gateway services went beyond simple email peering, such as allowing access to FTP sites via UUCP or e-mail.

Finally, the Internet's remaining centralized routing aspects were removed. The EGP routing protocol was replaced by a new protocol, the Border Gateway Protocol (BGP). This turned the Internet into a meshed topology and moved away from the centric architecture which ARPANET had emphasized. In 1994, Classless Inter-Domain Routing was introduced to support better conservation of address space which allowed use of route aggregation to decrease the size of routing tables.

TCP/IP goes Global

CERN, the European Internet, the link to the Pacific and beyond

Between 1984 and 1988 CERN began installation and operation of TCP/IP to interconnect its major internal computer systems, workstations, PCs and an accelerator control system. CERN continued to operate a limited self-developed system CERNET internally and several incompatible (typically proprietary) network protocols externally. There was considerable resistance in Europe towards more widespread use of TCP/IP and the CERN TCP/IP intranets remained isolated from the Internet until 1989.

In 1988 Daniel Karrenberg, from Centrum Wiskunde & Informatica (CWI) in Amsterdam, visited Ben Segal, CERN's TCP/IP Coordinator, looking for advice about the transition of the European side of the UUCP Usenet network (much of which ran over X.25 links) over to TCP/IP. In 1987, Ben Segal had met with Len Bosack from the then still small company Cisco about purchasing some TCP/IP routers for CERN, and was able to give Karrenberg advice and forward him on to Cisco for the appropriate hardware. This expanded the European portion of the Internet across the existing UUCP networks, and in 1989 CERN opened its first external TCP/IP connections. This coincided with the creation of Réseaux IP Européens (RIPE), initially a group of IP network administrators who met regularly to carry out co-ordination work together. Later, in 1992, RIPE was formally registered as a cooperative in Amsterdam.

At the same time as the rise of internetworking in Europe, ad hoc networking to ARPA and in-between Australian universities formed, based on various technologies such as X.25 and UUCPNet. These were limited in their connection to the global networks, due to the cost of making individual international UUCP dial-up or X.25 connections. In 1989, Australian universities joined the push towards using IP protocols to unify their networking infrastructures. AARNet was formed in 1989 by the Australian Vice-Chancellors' Committee and provided a dedicated IP based network for Australia.The Internet began to penetrate Asia in the late 1980s. Japan, which had built the UUCP-based network JUNET in 1984, connected to NSFNET in 1989. It hosted the annual meeting of the Internet Society, INET'92, in Kobe. Singapore developed TECHNET in 1990, and Thailand gained a global Internet connection between Chulalongkorn University and UUNET in 1992.

Global Digital Divide

While developed countries with technological infrastructures were joining the Internet, developing countries began to experience a digital divide separating them from the Internet. On an essentially continental basis, they are building organizations for Internet resource administration and sharing operational experience, as more and more transmission facilities go into place.

Africa

At the beginning of the 1990s, African countries relied upon X.25 IPSS and

2400 baud modem UUCP links for international and internetwork computer communications.

In August 1995, InfoMail Uganda, Ltd., a privately held firm in Kampala now known as InfoCom, and NSN Network Services of Avon, Colorado, sold in 1997 and now known as Clear Channel Satellite, established Africa's first native TCP/IP high-speed satellite Internet services. The data connection was originally carried by a C-Band RSCC Russian satellite which connected InfoMail's Kampala offices directly to NSN's MAE-West point of presence using a private network from NSN's leased ground station in New Jersey. InfoCom's first satellite connection was just 64 kbit/s, serving a Sun host computer and twelve US Robotics dial-up modems.

In 1996 a USAID funded project, the Leland initiative, started work on developing full Internet connectivity for the continent. Guinea, Mozambique, Madagascar and Rwanda gained satellite earth stations in 1997, followed by Côte d'Ivoire and Benin in 1998.

Africa is building an Internet infrastructure. AfriNIC, headquartered in Mauritius, manages IP address allocation for the continent. As do the other Internet regions, there is an operational forum, the Internet Community of Operational Networking Specialists.

There are a wide range of programs both to provide high-performance transmission plant, and the western and southern coasts have undersea optical cable. High-speed cables join North Africa and the Horn of Africa to intercontinental cable systems. Undersea cable development is slower for East Africa; the original joint effort between New Partnership for Africa's Development (NEPAD) and the East Africa Submarine System (Eassy) has broken off and may become two efforts.

Asia and Oceania

The Asia Pacific Network Information Centre (APNIC), headquartered in Australia, manages IP address allocation for the continent. APNIC sponsors an operational forum, the Asia-Pacific Regional Internet Conference on Operational Technologies (APRICOT).

In 1991, the People's Republic of China saw its first TCP/IP college network, Tsinghua University's TUNET. The PRC went on to make its first global Internet connection in 1994, between the Beijing Electro-Spectrometer Collaboration and Stanford University's Linear Accelerator

Center. However, China went on to implement its own digital divide by implementing a country-wide content filter.

Latin America

As with the other regions, the Latin American and Caribbean Internet Addresses Registry (LACNIC) manages the IP address space and other resources for its area. LACNIC, headquartered in Uruguay, operates DNS root, reverse DNS, and other key services.

Opening the network to commerce

The interest in commercial use of the Internet became a hotly debated topic. Although commercial use was forbidden, the exact definition of commercial use could be unclear and subjective. UUCPNet and the X.25 IPSS had no such restrictions, which would eventually see the official barring of UUCPNet use of ARPANET and NSFNET connections. Some UUCP links still remained connecting to these networks however, as administrators cast a blind eye to their operation.

During the late 1980s, the first Internet service provider (ISP) companies were formed. Companies like PSINet, UUNET, Netcom, and Portal Software were formed to provide service to the regional research networks and provide alternate network access, UUCP-based email and Usenet News to the public. The first commercial dialup ISP in the United States was The World, opened in 1989.

In 1992, the U.S. Congress passed the Scientific and Advanced-Technology Act, 42 U.S.C. § 1862(g), which allowed NSF to support access by the research and education communities to computer networks which were not used exclusively for research and education purposes, thus permitting NSFNET to interconnect with commercial networks. This caused controversy within the research and education community, who were concerned commercial use of the network might lead to an Internet that was less responsive to their needs, and within the community of commercial network providers, who felt that government subsidies were giving an unfair advantage to some organizations.

By 1990, ARPANET had been overtaken and replaced by newer networking technologies and the project came to a close. New network service providers including PSINet, Alternet, CERFNet, ANS CO+RE, and many others were offering network access to commercial customers.

NSFNET was no longer the de facto backbone and exchange point for Internet. The Commercial Internet eXchange (CIX), Metropolitan Area Exchanges (MAEs), and later Network Access Points (NAPs) were becoming the primary interconnections between many networks. The final restrictions on carrying commercial traffic ended on April 30, 1995 when the National Science Foundation ended its sponsorship of the NSFNET Backbone Service and the service ended. NSF provided initial support for the NAPs and interim support to help the regional research and education networks transition to commercial ISPs. NSF also sponsored the very high speed Backbone Network Service (vBNS) which continued to provide support for the supercomputing centers and research and education in the United States.

Beyond Earth and TCP/IP

The first live Internet link into low earth orbit was established on January 22, 2010 when astronaut T. J. Creamer posted the first unassisted update to his Twitter account from the International Space Station, marking the extension of the Internet into space. This personal Web access, which NASA calls the Crew Support LAN, uses the space station's high-speed Ku band microwave link. To surf the Web, astronauts can use a station laptop computer to control a desktop computer on Earth, and they can talk to their families and friends on Earth using Voice over IP equipment.

Communication with spacecraft beyond earth orbit has traditionally been over point-to-point links through the Deep Space Network. Each such data link must be manually scheduled and configured. In the late 1990s NASA and Google began working on a new network protocol, Delay-tolerant networking (DTN) which automates this process, allows networking of spaceborn transmission nodes, and takes the fact into account that spacecraft can temporarily lose contact because they move behind the Moon or planets, or because space "weather" disrupts the connection. Under such conditions, DTN retransmits data packages instead of dropping them, as the standard TCP/IP internet protocol does.

NASA conducted the first field test of what it calls the "deep space internet" in November 2008. Testing of DTN-based communications between the International Space Station and Earth (now termed Disruption-Tolerant Networking) has been ongoing since March 2009, and is scheduled to continue until March 2014.

This network technology is supposed to ultimately enable missions that involve multiple spacecraft where reliable inter-vessel communication might take precedence over vessel-to-earth downlinks. According to a February 2011 statement by Google's Vint Cerf, the so-called "Bundle protocols" have been uploaded to NASA's EPOXI mission spacecraft (which is in orbit around the sun) and communication with Earth has been tested at a distance of approximately 80 light seconds.

Internet Technology

Protocols

The communications infrastructure of the Internet consists of its hardware components and a system of software layers that control various aspects of the architecture. While the hardware can often be used to support other software systems, it is the design and the rigorous standardization process of the software architecture that characterizes the Internet and provides the foundation for its scalability and success. The responsibility for the architectural design of the Internet software systems has been delegated to the Internet Engineering Task Force (IETF). The IETF conducts standard-setting work groups, open to any individual, about the various aspects of Internet architecture. Resulting discussions and final standards are published in a series of publications, each called a Request for Comments (RFC), freely available on the IETF web site. The principal methods of networking that enable the Internet are contained in specially designated RFCs that constitute the Internet Standards. Other less rigorous documents are simply informative, experimental, or historical, or document the best current practices (BCP) when implementing Internet technologies.

The Internet standards describe a framework known as the Internet protocol suite. This is a model architecture that divides methods into a layered system of protocols (RFC 1122, RFC 1123). The layers correspond to the environment or scope in which their services operate. At the top is the application layer, the space for the application-specific networking methods used in software applications, e.g., a web browser program. Below this top layer, the transport layer connects applications on different hosts via the network (e.g., client–server model) with appropriate data exchange methods. Underlying these layers are the core networking technologies, consisting of two layers. The internet layer enables computers to identify and locate each other via Internet Protocol (IP) addresses, and allows them to connect to one another via intermediate (transit) networks. Last, at the bottom of the architecture, is a software layer, the link layer, that provides connectivity between hosts on the same local network link, such as a local area network (LAN) or a dial-up connection. The model, also known as TCP/IP, is designed to be independent of the underlying hardware, which the model therefore does not concern itself with in any detail. Other models have been developed, such as the Open Systems Interconnection (OSI) model, but they are not compatible in the details of description or implementation; many similarities exist and the TCP/IP protocols are usually included in the discussion of OSI networking.

The most prominent component of the Internet model is the Internet Protocol (IP), which provides addressing systems (IP addresses) for computers on the Internet. IP enables internetworking and in essence establishes the Internet itself. IP Version 4 (IPv4) is the initial version used on the first generation of today's Internet and is still in dominant use. It was designed to address up to ~4.3 billion (109) Internet hosts. However, the explosive growth of the Internet has led to IPv4 address exhaustion, which entered its final stage in 2011, when the global address allocation pool was exhausted. A new protocol version, IPv6, was developed in the mid-1990s, which provides vastly larger addressing capabilities and more efficient routing of Internet traffic. IPv6 is currently in growing deployment around the world, since Internet address registries (RIRs) began to urge all resource managers to plan rapid adoption and conversion.

IPv6 is not interoperable with IPv4. In essence, it establishes a parallel version of the Internet not directly accessible with IPv4 software. This means software upgrades or translator facilities are necessary for networking devices that need to communicate on both networks. Most modern computer operating systems already support both versions of the Internet Protocol. Network infrastructures, however, are still lagging in this development. Aside from the complex array of physical connections that make up its infrastructure, the Internet is facilitated by bi- or multi-lateral commercial contracts (e.g., peering agreements), and by technical specifications or protocols that describe how to exchange data over the network. Indeed, the Internet is defined by its interconnections and routing policies.

Routing

Internet Service Providers connect customers (thought of at the "bottom" of the routing hierarchy) to customers of other ISPs. At the "top" of the routing hierarchy are ten or so Tier 1 networks, large telecommunication companies which exchange traffic directly "across" to all other Tier 1 networks via unpaid peering agreements. Tier 2 networks buy Internet transit from other ISP to reach at least some parties on the global Internet, though they may also engage in unpaid peering (especially for local partners of a similar size). ISPs can use a single "upstream" provider for connectivity, or use multihoming to provide protection from problems with individual links. Internet exchange points create physical connections between multiple ISPs, often hosted in buildings owned by independent third parties.

Computers and routers use routing tables to direct IP packets among locally connected machines. Tables can be constructed manually or automatically via DHCP for an individual computer or a routing protocol for routers themselves. In single-homed situations, a default route usually points "up" toward an ISP providing transit. Higher-level ISPs use the Border Gateway Protocol to sort out paths to any given range of IP addresses across the complex connections of the global Internet.

Academic institutions, large companies, governments, and other organizations can perform the same role as ISPs, engaging in peering and purchasing transit on behalf of their internal networks of individual computers. Research networks tend to interconnect into large subnetworks such as GEANT, GLORIAD, Internet2, and the UK's national research and education network, JANET. These in turn are built around smaller networks.

Not all computer networks are connected to the Internet. For example, some classified United States websites are only accessible from separate secure networks.

General Structure

The Internet structure and its usage characteristics have been studied extensively. It has been determined that both the Internet IP routing structure and hypertext links of the World Wide Web are examples of scale-free networks.

Many computer scientists describe the Internet as a "prime example of a large-scale, highly engineered, yet highly complex system". The Internet is heterogeneous; for instance, data transfer rates and physical characteristics of connections vary widely. The Internet exhibits "emergent phenomena" that depend on its large-scale organization. For example, data transfer rates exhibit temporal self-similarity. The principles of the routing and addressing methods for traffic in the Internet reach back to their origins in the 1960s when the eventual scale and popularity of the network could not be anticipated. Thus, the possibility of developing alternative structures is investigated. The Internet structure was found to be highly robust to random failures and very vulnerable to high degree attacks.

Internet Governance

Internet governance is the development and application of shared principles, norms, rules, decision-making procedures, and programs that shape the evolution and use of the Internet. This article describes how the Internet was and is currently governed, some of the controversies that occurred along the way, and the ongoing debates about how the Internet should or should not be governed in the future. Internet governance should not be confused with E-Governance which refers to technology driven governance.

The Internet is a globally distributed network comprising many voluntarily interconnected autonomous networks. It operates without a central governing body. However, to help ensure interoperability, several key technical and policy aspects of the underlying core infrastructure and the principal namespaces are administered by the Internet Corporation for Assigned Names and Numbers (ICANN), headquartered in Marina del Rey, California. ICANN oversees the assignment of globally unique identifiers on the Internet, including domain names, Internet Protocol (IP) addresses, application port numbers in the transport protocols, and many other parameters. This seeks to create a globally unified namespace to ensure the global reach of the Internet. ICANN is governed by an international board of directors drawn from across the Internet technical, business, academic, and other non-commercial communities. However, the National Telecommunications and Information Administration, an agency of the United States Department of Commerce, continues to have final approval over changes to the DNS root zone. This authority over the root zone file makes ICANN one of a few bodies with global, centralized influence over the otherwise distributed Internet.

On 16 November 2005, the World Summit on the Information Society, held in Tunis, established the Internet Governance Forum (IGF) to open an ongoing, non-binding conversation among multiple stakeholders about the future of Internet governance. Since WSIS, the term "Internet governance" has been broadened beyond narrow technical concerns to include a wider range of Internet-related policy issues.

The definition of Internet governance has been contested by differing groups across political and ideological lines. One of the main debates concerns the authority and participation of certain actors, such as national governments, corporate entities and civil society, to play a role in the Internet's governance.

A Working group established after a United Nations-initiated World Summit on the Information Society (WSIS) proposed the following definition of Internet governance as part of its June 2005 report:

Internet governance is the development and application by Governments, the private sector and civil society, in their respective roles, of shared principles, norms, rules, decision-making procedures, and programmes that shape the evolution and use of the Internet.

Law professor Yochai Benkler developed a conceptualization of Internet governance by the idea of three "layers" of governance: the "physical infrastructure" layer through which information travels; the "code" or "logical" layer that controls the infrastructure; and the "content" layer, which contains the information that signals through the network.

Formation and Growth of the Network

The original ARPANET, one of the components which evolved eventually into the Internet, connected four Universities: University of California Los Angeles, University of California Santa Barbara, Stanford Research Institute and Utah University. The IMPs, interface minicomputers, were built during 1969 by Bolt, Beranek and Newman in accord with a proposal by the US Department of Defense Advanced Research Projects Agency, which funded the system as an experiment. By 1973 it connected many more systems and included satellite links to Hawaii and Scandinavia, and a further link from Norway to London. ARPANET continued to grow in size, becoming more a utility than a research project. For this reason, in 1975 it was transferred to the US Defense Communications Agency.

During the development of ARPANET, a numbered series of Request for Comments (RFCs) memos documented technical decisions and methods of working as they evolved. The standards of today's Internet are still documented by RFCs, produced through the very process which evolved on ARPANET.

Outside of the USA the dominant technology was X.25. The International Packet Switched Service, created during 1978, used X.25 and extended to Europe, Australia, Hong Kong, Canada, and the USA. It allowed individual users and companies to connect to a variety of mainframe systems, including Compuserve. Between 1979 and 1984, a system known as Unix to Unix Copy Program(UUCP) grew to connect 940 hosts, using methods like X.25 links, ARPANET connections, and leased lines. Usenet News, a distributed discussion system, was a major use of UUCP.

The Internet protocol suite, developed between 1973 and 1977 with funding from ARPA, was intended to hide the differences between different underlying networks and allow many different applications to be used over the same network.

RFC 801 describes how the US Department of Defense organized the replacement of ARPANET's Network Control Program by the new Internet Protocol during January 1983. During the same year, the military systems were removed to a distinct MILNET, and the Domain Name System was invented to manage the names and addresses of computers on the "ARPA Internet". The familiar top-level domains .gov, .mil, .edu, .org, .net, .com, and .int, and the two-letter country code top-level domains were deployed during 1984.

Between 1984 and 1986 the US National Science Foundation created the NSFNET backbone, using TCP/IP, to connect their supercomputing facilities. The combined network became generally known as the Internet.

By the end of 1989 Australia, Germany, Israel, Italy, Japan, Mexico, the Netherlands, New Zealand, and the United Kingdom had connected to the Internet, which now contained over 160,000 hosts.

During 1990, ARPANET formally terminated, and during 1991 the NSF ended its restrictions on commercial use of its part of the Internet. Commercial network providers began to interconnect, extending the Internet.

Today almost all Internet infrastructure is provided and owned by the private sector. Traffic is exchanged between these networks, at major interconnect points, in accordance with established Internet standards and commercial agreements.

Governors

During 1979 the Internet Configuration Control Board was founded by

DARPA to oversee the network's development. During 1984 it was renamed the Internet Advisory Board (IAB), and during 1986 it became the Internet Activities Board.

The Internet Engineering Task Force (IETF) was formed during 1986 by the US Government to develop and promote Internet standards. It consisted initially of researchers, but by the end of the year participation was available to anyone, and its business was performed largely by email.

From the early days of the network until his death during 1998, Jon Postel oversaw address allocation and other Internet protocol numbering and assignments in his capacity as Director of the Computer Networks Division at the Information Sciences Institute of the University of Southern California, under a contract from the Dept. of Defense. This function eventually became known as the Internet Assigned Numbers Authority (IANA), and as it expanded to include management of the global Domain Name System (DNS) root servers, a small organization grew. Postel also served as RFC Editor.

Allocation of IP addresses was delegated to four Regional Internet Registries (RIRs):

- American Registry for Internet Numbers (ARIN) for North America
- Réseaux IP Européens - Network Coordination Centre (RIPE NCC) for Europe, the Middle East, and Central Asia
- Asia-Pacific Network Information Centre (APNIC) for Asia and the Pacific region
- Latin American and Caribbean Internet Addresses Registry (LACNIC) for Latin America and the Caribbean region

In 2004 a new RIR, AfriNIC, was created to manage allocations for Africa.

After Jon Postel's death during 1998, the IANA became part of the Internet Corporation for Assigned Names and Numbers (ICANN), a newly created Californian non-profit corporation, initiated during September 1998 by the US Government and awarded a contract by the US Department of Commerce. Initially two board members were elected by the Internet community at large, though this was changed by the rest of the board during 2002 in a little- attended public meeting in Accra, Ghana.

During 1992 the Internet Society (ISOC) was founded, with a mission to "assure the open development, evolution and use of the Internet for the benefit of all people throughout the world". Its members include individuals (anyone may join) as well as corporations, organizations, governments, and universities. The IAB was renamed the Internet Architecture Board, and became part of ISOC. The Internet Engineering Task Force also became part of the ISOC. The IETF is overseen currently by the Internet Engineering Steering Group (IESG), and longer term research is carried on by the Internet Research Task Force and overseen by the Internet Research Steering Group.

At the first World Summit on the Information Society (WSIS) in Geneva 2003 the topic of Internet governance was discussed. ICANN's status as a private corporation under contract to the U.S. government created controversy among other governments, especially Brazil, China, South Africa and some Arab states. Since no general agreement existed even on the definition of what comprised Internet governance, United Nations Secretary General Kofi Annan initiated a Working Group on Internet Governance (WGIG) to clarify the issues and report before the second part of the World Summit on the Information Society in Tunis 2005. After much controversial debate, during which the US delegation refused to consider surrendering the US control of the Root Zone file, participants agreed on a compromise to allow for wider international debate on the policy principles. They agreed to establish an Internet Governance Forum, to be convened by United Nations Secretary General before the end of the second quarter of the year 2006. The Greek government volunteered to host the first such meeting.

Globalization and Governance Controversy

The position of the US Department of Commerce as the controller of the Internet gradually attracted criticism from those who felt that control should be more international. A hands-off philosophy by the US Dept. of Commerce helped limit this criticism, but this was undermined in 2005 when the Bush administration intervened to help kill the .xxx top level domain proposal.

When the IANA functions were given to a new US non-profit Corporation called ICANN, controversy increased. ICANN's decision-making process was criticised by some observers as being secretive and unaccountable. When the directors' posts which had previously been elected by the "at-large" community of Internet users were abolished, some feared that ICANN would become illegitimate and its qualifications questionable, due to the fact that it was now losing the aspect of being a neutral governing body. ICANN stated that they were merely streamlining decision-making processes, and developing a structure suitable for the modern Internet.

Other topics of controversy included the creation and control of generic top-level domains (.com, .org, and possible new ones, such as .biz or .xxx), the control of country-code domains, recent proposals for a large increase in ICANN's budget and responsibilities, and a proposed "domain tax" to pay for the increase.

There were also suggestions that individual governments should have more control, or that the International Telecommunication Union or the United Nations should have a function in Internet governance.

One such proposal, resulting from a September 2011 summit between India, Brazil, and South Africa (IBSA), would seek to move internet governance into their sphere of dominance. The move is a reaction to a perception that the principles of the 2005 Tunis Agenda for the Information Society have not been met. The statement calls for the subordination of independent technical organizations such as ICANN and the ITU to a political organization operating under the auspices of the United Nations.

Modern Uses

The Internet allows greater flexibility in working hours and location, especially with the spread of unmetered high-speed connections. The Internet can be accessed almost anywhere by numerous means, including through mobile Internet devices. Mobile phones, datacards, handheld game consoles and cellular routers allow users to connect to the Internet wirelessly. Within the limitations imposed by small screens and other limited facilities of such pocket-sized devices, the services of the Internet, including email and the web, may be available. Service providers may restrict the services offered and mobile data charges may be significantly higher than other access methods.

Educational material at all levels from pre-school to post-doctoral is available from websites. Examples range from CBeebies, through school and high-school revision guides and virtual universities, to access to top-end scholarly literature through the likes of Google Scholar. For distance education, help with homework and other assignments, self-guided learning, whiling away spare time, or just looking up more detail on an interesting fact, it has never been easier for people to access educational information at any level from anywhere. The Internet in general and the World Wide Web in particular are important enablers of both formal and informal education.

The low cost and nearly instantaneous sharing of ideas, knowledge, and skills has made collaborative work dramatically easier, with the help of collaborative software. Not only can a group cheaply communicate and share ideas but the wide reach of the Internet allows such groups more easily to form. An example of this is the free software movement, which has produced, among other things, Linux, Mozilla Firefox, and OpenOffice.org. Internet chat, whether using an IRC chat room, an instant messaging system, or a social networking website, allows colleagues to stay in touch in a very convenient way while working at their computers during the day. Messages can be exchanged even more quickly and conveniently than via email. These systems may allow files to be exchanged, drawings and images to be shared, or voice and video contact between team members.

Content management systems allow collaborating teams to work on shared sets of documents simultaneously without accidentally destroying each other's work. Business and project teams can share calendars as well as documents and other information. Such collaboration occurs in a wide variety of areas including scientific research, software development, conference planning, political activism and creative writing. Social and political collaboration is also becoming more widespread as both Internet access and computer literacy spread.

The Internet allows computer users to remotely access other computers and information stores easily, wherever they may be. They may do this with or without computer security, i.e. authentication and encryption technologies, depending on the requirements. This is encouraging new ways of working from home, collaboration and information sharing in many industries. An accountant sitting at home can audit the books of a company based in another country, on a server situated in a third country that is remotely maintained by IT specialists in a fourth. These accounts could have been created by home-working bookkeepers, in other remote locations, based on information emailed to them from offices all over the world. Some of these things were possible before the widespread use of the Internet, but the cost of private leased lines would have made many of them infeasible in practice. An office worker away from their desk, perhaps on the other side of the world on a business trip or a holiday, can access their emails, access their data using cloud computing, or open a remote desktop session into their office PC using a secure Virtual Private Network (VPN) connection on the Internet. This can give the worker complete access to all of their normal files and data, including email and other applications, while away from the office. It has been referred to among system administrators as the Virtual Private Nightmare, because it extends the secure perimeter of a corporate network into remote locations and its employees' homes.

Internet Services

World Wide Web

Many people use the terms Internet and World Wide Web, or just the Web, interchangeably, but the two terms are not synonymous. The World Wide Web is a global set of documents, images and other resources, logically interrelated by hyperlinks and referenced with Uniform Resource Identifiers (URIs). URIs symbolically identify services, servers, and other databases, and the documents and resources that they can provide. Hypertext Transfer Protocol (HTTP) is the main access protocol of the World Wide Web, but it is only one of the hundreds of communication protocols used on the Internet. Web services also use HTTP to allow software systems to communicate in order to share and exchange business logic and data.

World Wide Web browser software, such as Microsoft's Internet Explorer, Mozilla Firefox, Opera, Apple's Safari, and Google Chrome, lets users navigate from one web page to another via hyperlinks embedded in the documents. These documents may also contain any combination of computer data, including graphics, sounds, text, video, multimedia and interactive content that runs while the user is interacting with the page. Client-side software can include animations, games, office applications and scientific demonstrations. Through keyword-driven Internet research using search engines like Yahoo! and Google, users worldwide have easy, instant access to a vast and diverse amount of online information. Compared to printed media, books, encyclopedias and traditional libraries, the World Wide Web has enabled the decentralization of information on a large scale.

The Web has also enabled individuals and organizations to publish ideas and information to a potentially large audience online at greatly reduced expense and time delay. Publishing a web page, a blog, or building a website involves little initial cost and many cost-free services are available. Publishing and maintaining large, professional web sites with attractive, diverse and up-to-date information is still a difficult and expensive proposition, however. Many individuals and some companies and groups use web logs or blogs, which are largely used as easily updatable online diaries. Some commercial organizations encourage staff to communicate advice in their areas of specialization in the hope that visitors will be impressed by the expert knowledge and free information, and be attracted to the corporation as a result. One example of this practice is Microsoft, whose product developers publish their personal blogs in order to pique the public's interest in their work. Collections of personal web pages published by large service providers remain popular, and have become increasingly sophisticated. Whereas operations such as Angelfire and GeoCities have existed since the early days of the Web, newer offerings from, for example, Facebook and Twitter currently have large followings. These operations often brand themselves as social network services rather than simply as web page hosts.

Advertising on popular web pages can be lucrative, and e-commerce or the sale of products and services directly via the Web continues to grow.

When the Web began in the 1990s, a typical web page was stored in completed form on a web server, formatted in HTML, ready to be sent to a user's browser in response to a request. Over time, the process of creating and serving web pages has become more automated and more dynamic. Websites are often created using content management or wiki software with, initially, very little content. Contributors to these systems, who may be paid staff, members of a club or other organization or members of the public, fill underlying databases with content using editing pages designed for that purpose, while casual visitors view and read this content in its final HTML form. There may or may not be editorial, approval and security systems built into the process of taking newly entered content and making it available to the target visitors.

Communication

Email is an important communications service available on the Internet. The concept of sending electronic text messages between parties in a way analogous to mailing letters or memos predates the creation of the Internet. Pictures, documents and other files are sent as email attachments. Emails can be cc-ed to multiple email addresses.

Internet telephony is another common communications service made possible by the creation of the Internet. VoIP stands for Voice-over-Internet Protocol, referring to the protocol that underlies all Internet communication.

The idea began in the early 1990s with walkie-talkie-like voice applications for personal computers. In recent years many VoIP systems have become as easy to use and as convenient as a normal telephone. The benefit is that, as the Internet carries the voice traffic, VoIP can be free or cost much less than a traditional telephone call, especially over long distances and especially for those with always-on Internet connections such as cable or ADSL. VoIP is maturing into a competitive alternative to traditional telephone service. Interoperability between different providers has improved and the ability to call or receive a call from a traditional telephone is available. Simple, inexpensive VoIP network adapters are available that eliminate the need for a personal computer.

Voice quality can still vary from call to call, but is often equal to and can even exceed that of traditional calls. Remaining problems for VoIP include emergency telephone number dialing and reliability. Currently, a few VoIP providers provide an emergency service, but it is not universally available. Traditional phones are line-powered and operate during a power failure; VoIP does not do so without a backup power source for the phone equipment and the Internet access devices. VoIP has also become increasingly popular for gaming applications, as a form of communication between players. Popular VoIP clients for gaming include Ventrilo and Teamspeak. Wii, PlayStation 3, and Xbox 360 also offer VoIP chat features.

Data Transfer

File sharing is an example of transferring large amounts of data across the Internet. A computer file can be emailed to customers, colleagues and friends as an attachment. It can be uploaded to a website or FTP server for easy download by others. It can be put into a "shared location" or onto a file server for instant use by colleagues. The load of bulk downloads to many users can be eased by the use of "mirror" servers or peer-to-peer networks. In any of these cases, access to the file may be controlled by user authentication, the transit of the file over the Internet may be obscured by encryption, and money may change hands for access to the file. The price can be paid by the remote charging of funds from, for example, a credit card whose details are also passed – usually fully encrypted – across the Internet. The origin and authenticity of the file received may be checked by digital signatures or by MD5 or other message digests. These simple features of the Internet, over a worldwide basis, are changing the production, sale, and distribution of anything that can be reduced to a computer file for transmission. This includes all manner of print publications, software products, news, music, film, video, photography, graphics and the other arts. This in turn has caused seismic shifts in each of the existing industries that previously controlled the production and distribution of these products.

Streaming media is the real-time delivery of digital media for the immediate consumption or enjoyment by end users. Many radio and television broadcasters provide Internet feeds of their live audio and video productions. They may also allow time-shift viewing or listening such as Preview, Classic Clips and Listen Again features. These providers have been joined by a range of pure Internet "broadcasters" who never had on-air licenses. This means that an Internet-connected device, such as a computer or something more specific, can be used to access on-line media in much the same way as was previously possible only with a television or radio receiver. The range of available types of content is much wider, from specialized technical webcasts to on-demand popular multimedia services. Podcasting is a variation on this theme, where – usually audio – material is downloaded and played back on a computer or shifted to a portable media player to be listened to on the move. These techniques using simple equipment allow anybody, with little censorship or licensing control, to broadcast audio-visual material worldwide.

Digital media streaming increases the demand for network bandwidth. For example, standard image quality needs 1 Mbit/s link speed for SD 480p, HD 720p quality requires 2.5 Mbit/s, and the top-of-the-line HDX quality needs 4.5 Mbit/s for 1080p.

Webcams are a low-cost extension of this phenomenon. While some webcams can give full-frame-rate video, the picture either is usually small or updates slowly. Internet users can watch animals around an African waterhole, ships in the Panama Canal, traffic at a local roundabout or monitor their own premises, live and in real time. Video chat rooms and video conferencing are also popular with many uses being found for personal webcams, with and without two-way sound. YouTube was founded on 15 February 2005 and is now the leading website for free streaming video with a vast number of users. It uses a flash-based web player to stream and show video files. Registered users may upload an unlimited amount of video and build their own personal profile. YouTube claims that its users watch hundreds of millions, and upload hundreds of thousands of videos daily.

References

Berdal, S.R.B. (2004) (PDF), *Public deliberation on the Web: A Habermasian inquiry into online discourse*, Oslo: University of Oslo.

Comer, Douglas (2006). *The Internet book.* Prentice Hall. p. 64.

Hafner, Katie (1998). *Where Wizards Stay Up Late: The Origins Of The Internet.* Simon & Schuster.

Julie Rehmeyer, (2007). "The Internet spreads its tentacles", *Science News*, Vol. 171, No. 25, pp. 387–388, 23 June.

Lorenzo Cantoni & Stefano Tardini, (2006). *Internet*, Routledge.

Ronda Hauben (2001). *From the ARPANET to the Internet.* Retrieved 28 May 2009.

7

Access to Internet

Internet access is the means by which individual terminals, computers, mobile devices, and local area networks are connected to the global Internet. Internet access is usually sold by Internet Service Providers (ISPs) that use many different technologies offering a wide range of data rates to the end user. Consumer use first became popular through dial-up connections in the 1980s and 1990s. By the first decade of the 21st century, many consumers had switched away from dial-up to dedicated connections, most Internet access products were being marketed using the term "broadband", and broadband penetration was being treated as a key economic indicator.

The Internet began as a network funded by the U.S. government to support projects within the government and at universities and research laboratories in the US - but grew over time to include most of the world's large universities and the research arms of many technology companies. Use by a wider audience only came in 1995 when restrictions on the use of the Internet to carry commercial traffic were lifted.

In the early to mid-1980s, most Internet access was from personal computers and workstations directly connected to local area networks or from dial-up connections using modems and analog telephone lines. LANs typically operated at 10 Mbit/s and grew to support 100 and 1000 Mbit/s, while modem data rates grew from 1200 and 2400 bit/s in the 1980s, to 28 and 56 kbit/s by the mid to late 1990s. Initially dial-up connections were made from terminals or computers running terminal emulation software to terminal servers on LANs. These dial-up connections did not support end-to-end use of the Internet protocols and only provided terminal to host connections. The introduction of network access servers (NASs) supporting the Serial Line Internet Protocol (SLIP) and later the Point-to-point protocol (PPP) extended the Internet protocols and made the full range of Internet services available to dial-up users, subject only to limitations imposed by the lower data rates available using dial-up.

Broadband Internet access, often shortened to just broadband and also known as high-speed Internet access, are services that provide bit-rates considerably higher than that available using a 56 kbit/s modem. In the U.S. National Broadband Plan of 2009, the Federal Communications Commission (FCC) defined broadband access as "Internet access that is always on and faster than the traditional dial-up access", although the FCC has defined it differently through the years. The term broadband was originally a reference to multi-frequency communication, as opposed to narrowband or baseband. Broadband is now a marketing term that telephone, cable, and other companies use to sell their more expensive higher data rate products.

Most broadband services provide a continuous "always on" connection; there is no dial-in process required, and it does not "hog" phone lines. Broadband provides improved access to Internet services such as:

- Faster world wide web browsing
- Faster downloading of documents, photographs, videos, and other large files
- Telephony, radio, television, and videoconferencing
- Virtual private networks and remote system administration
- Online gaming, especially massively multiplayer online role-playing games which are interaction-intensive

In the 1990s, the National Information Infrastructure initiative in the U.S. made broadband Internet access a public policy issue. In 2000, most Internet access to homes was provided using dial-up, while many businesses and schools were using broadband connections. In 2000 there were just under 150 million dial-up subscriptions in the 34 OECD countries and fewer than 20 million broadband subscriptions. By 2004, broadband had grown and dial-up had declined so that the number of subscriptions were roughly equal at 130 million each. In 2010, in the OECD countries, over 90% of the Internet access subscriptions used broadband, broadband had grown to more than

300 million subscriptions, and dial-up subscriptions had declined to fewer than 30 million.

The broadband technologies in widest use are ADSL and cable Internet access. Newer technologies include VDSL and optical fibre extended closer to the subscriber in both telephone and cable plants. Fibre-optic communication, while only recently being used in premises and to the curb schemes, has played a crucial role in enabling broadband Internet access by making transmission of information at very high data rates over longer distances much more cost-effective than copper wire technology.

In areas not served by ADSL or cable, some community organizations and local governments are installing Wi-Fi networks. Wireless and satellite Internet are often used in rural, undeveloped, or other hard to serve areas where wired Internet is not readily available.

Newer technologies being deployed for fixed (stationary) and mobile broadband access include WiMAX, LTE, and fixed wireless, e.g., Motorola Canopy.

Starting in roughly 2006, mobile broadband access is increasingly available at the consumer level using "3G" and "4G" technologies such as HSPA, EV-DO, HSPA+, and LTE.

Availability of Internet

In addition to access from home, school, and the workplace Internet access may be available from public places such as libraries and Internet cafes, where computers with Internet connections are available. Some libraries provide stations for connecting users' laptops to local area networks (LANs).

Wireless Internet access points are available in public places such as airport halls, in some cases just for brief use while standing. Some access points may also provide coin operated computers. Various terms are used, such as "public Internet kiosk", "public access terminal", and "Web payphone". Many hotels also have public terminals, usually fee based.

Coffee shops, shopping malls, and other venues increasingly offer wireless access to computer networks, referred to as hotspots, for users who bring their own wireless-enabled devices such as a laptop or PDA. These services may be free to all, free to customers only, or fee-based. A hotspot need not be limited to a confined location. A whole campus or park, or even an entire city can be enabled. Grassroots efforts have led to wireless community networks.

And Mobile broadband access allows smart phones and other digital devices to connect to the Internet from any location from which a mobile phone call can be made.

Data Rates

The bit rates for dial-up modems range from as little as 110 bit/s in the late 1950s, to a maximum of from 33 to 64 kbit/s (V.90 and V.92) in the late 1990s. Dial-up connections generally require the dedicated use of a telephone line. Data compression can boost the effective bit rate for a dial-up modem connection to from 220 (V.42bis) to 320 (V.44) kbit/s. However, the effectiveness of data compression is quite variable, depending on the type of data being sent, the condition of the telephone line, and a number of other factors. In reality, the overall data rate rarely exceeds 150 kbit/s.

Broadband technologies supply considerably higher bit rates than dial-up, generally without disrupting regular telephone use. Various minimum data rates and maximum latencies have been used in definitions of broadband, ranging from 64 kbit/s up to 4.0 Mbit/s. In 1988 the CCITT standards body defined "broadband service" as requiring transmission channels capable of supporting bit rates greater than the primary rate which ranged from about 1.5 to 2 Mbit/s. A 2006 Organization for Economic Co-operation and Development (OECD) report defined broadband as having download data transfer rates equal to or faster than 256 kbit/s. And in 2010 the U.S. Federal Communications Commission (FCC) defined "Basic Broadband" as data transmission speeds of at least 4 Mbit/s downstream (from the Internet to the user's computer) and 1 Mbit/s upstream (from the user's computer to the Internet). The trend is to raise the threshold of the broadband definition as higher data rate services become available.

The higher data rate dial-up modems and many broadband services are "asymmetric"—supporting much higher data rates for download (toward the user) than for upload (toward the Internet).

Data rates, including those given in this article, are usually defined and advertised in terms of the maximum or peak download rate. In practice, these maximum data rates are not always reliably available to the customer. Actual end-to-end data rates can be lower due to a number of factors. Physical link quality can vary with distance and for wireless access with terrain, weather, building construction, antenna placement, and interference from other radio sources. Network bottlenecks may exist at points anywhere on the path from the end-user to the remote server or service being used and not just on the first or last link providing Internet access to the end-user.

Users may share access over a common network infrastructure. Since most users do not use their full connection capacity all of the time, this aggregation strategy (known as contended service) usually works well and users can burst to their full data rate at least for brief periods. However, peer-to-peer (P2P) file sharing and high quality streaming video can require high data rates for extended periods, which violates these assumptions and can cause a service to become oversubscribed, resulting in congestion and poor performance. The TCP protocol includes flow-control mechanisms that automatically throttle back on the bandwidth being used during periods of network congestion. This is fair in the sense that all users that experience congestion receive less bandwidth, but it can be frustrating for customers and a major problem for ISPs. In some cases the amount of bandwidth actually available may fall below the threshold required to support a particular service such as video conferencing or streaming live video–effectively making the service unavailable.

When traffic is particularly heavy, an ISP can deliberately throttle back the bandwidth available to classes of users or for particular services. This is known as traffic shaping and careful use can ensure a better quality of service for time critical services even on extremely busy networks. However, overuse can lead to concerns about fairness and network neutrality or even charges of censorship, when some types of traffic are severely or completely blocked.

Access Technologies

Access technologies generally use a modem, which converts digital data to analog for transmission over analog networks such as the telephone and cable networks.

Local Area Networks

Local area networks (LANs) provide Internet access to computers and other devices in a limited area such as a home, school, computer laboratory, or office building, usually at relatively high data rates that typically range from 10 to 1000 Mbit/s. There are wired and wireless LANs. Ethernet over twisted pair cabling and Wi-Fi are the two most common technologies used to build LANs today, but ARCNET, Token Ring, Localtalk, FDDI, and other technologies were used in the past.

Most Internet access today is through a LAN, often a very small LAN with just one or two devices attached. And while LANs are an important form of Internet access, this begs the question of how and at what data rate the LAN itself is connected to the rest of the global Internet. The technologies described below are used to make these connections.

Dial-up Access

Dial-up access uses a modem and a phone call placed over the public switched telephone network (PSTN) to connect to a pool of modems operated by an ISP. The modem converts a computer's digital signal into an analog signal that travels over a phone line's local loop until it reaches a telephone company's switching facilities or central office (CO) where it is switched to another phone line that connects to another modem at the remote end of the connection. Operating on a single channel, a dial-up connection monopolizes the phone line and is one of the slowest methods of accessing the Internet. Dial-up is often the only form of Internet access available in rural areas as it requires no new infrastructure beyond the already existing telephone network, to connect to the Internet. Typically, dial-up connections do not exceed a speed of 56 kbit/s, as they are primarily made using modems that operate at a maximum data rate of 56 kbit/s downstream (towards the end user) and 34 or 48 kbit/s upstream (toward the global Internet).

Broadband Access

The term broadband includes a broad range of technologies, all of which provide higher data rate access to the Internet. These technologies use wires or fiber optic cables in contrast to wireless broadband described later.

Multilink dial-up

Multilink dial-up provides increased bandwidth by bonding two or more dial-up connections together and treating them as a single data channel. It requires two or more modems, phone lines, and dial-up accounts, as well as an ISP that supports multilinking - and of course any line and data charges are also doubled. This inverse multiplexing option was briefly popular with some high-end users before ISDN, DSL and other technologies became available. Diamond and other vendors created special modems to support multilinking.

Integrated Services Digital Network (ISDN)

Integrated Services Digital Network (ISDN), a switched telephone service capable of transporting voice and digital data, is one of the oldest Internet access methods. ISDN has been used for voice, video conferencing, and broadband data applications. ISDN was very popular in Europe, but less common in North America. Its use peaked in the late 1990s before the availability of DSL and cable modem technologies.

Basic rate ISDN, known as ISDN-BRI, has two 64 kbit/s "bearer" or "B" channels. These channels can be used separately for voice or data calls or bonded together to provide a 128 kbit/s service. Multiple ISDN-BRI lines can be bonded together to provide data rates above 128 kbit/s. Primary rate ISDN, known as ISDN-PRI, has 23 bearer channels (64 kbit/s each) for a combined data rate of 1.5 Mbit/s (US standard). An ISDN E1 (European standard) line has 30 bearer channels and a combined data rate of 1.9 Mbits.

Leased lines

Leased lines are dedicated lines used primarily by ISPs, business, and other large enterprises to connect LANs and campus networks to the Internet using the existing infrastructure of the public telephone network or other providers. Delivered using wire, optical fiber, and radio, leased lines are used to provide Internet access directly as well as the building blocks from which several other forms of Internet access are created.

T-carrier technology dates to 1957 and provides data rates that range from 56 and 64 kbit/s (DS0) to 1.5 Mbit/s (DS1 or T1), to 45 Mbit/s (DS3 or T3). A T1 line carries 24 voice or data channels (24 DS0s), so customers may use some channels for data and others for voice traffic or use all 24 channels for clear channel data. A DS3 (T3) line carries 28 DS1 (T1) channels. Fractional T1 lines are also available in multiples of a DS0 to provide data rates between 56 and 1,500 kbit/s. T-carrier lines require special termination equipment that may be separate from or integrated into a router or switch and which may be purchased or leased from an ISP. In Japan the equivalent standard is J1/J3. In Europe, a slightly different standard, E-carrier, provides 32 user channels (64 kbit/s) on an E1 (2.0 Mbit/s) and 512 user channels or 16 E1s on an E3 (34.4 Mbit/s).

Synchronous Optical Networking (SONET, in the U.S. and Canada) and Synchronous Digital Hierarchy (SDH, in the rest of the world) are the standard multiplexing protocols used to carry high data rate digital bit streams over optical fiber using lasers or highly coherent light from light-emitting diodes (LEDs). At lower transmission rates data can also be transferred via an electrical interface. The basic unit of framing is an OC-3c (optical) or STS-3c (electrical) which carries 155.520 Mbit/s. Thus an OC-3c will carry three OC-1 (51.84 Mbit/s) payloads each of which has enough capacity to include a full DS3. Higher data rates are delivered in OC-3c multiples of four providing OC-12c (622.080 Mbit/s), OC-48c (2.488 Gbit/s), OC-192c (9.953 Gbit/s), and OC-768c (39.813 Gbit/s). The "c" at the end of the OC labels stands for "concatenated" and indicates a single data stream rather than several multiplexed data streams.

The 1, 10, 40, and 100 Gigabit Ethernet (GbE, 10GbE, 40GbE, and 100GbE) IEEE standards (802.3) allow digital data to be delivered over copper wiring at distances to 100 m and over optical fiber at distances to 40 km.

Cable Internet Access

Cable Internet or cable modem access provides Internet access via Hybrid Fiber Coaxial wiring originally developed to carry television signals. Either fiber-optic or coaxial copper cable may connect a node to a customer's location at a connection known as a cable drop. In a cable modem termination system, all nodes for cable subscribers in a neighborhood connect to a cable company's central office, known as the "head end." The cable company then connects to the Internet using a variety of means – usually fiber optic cable or digital satellite and microwave transmissions. Like DSL, broadband cable provides a continuous connection with an ISP.

Downstream, the direction toward the user, bit rates can be as much as 400 Mbit/s for business connections, and 100 Mbit/s for residential service in some countries. Upstream traffic, originating at the user, ranges from 384 kbit/s to more than 20 Mbit/s. Broadband cable access tends to service fewer business customers because existing television cable networks tend to service residential buildings and commercial buildings do not always include wiring for coaxial cable networks. In addition, because broadband cable subscribers share the same local line, communications may be intercepted by neighboring subscribers. Cable networks regularly provide encryption schemes for data traveling to and from customers, but these schemes may be thwarted.

Digital subscriber line (DSL, ADSL, SDSL, and VDSL)

Digital Subscriber Line (DSL) service provides a connection to the Internet through the telephone network. Unlike dial-up, DSL can operate using a single phone line without preventing normal use of the telephone line for voice phone calls. DSL uses the high frequencies, while the low (audible) frequencies of the line are left free for regular telephone communication. These frequency bands are subsequently separated by filters installed at the customer's premises.

DSL originally stood for "digital subscriber loop". In telecommunications marketing, the term digital subscriber line is widely understood to mean Asymmetric Digital Subscriber Line (ADSL), the most commonly installed variety of DSL. The data throughput of consumer DSL services typically ranges from 256 kbit/s to 20 Mbit/s in the direction to the customer (downstream), depending on DSL technology, line conditions, and service-level implementation. In ADSL, the data throughput in the upstream direction, (i.e. in the direction to the service provider) is lower than that in the downstream direction (i.e. to the customer), hence the designation of asymmetric. With a symmetric digital subscriber line (SDSL), the downstream and upstream data rates are equal.

Very-high-bit-rate digital subscriber line (VDSL or VHDSL, ITU G.993.1) is a digital subscriber line (DSL) standard approved in 2001 that provides data rates up to 52 Mbit/s downstream and 16 Mbit/s upstream over copper wires and up to 85 Mbit/s down- and upstream on coaxial cable. VDSL is capable of supporting applications such as high-definition television, as well as telephone services (voice over IP) and general Internet access, over a single physical connection.

VDSL2 (ITU-T G.993.2) is a second-generation version and an enhancement of VDSL. Approved in February 2006, it is able to provide data rates exceeding 100 Mbit/s simultaneously in both the upstream and downstream directions. However, the maximum data rate is achieved at a range of about 300 meters and performance degrades as distance and loop attenuation increases.

DSL Rings

DSL Rings (DSLR) or Bonded DSL Rings is a ring topology that uses DSL technology over existing copper telephone wires to provide data rates of up to 400 Mbit/s.

Fiber to the home

Fiber-to-the-home (FTTH) is one member of the Fiber-to-the-x (FTTx) family that includes Fiber-to-the-building or basement (FTTB), Fiber-to-the-premises (FTTP), Fiber-to-the-desk (FTTD), Fiber-to-the-curb (FTTC), and Fiber-to-the-node (FTTN). These methods all bring data closer to the end user on optical fibers. The differences between the methods have mostly to do with just how close to the end user the delivery on fiber comes. All of these delivery methods are similar to hybrid fiber-coaxial (HFC) systems used to provide cable Internet access.

The use of optical fiber offers much higher data rates over relatively longer distances. Most high-capacity Internet and cable television backbones already use fiber optic technology, with data switched to other technologies (DSL, cable, POTS) for final delivery to customers.

Australia has already begun rolling out its National Broadband Network across the country using fiber-optic cables to 93 percent of Australian homes, schools, and businesses. Similar efforts are underway in Italy, Canada, India, and many other countries.

Power-line Internet

Power-line Internet, also known as Broadband over power lines (BPL), carries Internet data on a conductor that is also used for electric power transmission. Because of the extensive power line infrastructure already in place, this technology can provide people in rural and low population areas access the Internet with little cost in terms of new transmission equipment, cables, or wires. Data rates are asymmetric and generally range from 256 kbit/s to 2.7 Mbit/s.

Because these systems use parts of the radio spectrum allocated to other over-the-air communication services, interference between the services is a limiting factor in the introduction of power-line Internet systems. The IEEE P1901 standard specifies that all powerline protocols must detect existing usage and avoid interfering with it.

Power-line Internet has developed faster in Europe than in the U.S. due to a historical difference in power system design philosophies. Data signals cannot pass through the step-down transformers used and so a repeater must be installed on each transformer. In the U.S. a transformer serves a small clusters of from one to a few houses. In Europe, it is more common for a somewhat larger transformer to service larger clusters of from 10 to 100 houses. Thus a typical U.S. city requires an order of magnitude more repeaters than in a comparable European city.

ATM and Frame Relay

Asynchronous Transfer Mode (ATM) and Frame Relay are wide area networking standards that can be used to provide Internet access directly or as building blocks of other access technologies. For example many DSL implementations use an ATM layer over the low-level bitstream layer to enable a number of different technologies over the same link. Customer LANs are typically connected to an ATM switch or a Frame Relay node using leased lines at a wide range of data rates.

While still widely used, with the advent of Ethernet over optical fiber, MPLS, VPNs and broadband services such as cable modem and DSL, ATM and Frame Relay no longer play the prominent role they once did.

Wireless Broadband Access

Wireless broadband is used to provide both fixed and mobile Internet access.

Wi-Fi

Wi-Fi is the popular name for a "wireless local area network" that uses one of the IEEE 802.11 standards. It is a trademark of the Wi-Fi Alliance. Individual homes and businesses often use Wi-Fi to connect laptops and smart phones to the Internet. Wi-Fi Hotspots may be found in coffee shops and various other public establishments. Wi-Fi is used to create campus-wide and city-wide wireless networks.

Wi-Fi networks are built using one or more wireless routers called Access Points. "Ad hoc" computer to computer Wi-Fi" networks are also possible. The Wi-Fi network is connected to the larger Internet using DSL, cable modem, and other Internet access technologies. Data rates range from 6 to 600 Mbit/s. Wi-Fi service range is fairly short, typically 20 to 250 meters or from 65 to 820 feet. Both data rate and range are quite variable depending on the Wi-Fi protocol, location, frequency, building construction, and interference from other devices. Using directional antennas and with careful engineering Wi-Fi can be extended to operate over distances of up to several kilometers.

Wireless ISP

Wireless ISPs typically employ low-cost 802.11 Wi-Fi radio systems to link up remote locations over great distances, but may use other higher-power radio communications systems as well.

Traditional 802.11b is an unlicensed omnidirectional service designed to span between 100 and 150 meters (300 to 500 ft). By focusing the radio signal using a directional antenna 802.11b can operate reliably over a distance of many kilometres (miles), although the technology's line-of-sight requirements hamper connectivity in areas with hilly or heavily foliated terrain. In addition, compared to hard-wired connectivity, there are security risks (unless robust security protocols are enabled); data rates are significantly slower (2 to 50 times slower); and the network can be less stable, due to interference from other wireless devices and networks, weather and line-of-sight problems.

Rural Wireless-ISP installations are typically not commercial in nature and are instead a patchwork of systems built up by hobbyists mounting antennas on radio masts and towers, agricultural storage silos, very tall trees, or whatever other tall objects are available. There are currently a number of companies that provide this service.

Motorola Canopy and other proprietary technologies offer wireless access to rural and other markets that are hard to reach using Wi-Fi or WiMAX.

WiMAX

WiMAX (Worldwide Interoperability for Microwave Access) is a set of interoperable implementations of the IEEE 802.16 family of wireless-network standards certified by the WiMAX Forum. WiMAX enables "the delivery of last mile wireless broadband access as an alternative to cable and DSL". The original IEEE 802.16 standard, now called "Fixed WiMAX", was published in 2001 and provided 30 to 40 megabit-per-second data rates. Mobility support was added in 2005. A 2011 update provides data rates up to 1 Gbit/s for fixed stations. WiMax offers a metropolitan area network with a signal radius of about 50 km (30 miles), far surpassing the 30-metre (100-foot) wireless range of a conventional Wi-Fi local area network (LAN). WiMAX signals also penetrate building walls much more effectively than Wi-Fi.

Satellite broadband

Satellites can provide fixed, portable, and mobile Internet access. It is among the most expensive forms of broadband Internet access, but may be the only choice available in remote areas. Data rates range from 2 kbit/s to 1 Gbit/s downstream and from 2 kbit/s to 10 Mbit/s upstream. Satellite communication typically requires a clear line of sight, will not work well through trees and other vegetation, is adversely affected by moisture, rain, and snow (known as rain fade), and may require a fairly large, carefully aimed, directional antenna.

Satellites in geostationary Earth orbit (GEO) operate in a fixed position 35,786 km (22,236 miles) above the earth's equator. Even at the speed of light (about 300,000 km/s or 186,000 miles per second), it takes a quarter of a second for a radio signal to travel from the earth to the satellite and back. When other switching and routing delays are added and the delays are doubled to allow for a full round-trip transmission, the total delay can be 0.75 to 1.25 seconds. This latency is large when compared to other forms of Internet access with typical latencies that range from 0.015 to 0.2 seconds. Long latencies can make some applications, such as video conferencing, voice over IP, multiplayer games, and remote control of equipment, that require a real-time response impracticable via satellite. TCP tuning and TCP acceleration techniques can mitigate some of these problems. GEO satellites do not cover the earth's polar regions. HughesNet and ViaSat are GEO systems.

Satellites in Low Earth orbit (LEO, below 2000 km or 1243 miles) and Medium earth orbit (MEO, between 2000 and 35,786 km or 1,243 and 22,236 miles) are less common, operate at lower altitudes, and are not fixed in their position above the earth. Lower altitudes allow lower latencies and make real-time interactive Internet applications feasible. LEO systems include Globalstar and Iridium. The O3b Satellite Constellation is a proposed MEO system with a latency of 125 ms. COMMStellation™ is a LEO system, scheduled for launch in 2015, that is expected to have a latency of just 7 ms.

Mobile broadband

Mobile broadband is the marketing term for wireless Internet access delivered through mobile phone towers to computers, mobile phones (called "cell phones" in North America and South Africa), and other digital devices using portable modems. Some mobile services allow more than one device to be connected to the Internet using a single cellular connection using a process called tethering. The modem may be built into laptop computers, tablets, mobile phones, and other devices, added to some devices using PC cards, USB modems, and USB sticks or dongles, or separate wireless modems can be used. Roughly every ten years new mobile phone technology and infrastructure involving a change in the fundamental nature of the service, non-backwards-compatible transmission technology, higher peak data rates, new frequency bands, wider channel frequency bandwidth in Hertz becomes available

Pricing

Dial-up users pay the costs for making local or long distance phone calls, usually pay a monthly subscription fee, and may be subject to additional per minute or traffic based charges, and connect time limits by their ISP. Though less common today than in the past, some dial-up access is offered for "free" in return for watching banner ads as part of the dial-up service. NetZero, BlueLight, Juno, Freenet (NZ), and Free-nets are examples of services providing free access. Some Wireless community networks continue the tradition of providing free Internet access.

Fixed broadband Internet access is often sold under an "unlimited" or flat rate pricing model, with price determined by the maximum data rate chosen by the customer, rather than a per minute or traffic based charge. Per minute and traffic based charges and traffic caps are common for mobile broadband Internet access.

With increased consumer demand for streaming content such as video on demand and peer-to-peer file sharing, demand for bandwidth has increased rapidly and for some ISPs the flat rate pricing model may become unsustainable. However, with fixed costs estimated to represent 80-90% of the cost of providing broadband service, the marginal cost to carry additional traffic is low. Most ISPs do not disclose their costs, but the cost to transmit a gigabyte of data in 2011 was estimated to be about $0.03.

Some ISPs estimate that about 5% of their users consume about 50% of the total bandwidth. To ensure these high-bandwidth users do not slow down the network for everyone, some ISPs are considering, are experimenting with, or have implemented combinations of traffic based pricing, time of day or "peak" and "off peak" pricing, and bandwidth or traffic caps.

In Canada, Rogers Hi-Speed Internet and Bell Canada have imposed bandwidth caps. Time Warner experimented with usage-based pricing in Beaumont, Texas. An effort by Time Warner to expand usage-based pricing into the Rochester, New York area met with public resistance, however, and was abandoned.

Growth in Number of Users

Access to the Internet grew from an estimated 10 million people in 1993, to almost 40 million in 1995, to 670 million in 2002, and to 2.45 billion in 2011. With market saturation, growth in the number of Internet users is slowing in industrialized countries, but continues in Asia, Africa, Latin America, the Caribbean, and the Middle East.

There were roughly 0.6 billion fixed broadband subscribers and almost 1.2 billion mobile broadband subscribers in 2011. In developed countries people frequently use both fixed and mobile broadband networks. In developing countries mobile broadband is often the only access method available.

Digital Divide

Despite its tremendous growth, Internet access is not distributed equally within or between countries.

The digital divide refers to "the gap between people with effective access to information and communications technology (ICT), and those with very limited or no access". The gap between people with Internet access and those without is one of many aspects of the digital divide. Whether someone has access to the Internet can depend greatly on financial status, geographical location as well as government policies. "Low-income, rural, and minority populations have received special scrutiny as the technological "have-nots."

Government policies play a tremendous role in bringing Internet access to or limiting access for underserved groups, regions, and countries. For example in Pakistan, which is pursuing an aggressive IT policy aimed at boosting its drive for economic modernization, the number of Internet users grew from 133,900 (0.1% of the population) in 2000 to 31 million (17.6% of the population) in 2011. In countries such as North Korea and Cuba there is relatively little access to the Internet due to the governments' fear of political instability that might accompany the benefits of access to the global Internet. The U.S. trade embargo is another barrier limiting Internet access in Cuba.

In the United States, billions of dollars has been invested in efforts to narrow the digital divide and bring Internet access to more people in low-income and rural areas of the United States. The Obama administration has continued this commitment to narrowing the digital divide through the use of stimulus funding. The National Center for Education Statistics reported that 98% of all U.S. classroom computers had Internet access in 2008 with roughly one computer with Internet access available for every three students. The percentage and ratio of students to computers was the same for rural schools (98% and 1 computer for every 2.9 students).

Access to computers is a dominant factor in determining the level of Internet access. In 2011, in developing countries, 25% of households had a computer and 20% had Internet access, while in developed countries the figures were 74% of households had a computer and 71% had Internet access. When buying computers was legalized in Cuba in 2007, the private ownership of computers soared (there were 630,000 computers available on the island in 2008, a 23% increase over 2007).

Internet access has changed the way in which many people think and has become an integral part of peoples economic, political, and social lives. Providing Internet access to more people in the world allow will them to take advantage of the "political, social, economic, educational, and career opportunities" available over the Internet. Several of the 67 principles adopted at the World Summit on the Information Society convened by the United Nations in Geneva in 2003, directly address the digital divide. To promote economic development and a reduction of the digital divide, national broadband plans have been and are being developed to increase the availability of affordable high-speed Internet access throughout the world.

Rural Access

One of the great challenges for Internet access in general and for broadband access in particular is to provide service to potential customers in areas of low population density, such as to farmers, ranchers, and small towns. In cities where the population density is high, it is easier for a service provider to recover equipment costs, but each rural customer may require expensive equipment to get connected. While 66% of Americans had an Internet connection in 2010, that figure was only 50% in rural areas, according to the Pew Internet & American Life Project. Virgin Media advertised over 100 towns across the United Kingdom "from Cwmbran to Clydebank" that have access to their 100 Mbit/s service.

Wireless Internet Service Provider (WISPs) are rapidly becoming a popular broadband option for rural areas. The technology's line-of-sight requirements may hamper connectivity in some areas with hilly and heavily foliated terrain. However, the Tegola project, a successful pilot in remote Scotland, demonstrates that wireless can be a viable option.

The Broadband for Rural Nova Scotia initiative is the first program in North America to guarantee access to "100% of civic addresses" in a region. It is based on Motorola Canopy technology. As of November 2011, under 1000 households have reported access problems. Deployment of a new cell network by one Canopy provider (Eastlink) was expected to provide the alternative of 3G/4G service, possibly at a special unmetered rate, for areas harder to serve by Canopy.

Access as a Human Right

Several countries have adopted laws that make Internet access a right by requiring the state to work to ensure that Internet access is broadly available and/or preventing states from unreasonably restricting an individual's access to information and the Internet:

— Costa Rica: A 30 July 2010 ruling by the Supreme Court of Costa Rica stated: "Without fear of equivocation, it can be said that these technologies [information technology and communication] have impacted the way humans communicate, facilitating the connection between people and institutions worldwide and eliminating barriers of space and time. At this time, access to these technologies becomes a basic tool to facilitate the exercise of fundamental rights and democratic participation (e-democracy) and citizen control, education, freedom of thought and expression, access to information and public services online, the right to communicate with government electronically and administrative transparency, among others. This includes the fundamental right of access to these technologies, in particular, the right of access to the Internet or World Wide Web."

— Estonia: In 2000, the parliament passed a law declaring Internet access a fundamental human right and launched a massive program to expand access to the countryside. The Internet, the government argues, is essential for life in the 21st century.

— Finland: By July 2010, every person in Finland was to have the right to a one-megabit per second broadband connection, according to the

Ministry of Transport and Communications. And by 2015, access to a 100 Mbit/s connection will be a legal right.

— France: In June 2009, the Constitutional Council, France's highest court, declared access to the Internet to be a basic human right in a strongly-worded decision that struck down portions of the HADOPI law, a law that would have tracked abusers and without judicial review automatically cut off network access to those who continued to download illicit material after two warnings

— Greece: Article 5A of the Constitution of Greece states that all persons has a right to participate in the Information Society and that the state has an obligation to facilitate the production, exchange, diffusion, and access to electronically transmitted information.

— Spain: Starting in 2011, Telefónica, the former state monopoly that holds the country's "universal service" contract, has to guarantee to offer "reasonably" priced broadband of at least one megabyte per second throughout Spain.

In December 2003, the World Summit on the Information Society (WSIS) was convened under the auspice of the United Nations. After lengthy negotiations between governments, businesses and civil society representatives the WSIS Declaration of Principles was adopted reaffirming the importance of the Information Society to maintaining and strengthening human rights:

1. We, the representatives of the peoples of the world, assembled in Geneva from 10–12 December 2003 for the first phase of the World Summit on the Information Society, declare our common desire and commitment to build a people-centred, inclusive and development-oriented Information Society, where everyone can create, access, utilize and share information and knowledge, enabling individuals, communities and peoples to achieve their full potential in promoting their sustainable development and improving their quality of life, premised on the purposes and principles of the Charter of the United Nations and respecting fully and upholding the Universal Declaration of Human Rights.

3. We reaffirm the universality, indivisibility, interdependence and interrelation of all human rights and fundamental freedoms, including the right to development, as enshrined in the Vienna Declaration. We

also reaffirm that democracy, sustainable development, and respect for human rights and fundamental freedoms as well as good governance at all levels are interdependent and mutually reinforcing. We further resolve to strengthen the rule of law in international as in national affairs.

The WSIS Declaration of Principles makes specific reference to the importance of the right to freedom of expression in the "Information Society" in stating:

4. We reaffirm, as an essential foundation of the Information Society, and as outlined in Article 19 of the Universal Declaration of Human Rights, that everyone has the right to freedom of opinion and expression; that this right includes freedom to hold opinions without interference and to seek, receive and impart information and ideas through any media and regardless of frontiers. Communication is a fundamental social process, a basic human need and the foundation of all social organisation. It is central to the Information Society. Everyone, everywhere should have the opportunity to participate and no one should be excluded from the benefits of the Information Society offers."

A poll of 27,973 adults in 26 countries, including 14,306 Internet users, conducted for the BBC World Service between 30 November 2009 and 7 February 2010 found that almost four in five Internet users and non-users around the world felt that access to the Internet was a fundamental right. 50% strongly agreed, 29% somewhat agreed, 9% somewhat disagreed, 6% strongly disagreed, and 6% gave no opinion.

The 88 recommendations made by the Special Rapporteur on the promotion and protection of the right to freedom of opinion and expression in a May 2011 report to the Human Rights Council of the United Nations General Assembly include several that bear on the question of the right to Internet access:

67. Unlike any other medium, the Internet enables individuals to seek, receive and impart information and ideas of all kinds instantaneously and inexpensively across national borders. By vastly expanding the capacity of individuals to enjoy their right to freedom of opinion and expression, which is an "enabler" of other human rights, the Internet boosts economic, social and political development, and contributes to the progress of humankind as a whole. In this regard, the Special

Rapporteur encourages other Special Procedures mandate holders to engage on the issue of the Internet with respect to their particular mandates.

78. While blocking and filtering measures deny users access to specific content on the Internet, States have also taken measures to cut off access to the Internet entirely. The Special Rapporteur considers cutting off users from Internet access, regardless of the justification provided, including on the grounds of violating intellectual property rights law, to be disproportionate and thus a violation of article 19, paragraph 3, of the International Covenant on Civil and Political Rights.
79. The Special Rapporteur calls upon all States to ensure that Internet access is maintained at all times, including during times of political unrest.
85. Given that the Internet has become an indispensable tool for realizing a range of human rights, combating inequality, and accelerating development and human progress, ensuring universal access to the Internet should be a priority for all States. Each State should thus develop a concrete and effective policy, in consultation with individuals from all sections of society, including the private sector and relevant Government ministries, to make the Internet widely available, accessible and affordable to all segments of population.

These statements, opinions, and recommendations have led to the suggestion that Internet access itself is or should become a fundamental human right.

Users of Internet

Overall Internet usage has seen tremendous growth. From 2000 to 2009, the number of Internet users globally rose from 394 million to 1.858 billion. By 2010, 22 percent of the world's population had access to computers with 1 billion Google searches every day, 300 million Internet users reading blogs, and 2 billion videos viewed daily on YouTube.

The prevalent language for communication on the Internet has been English. This may be a result of the origin of the Internet, as well as the language's role as a lingua franca. Early computer systems were limited to the characters in the American Standard Code for Information Interchange (ASCII), a subset of the Latin alphabet.

After English (27%), the most requested languages on the World Wide Web are Chinese (23%), Spanish (8%), Japanese (5%), Portuguese and German (4% each), Arabic, French and Russian (3% each), and Korean (2%). By region, 42% of the world's Internet users are based in Asia, 24% in Europe, 14% in North America, 10% in Latin America and the Caribbean taken together, 6% in Africa, 3% in the Middle East and 1% in Australia/ Oceania. The Internet's technologies have developed enough in recent years, especially in the use of Unicode, that good facilities are available for development and communication in the world's widely used languages. However, some glitches such as mojibake (incorrect display of some languages' characters) still remain.

In an American study in 2005, the percentage of men using the Internet was very slightly ahead of the percentage of women, although this difference reversed in those under 30. Men logged on more often, spent more time online, and were more likely to be broadband users, whereas women tended to make more use of opportunities to communicate (such as email). Men were more likely to use the Internet to pay bills, participate in auctions, and for recreation such as downloading music and videos. Men and women were equally likely to use the Internet for shopping and banking. More recent studies indicate that in 2008, women significantly outnumbered men on most social networking sites, such as Facebook and Myspace, although the ratios varied with age. In addition, women watched more streaming content, whereas men downloaded more. In terms of blogs, men were more likely to blog in the first place; among those who blog, men were more likely to have a professional blog, whereas women were more likely to have a personal blog.

References

Coffman, K. G; Odlyzko, A. M. (1998). *The size and growth rate of the Internet.* AT&T Labs. Retrieved 21 May.

John Mulcahy, (1989). *A Chronicle of Merit's Early History*, Merit Network, Ann Arbor, Michigan.

Karen D. Frazer, (1995). *NSFNET: A Partnership for High-Speed Networking, Final Report 1987-1995*, Merit Network, Inc.

Ronald J. Deibert, John G. Palfrey, Rafal Rohozinski, and Jonathan Zittrain (eds), *(2010) Access Controlled: The Shaping of Power, Rights, and Rule in Cyberspace*, MIT Press.

8

Sociology of the Internet

The sociology of the Internet involves the application of sociological theory and method to the Internet as a source of information and communication. Sociologists are concerned with the social implications of the technology; new social networks, virtual communities and ways of interaction that have arisen, as well as issues related to cyber crime, etc.

The Internet—the newest in a series of major information breakthroughs—is of interest for sociologists in various ways: as a tool for research, for example, in using online questionnaires instead of paper ones, as a discussion platform, and as a research topic. The sociology of the Internet in the stricter sense concerns the analysis of online communities (e.g. as found in newsgroups), virtual communities and virtual worlds, organizational change catalyzed through new media such as the Internet, and social change at-large in the transformation from industrial to informational society (or to information society). Online communities can be studied statistically through network analysis and at the same time interpreted qualitatively, such as through virtual ethnography. Social change can be studied through statistical demographics or through the interpretation of changing messages and symbols in online media studies.

The Internet is a relatively new phenomenon. As Robert Darnton wrote, it is a revolutionary change that "took place yesterday, or the day before, depending on how you measure it." The Internet developed from the ARPANET, dating back to 1969; as a term it was coined in 1974. The World Wide Web as we know it was shaped in the mid 1990s, when graphical interface and services like email became popular and reached wider (non-scientific and non-military) audiences and commerce. Internet Explorer was first released in 1995; Netscape a year earlier. Google was founded in 1998. Wikipedia was founded in 2001. Facebook, MySpace, and YouTube in the mid-2000s. Web 2.0 is still emerging. Steadily, the amount of information available on the net and the number of Internet users worldwide has continued to grow rapidly.

According to DiMaggio et al., research tends to focus on the Internet's implications in five domains:

- inequality (the issues of digital divide)
- community and social capital (the issues of time displacement)
- political participation (the issues of public sphere, deliberative democracy and civil society)
- organizations and other economic institutions
- cultural participation and cultural diversity

Early on there were predictions that the Internet would change everything (or nothing); over time, however, a consensus emerged that the Internet, at least in the current phase of development, complements rather than displaces previously implemented media. This has meant a rethinking of the 1990s ideas of "convergence of new and old media". Further, the Internet offers a rare opportunity to study changes caused by the newly emerged - and likely, still evolving - information and communication technology (ICT).

Social Impact

The Internet has created new forums of social interaction and social relations including social networking websites such as Facebook and MySpace and sites such as meetup.com and Couchsurfing which facilitate offline interaction.

Though virtual communities were once thought to be composed of strictly virtual social ties, researchers often find that even those social ties formed in virtual spaces are often maintained both online and offline

There are ongoing debates about the impact of the Internet on strong and weak ties, whether the internet is creating more or less social capital, the internet's role in trends towards social isolation, and whether it creates a more or less diverse social environment.

Political Organization and Censorship

The Internet has achieved new relevance as a political tool. The presidential campaign of Howard Dean in 2004 in the United States became famous for its ability to generate donations via the Internet, and the 2008 campaign of Barack Obama became even more so. Increasingly, social movements and other organizations use the Internet to carry out both traditional and the new Internet activism.

Governments are also getting on-line. Some countries, such as those of Cuba, Iran, North Korea, Myanmar, the People's Republic of China, and Saudi Arabia, use filtering and censoring software to restrict what people in their countries can access on the Internet. With United Kingdom, they also use software to locate and arrest various individuals they perceive as a threat. Other countries, including the United States, have enacted laws making the possession or distribution of certain material, such as child pornography, illegal, but do not use filtering software. In some countries Internet service providers have agreed to restrict access to sites listed by police.

Philanthropy

The spread of low-cost internet access in developing countries has opened up new possibilities for peer-to-peer charities, which allow individuals to contribute small amounts to charitable projects for other individuals. Websites such as Donors Choose and Global Giving now allow small-scale donors to direct funds to individual projects of their choice.

A popular twist on internet-based philanthropy is the use of peer-to-peer lending for charitable purposes. Kiva pioneered this concept in 2005, offering the first web-based service to publish individual loan profiles for funding. Kiva raises funds for local intermediary microfinance organizations which post stories and updates on behalf of the borrowers. Lenders can contribute as little as $25 to loans of their choice, and receive their money back as borrowers repay. Kiva falls short of being a pure peer-to-peer charity, in that loans are disbursed before being funded by lenders and borrowers do not communicate with lenders themselves. However, the recent spread of cheap internet access in developing countries has made genuine peer-to-peer connections increasingly feasible. In 2009 the US-based nonprofit Zidisha tapped into this trend to offer the first peer-to-peer microlending platform to link lenders and borrowers across international borders without local intermediaries. Inspired by interactive websites such as Facebook and eBay, Zidisha's microlending platform facilitates direct dialogue between lenders and borrowers and a performance rating system for borrowers. Web users worldwide can fund loans for as little as a dollar.

Leisure

The Internet has been a major source of leisure since before the World Wide Web, with entertaining social experiments such as MUDs and MOOs being conducted on university servers, and humor-related Usenet groups receiving much of the main traffic. Today, many Internet forums have sections devoted to games and funny videos; short cartoons in the form of Flash movies are also popular. Over 6 million people use blogs or message boards as a means of communication and for the sharing of ideas.

The pornography and gambling industries have both taken full advantage of the World Wide Web, and often provide a significant source of advertising revenue for other websites. Although governments have made attempts to censor internet porn, internet service providers have told governments that these plans are not feasible. Also many governments have attempted to put restrictions on both industries' use of the Internet, this has generally failed to stop their widespread popularity.

One area of leisure on the Internet is multiplayer gaming. This form of leisure creates communities, bringing people of all ages and origins to enjoy the fast-paced world of multiplayer games. These range from MMORPG to first-person shooters, from role-playing video games to online gambling. This has revolutionized the way many people interact and spend their free time on the Internet.

While online gaming has been around since the 1970s, modern modes of online gaming began with services such as GameSpy and MPlayer, to which players of games would typically subscribe. Non-subscribers were limited to certain types of gameplay or certain games.

Many use the Internet to access and download music, movies and other works for their enjoyment and relaxation. As discussed above, there are paid and unpaid sources for all of these, using centralized servers and distributed peer-to-peer technologies. Discretion is needed as some of these sources take more care over the original artists' rights and over copyright laws than others.

Many use the World Wide Web to access news, weather and sports reports, to plan and book holidays and to find out more about their random ideas and casual interests.

People use chat, messaging and e-mail to make and stay in touch with friends worldwide, sometimes in the same way as some previously had pen pals. Social networking websites like MySpace, Facebook and many others like them also put and keep people in contact for their enjoyment.

The Internet has seen a growing number of Web desktops, where users can access their files, folders, and settings via the Internet.

Cyberslacking has become a serious drain on corporate resources; the average UK employee spends 57 minutes a day surfing the Web at work, according to a study by Peninsula Business Services.

Social Networking

A social networking service is an online service, platform, or site that focuses on facilitating the building of social networks or social relations among people who, for example, share interests, activities, backgrounds, or real-life connections. A social network service consists of a representation of each user (often a profile), his/her social links, and a variety of additional services. Most social network services are web-based and provide means for users to interact over the Internet, such as e-mail and instant messaging. Online community services are sometimes considered as a social network service, though in a broader sense, social network service usually means an individual-centered service whereas online community services are group-centered. Social networking sites allow users to share ideas, activities, events, and interests within their individual networks.

The main types of social networking services are those that contain category places (such as former school year or classmates), means to connect with friends (usually with self-description pages), and a recommendation system linked to trust. Popular methods now combine many of these, with American-based services Facebook, Google+, and Twitter widely used worldwide; Nexopia in Canada; Badoo, Bebo, VKontakte, Draugiem.lv (mostly in Latvia), Hi5, Hyves (mostly in The Netherlands), iWiW (mostly in Hungary), Nasza-Klasa (mostly in Poland), Skyrock, The Sphere, StudiVZ (mostly in Germany), Tagged, Tuenti (mostly in Spain), and XING in parts of Europe; Hi5 and Orkut in South America and Central America; LAGbook in Africa; and Cyworld, Mixi, Orkut, renren,weibo and Wretch in Asia and the Pacific Islands.

There have been attempts to standardize these services to avoid the need to duplicate entries of friends and interests. A 2011 survey found that 47% of American adults use a social networking service.

History

The potential for computer networking to facilitate newly improved forms of computer-mediated social interaction was suggested early on. Efforts to support social networks via computer-mediated communication were made in many early online services, including Usenet, ARPANET, LISTSERV, and bulletin board services (BBS). Many prototypical features of social networking sites were also present in online services such as America Online, Prodigy, CompuServe, ChatNet, and The WELL. Early social networking on the World Wide Web began in the form of generalized online communities such as Theglobe.com (1995), Geocities (1994) and Tripod.com (1995).

Many of these early communities focused on bringing people together to interact with each other through chat rooms, and encouraged users to share personal information and ideas via personal webpages by providing easy-to-use publishing tools and free or inexpensive webspace. Some communities - such as Classmates.com - took a different approach by simply having people link to each other via email addresses. In the late 1990s, user profiles became a central feature of social networking sites, allowing users to compile lists of "friends" and search for other users with similar interests. New social networking methods were developed by the end of the 1990s, and many sites began to develop more advanced features for users to find and manage friends.

This newer generation of social networking sites began to flourish with the emergence of SixDegrees.com in 1997, followed by Makeoutclub in 2000, Hub Culture and Friendster in 2002, and soon became part of the Internet mainstream. Friendster was followed by MySpace and LinkedIn a year later, and eventually Bebo. Attesting to the rapid increase in social networking sites' popularity, by 2005, it was reported that MySpace was getting more page views than Google. Facebook, launched in 2004, became the largest social networking site in the world in early 2009.

Social Networking and Entertainment

Web-based social networking services make it possible to connect people who share interests and activities across political, economic, and geographic borders. Through e-mail and instant messaging, online communities are created where a gift economy and reciprocal altruism are encouraged through cooperation. Information is particularly suited to gift economy, as information is a nonrival good and can be gifted at practically no cost.

Facebook and other social networking tools are increasingly the object of scholarly research. Scholars in many fields have begun to investigate the impact of social-networking sites, investigating how such sites may play into issues of identity, privacy, social capital, youth culture, and education.

Several websites are beginning to tap into the power of the social networking model for philanthropy. Such models provide a means for connecting otherwise fragmented industries and small organizations without the resources to reach a broader audience with interested users. Social networks are providing a different way for individuals to communicate digitally. These communities of hypertexts allow for the sharing of information and ideas, an old concept placed in a digital environment.

In 2011, HCL Technologies conducted research that showed that 50% of British employers had banned the use of social networking sites/services during office hours.

Typical Features

According to Boyd and Ellison's (2007) article, "Why Youth (Heart) Social Network Sites: The Role of Networked Publics in Teenage Social Life", social networking sites (SNSs) share a variety of technical features that allows individuals to: construct a public/semi-public profile, articulate list of other users that they share a connection with, and view their list of connections within the system (6). The most basic of these are visible profiles with a list of "friends" who are also users of the site. In an article entitled "Social Network Sites: Definition, History, and Scholarship," Boyd and Ellison adopt Sunden's (2003) description of profiles as unique pages where one can "type oneself into being." A profile is generated from answers to questions, such as age, location, interests, etc. Some sites allow users to upload pictures, add multimedia content or modify the look and feel of the profile. Others, e.g., Facebook, allow users to enhance their profile by adding modules or "Applications." Many sites allow users to post blog entries, search for others with similar interests and compile and share lists of contacts. User profiles often have a section dedicated to comments from friends and other users. To protect user privacy, social networks typically have controls that allow users to choose who can view their profile, contact them, add them to their list of contacts, and so on.

Additional Features

Some social networks have additional features, such as the ability to create groups that share common interests or affiliations, upload or stream live videos, and hold discussions in forums. Geosocial networking co-opts Internet mapping services to organize user participation around geographic features and their attributes.

There is a trend towards more interoperability between social networks led by technologies such as OpenID and OpenSocial. In most mobile communities, mobile phone users can now create their own profiles, make friends, participate in chat rooms, create chat rooms, hold private conversations, share photos and videos, and share blogs by using their mobile phone. Some companies provide wireless services that allow their customers to build their own mobile community and brand it; one of the most popular wireless services for social networking in North America is Facebook Mobile.

Emerging Trends

As the increase in popularity of social networking is on a constant rise, new uses for the technology are constantly being observed.

At the forefront of emerging trends in social networking sites is the concept of "real-time web" and "location-based." Real-time allows users to contribute content, which is then broadcast as it is being uploaded - the concept is analogous to live radio and television broadcasts. Twitter set the trend for "real-time" services, wherein users can broadcast to the world what they are doing, or what is on their minds within a 140-character limit. Facebook followed suit with their "Live Feed" where users' activities are streamed as soon as it happens. While Twitter focuses on words, Clixtr, another real-time service, focuses on group photo sharing wherein users can update their photo streams with photos while at an event. Facebook, however, remains the largest photo sharing site - Facebook application and photo aggregator Pixable estimates that Facebook will have 100 billion photos by Summer 2011. In April, 2012, the image-based social media network Pinterest had become the third largest social network in the United States.

Companies have begun to merge business technologies and solutions, such as cloud computing, with social networking concepts. Instead of connecting individuals based on social interest, companies are developing interactive communities that connect individuals based on shared business needs or experiences. Many provide specialized networking tools and applications that can be accessed via their websites, such as LinkedIn. Others companies, such as Monster.com, have been steadily developing a more "socialized" feel to their career center sites to harness some of the power of social networking sites. These more business related sites have their own nomenclature for the most part but the most common naming conventions are "Vocational Networking Sites" or "Vocational Media Networks", with the former more closely tied to individual networking relationships based on social networking principles.

Foursquare gained popularity as it allowed for users to "check-in" to places that they are frequenting at that moment. Gowalla is another such service that functions in much the same way that Foursquare does, leveraging the GPS in phones to create a location-based user experience. Clixtr, though in the real-time space, is also a location-based social networking site, since events created by users are automatically geotagged, and users can view events occurring nearby through the Clixtr iPhone app. Recently, Yelp announced its entrance into the location-based social networking space through check-ins with their mobile app; whether or not this becomes detrimental to Foursquare or Gowalla is yet to be seen, as it is still considered a new space in the Internet technology industry.

One popular use for this new technology is social networking between businesses. Companies have found that social networking sites such as Facebook and Twitter are great ways to build their brand image. According to Jody Nimetz, author of Marketing Jive, there are five major uses for businesses and social media: to create brand awareness, as an online reputation management tool, for recruiting, to learn about new technologies and competitors, and as a lead generation tool to intercept potential prospects. These companies are able to drive traffic to their own online sites while encouraging their consumers and clients to have discussions on how to improve or change products or services.

Social Networks and Science

One other use that is being discussed is the use of social networks in the science communities. Julia Porter Liebeskind et al. have published a study on how new biotechnology firms are using social networking sites to share exchanges in scientific knowledge. They state in their study that by sharing information and knowledge with one another, they are able to "increase both their learning and their flexibility in ways that would not be possible within a self-contained hierarchical organization." Social networking is allowing scientific groups to expand their knowledge base and share ideas, and without these new means of communicating their theories might become "isolated and irrelevant".

Social Networks and Education

Social networks are also being used by teachers and students as a communication tool. Because many students are already using a wide range of social networking sites, teachers have begun to familiarize themselves with this trend in order to leverage student interest in relation to curriculum content. Some of this includes creating chat-room forums and groups to extend classroom discussion to posting assignments, tests and quizzes, through to assisting with homework outside of the classroom setting. Social network services are also being used to foster teacher-parent communication. These services make it possible and more convenient for parents to ask questions and voice concerns without having to meet face-to-face with their children's teachers.

The advent of social networking platforms may also be impacting the way(s) in which learners engage with technology in general. For a number of years, Prensky's (2001) dichotomy between Digital Natives and Digital Immigrants has been considered a relatively accurate representation of the ease with which people of a certain age range—in particular those born before and after 1980—use technology. Prensky's theory has been largely disproved, however, and not least on account of the burgeoning popularity of social networking sites and other metaphors such as White and Le Cornu's "Visitors" and "Residents" (2011) are greater currency.

The use of online social networks by school libraries is also increasingly prevalent and they are being used to communicate with potential library users, as well as extending the services provided by individual school libraries.

Social networks and their educational uses are of interest to many researchers. According to Livingstone and Brake (2010), "Social networking sites, like much else on the internet, represent a moving target for researchers and policy makers." Recent trends indicate that 47% of American adults use a social network. A national survey in 2009 found that 73% of online teenagers use SNS, which is an increase from 55% three years earlier. (Lenhart, Purcell, Smith, & Zickuhr, 2010) Recent studies have shown that social network services provide opportunities within professional education, curriculum education, and learning. However, there are constraints in this area.

Professional Uses within Education

Professional use of social networking services refers to the employment of a network site to connect with other professionals within a given field of interest. SNSs like LinkedIn, a social networking website geared towards companies and industry professionals looking to make new business contacts or keep in touch with previous co-workers, affiliates, and clients. Other network sites are now being used in this manner, Twitter has become [a] mainstay for professional development as well as promotion and online SNSs support both the maintenance of existing social ties and the formation of new connections.

Much of the early research on online communities assume that individuals using these systems would be connecting with others outside their preexisting social group or location, liberating them to form communities around shared interests, as opposed to shared geography. Other researchers have suggested that the professional use of network sites produce "social capital." For individuals, social capital allows a person to draw on resources from other members of the networks to which he or she belongs. These resources can take the form of useful information, personal relationships, or the capacity to organize groups.

As well, networks within these services also can be established or built by joining special interest groups that others have made, or creating one and asking others to join.

Curriculum Uses within Education

According to Doering, Beach and O'Brien, a future English curriculum needs to recognize a major shift in how adolescents are communicating with each other. Curriculum uses of social networking services also can include sharing curriculum-related resources. Educators tap into user-generated content to find and discuss curriculum-related content for students. Responding to the popularity of social networking services among many students, teachers are increasingly using social networks to supplement teaching and learning in traditional classroom environments as they can provide new opportunities for enriching existing curriculum through creative, authentic and/or flexible, non-linear learning experiences. Some social networks, such as English, baby! and LiveMocha, are explicitly education-focused and couple instructional content with an educational peer environment. The new Web 2.0 technologies built into most social networking services promote conferencing, interaction, creation, research on a global scale, enabling educators to share, remix, and repurpose curriculum resources. In short, social networking services can become research networks as well as learning networks.

Learning Uses within Education

Educators and advocates of new digital literacies are confident that social networking encourages the development of transferable, technical, and social skills of value in formal and informal learning. In a formal learning environment, goals or objectives are determined by an outside department or agency. Tweeting, instant messaging, or blogging enhances student involvement. Students who would not normally participate in class are more apt to partake through social network services. Networking allows participants the opportunity for just-in-time learning and higher levels of engagement. The use of SNSs allow educators to enhance the prescribed curriculum. When learning experiences are infused into a website, students utilize everyday for fun, students realize that learning can and should be a part of everyday life. It does not have to be separate and unattached. Informal learning consists of the learner setting the goals and objectives. It has been claimed that media no longer just influence our culture. They are our culture. With such a high number of users between the ages of 13-18, a number of skills are developed. Participants hone technical skills in choosing to navigate through social networking services. This includes elementary items such as sending an instant message or updating a status. The development of new media skills are paramount in helping youth navigate the digital world with confidence. Social networking services foster learning through what Jenkins (2006) describes as a "Participatory Culture." A participatory culture consists of a space that allows engagement, sharing, mentoring, and an opportunity for social interaction. Participants of social network services avail of this opportunity. Informal learning, in the forms of participatory and social learning online, is an excellent tool for teachers to sneak in material and ideas that students will identify with and therefore, in a secondary manner, students will learn skills that would normally be taught in a formal setting in the more interesting and engaging environment of social learning. Sites like Twitter provide students with the opportunity to converse and collaborate with others in real time. Social networking services provide a virtual "space" for learners. James Gee (2004) suggests that affinity spaces instantiate participation, collaboration, distribution, and dispersion of expertise, and relatedness. Registered users share and search for knowledge which contributes to informal learning.

Constraints of Social Networking Services in Education

In the past social networking services were viewed as a distraction and offered no educational benefit. Blocking these social networks was a form of protection for students against wasting time, bullying, and privacy protection. In an education setting, Facebook is seen by many instructors and educators as a frivolous, time-wasting distraction from schoolwork, and it is not uncommon to have Facebook banned at junior high or high school computer labs. Cyberbullying has become an issue of concern with social networking services. According to the UK Children Go Online survey of 9-19 year olds found that a third have received bullying comments online. To avoid this problem, many school districts/boards have blocked access to social networking services like Facebook, MySpace, Twitter, and so on, within the school environment. Social networking services often include a lot of personal information posted publicly and many believe that sharing personal information is a window into privacy theft. Schools have taken action to protect students from this. It is believed that this outpouring of identifiable information and the easy communication vehicle that social networking services opens the door to sexual predators, cyberbullying, and cyberstalking. However, there is evidence to contradict this. 69% of social media using teens and 85% of adults believe that people are mostly kind to one another on social network sites Recent research suggests that there has been a shift in blocking the use of social networking services. In many cases, the opposite is occurring as the potential of online networking services is being realized. It has been suggested that if schools block them [social networking services], they're preventing students from learning the skills they need. Banning social networking [...] is not only inappropriate but also borderline irresponsible when it comes to providing the best educational experiences for students. Schools and school districts have the option of educating safe media usage as well as incorporating digital media into the classroom experience, thus preparing students for the literacy they will encounter in the future.

Social Networks and Grassroots Organizing

Social networks are being used by activists as a means of low-cost grassroots organizing. Extensive use of an array of social networking sites enabled organizers of the 2009 National Equality March to mobilize an estimated 200,000 participants to march on Washington with a cost savings of up to 85% per participant over previous methods. The August 2011 England riots were similarly considered to have escalated and been fuelled by this type of grassroots organization.

Social Networks and Employment

A final rise in social network use is being driven by college students using the services to network with professionals for internship and job opportunities. Many studies have been done on the effectiveness of networking online in a college setting, and one notable one is by Phipps Arabie and Yoram Wind published in Advances in Social Network Analysis. Many schools have implemented online alumni directories which serve as makeshift social networks that current and former students can turn to for career advice. However, these alumni directories tend to suffer from an oversupply of advice-seekers and an undersupply of advice providers. One new social networking service, Ask-a-peer, aims to solve this problem by enabling advice seekers to offer modest compensation to advisers for their time.

Social Network Hosting Service

A social network hosting service is a web hosting service that specifically hosts the user creation of web-based social networking services, alongside related applications. Such services are also known as vertical social networks due to the creation of SNSes that cater to specific user interests and niches; like larger, interest-agnostic SNSes, such niche networking services may also possess the ability to create increasingly niche groups of users. An example for this is Ning.

Business Model

Few social networks currently charge money for membership. In part, this may be because social networking is a relatively new service, and the value of using them has not been firmly established in customers' minds. Companies such as MySpace and Facebook sell online advertising on their site. Their business model is based upon large membership count, and charging for membership would be counterproductive. Some believe that the deeper information that the sites have on each user will allow much better targeted advertising than any other site can currently provide.

Social networks operate under an autonomous business model, in which a social network's members serve dual roles as both the suppliers and the consumers of content. This is in contrast to a traditional business model, where the suppliers and consumers are distinct agents. Revenue is typically gained in the autonomous business model via advertisements, but subscription-based revenue is possible when membership and content levels are sufficiently high.

Social Interaction

Put simply, social networking is a way for one person to meet up with other people on the net. People use social networking sites for meeting new friends, finding old friends, or locating people who have the same problems or interests they have, called niche networking.

More and more relationships and friendships are being formed online and then carried to an offline setting. Psychologist and University of Hamburg professor Erich H. Witte says that relationships which start online are much more likely to succeed. Witte has said that in less than 10 years, online dating will be the predominant way for people to start a relationship. One online dating site claims that 2% of all marriages begin at its site, the equivalent of 236 marriages a day. Other sites claim 1 in 5 relationships begin online.

Social networking sites play a vital role in this area as well. Being able to meet someone as a "friend" and see what common interests you share and how you have built up your friend base and "likes" you can truly see a fuller picture of the person you are talking with. Most sites are free instead of being pay based which allows younger people with stricter budgets to enjoy some of the same features as those of adults who are more likely to be able to afford pay based sites. While not the intended or original use for these social sites, a large area of their current function has stemmed from people wanting to meet other people in person and with the extremely busy schedules of most people, it is a fast, reliable and easy way in which to do so that costs you little time and money (if any). Users do not necessarily share with others the content which is of most interest to them, but rather that which projects a good impression of themselves.

New Trends in Social Networking

Nextdoor is a new private social networking site aimed at neighborhoods to help strength and enhance social ties. This SNS will help to bring together communities since neighbors drifted away because of the digital era.

More and more Americans are using social networking sites as their primary sources for information. The percentage of those who have used social networking sites to find news has increased, and nearly doubled, from 9% to 19% since 2010. This percentage is higher than those who get their news from other social media sites, new blogs and news podcasts.

Issues in Social Networking

Privacy

Privacy concerns with social networking services have been raised growing concerns amongst users on the dangers of giving out too much personal information and the threat of sexual predators. Users of these services also need to be aware of data theft or viruses. However, large services, such as MySpace and Netlog, often work with law enforcement to try to prevent such incidents.

In addition, there is a perceived privacy threat in relation to placing too much personal information in the hands of large corporations or governmental bodies, allowing a profile to be produced on an individual's behavior on which decisions, detrimental to an individual, may be taken.

Furthermore, there is an issue over the control of data—information that was altered or removed by the user may in fact be retained and/or passed to third parties. This danger was highlighted when the controversial social networking site Quechup harvested e-mail addresses from users' e-mail accounts for use in a spamming operation.

In medical and scientific research, asking subjects for information about their behaviors is normally strictly scrutinized by institutional review boards, for example, to ensure that adolescents and their parents have informed consent. It is not clear whether the same rules apply to researchers who collect data from social networking sites. These sites often contain a great deal of data that is hard to obtain via traditional means. Even though the data are public, republishing it in a research paper might be considered invasion of privacy.

Privacy on social networking sites can be undermined by many factors. For example, users may disclose personal information, sites may not take adequate steps to protect user privacy, and third parties frequently use information posted on social networks for a variety of purposes. "For the Net generation, social networking sites have become the preferred forum for social interactions, from posturing and role playing to simply sounding off. However, because such forums are relatively easy to access, posted content can be reviewed by anyone with an interest in the users' personal information".

Following plans by the UK government to monitor traffic on social networks schemes similar to E-mail jamming have been proposed for networks such as Twitter and Facebook. These would involve "friending" and "following" large numbers of random people to thwart attempts at network analysis.

Data Mining

Through data mining, companies are able to improve their sales and profitability. With this data, companies create customer profiles that contain customer demographics and online behavior. A recent strategy has been the purchase and production of "network analysis software". This software is able to sort out through the influx of social networking data for any specific company. Facebook has been especially important to marketing strategists. Facebook's controversial and new "Social Ads" program gives companies access to the millions of profiles in order to tailor their ads to a Facebook user's own interests and hobbies. However, rather than sell actual user information, Facebook sells tracked "social actions". That is, they track the websites a user uses outside of Facebook through a program called Facebook Beacon.

Notifications on Websites

There has been a trend for social networking sites to send out only 'positive' notifications to users. For example sites such as Bebo, Facebook, and MySpace will not send notifications to users when they are removed from a person's friends list. Likewise, Bebo will send out a notification if a user is moved to the top of another user's friends list but no notification is sent if they are moved down the list.

This allows users to purge undesirables from their list extremely easily and often without confrontation since a user will rarely notice if one person disappears from their friends list. It also enforces the general positive atmosphere of the website without drawing attention to unpleasant happenings such as friends falling out, rejection and failed relationships.

Access to Information

Many social networking services, such as Facebook, provide the user with a choice of who can view their profile. This prevents unauthorized user(s) from accessing their information. Parents who want to access their child's MySpace or Facebook account have become a big problem for teenagers who do not want their profile seen by their parents. By making their profile private, teens can select who may see their page, allowing only people added as "friends" to view their profile and preventing unwanted viewing of the profile by parents. Most teens are constantly trying to create a structural barrier between their private life and their parents.

To edit information on a certain social networking service account, the social networking sites require you to login or provide a password. This prevents unauthorized user(s) from adding, changing, or removing personal information, pictures, and/or other data.

Potential for Misuse

The relative freedom afforded by social networking services has caused concern regarding the potential of its misuse by individual patrons. In October 2006, a fake MySpace profile created in the name of Josh Evans by Lori Janine Drew led to the suicide of Megan Meier.[not in citation given]

The event incited global concern regarding the use of social networking services for bullying purposes.In July 2008, a Briton, Grant Raphael, was ordered to pay a total of GBP £22,000 (about USD $44,000) for libel and breach of privacy. Raphael had posted a fake page on Facebook purporting to be that of a former schoolfriend Matthew Firsht, with whom Raphael had fallen out in 2000. The page falsely claimed that Firsht was homosexual and that he was dishonest.

At the same time, genuine use of social networking services has been treated with suspicion on the ground of the services' misuse. In September 2008, the profile of Australian Facebook user Elmo Keep was banned by the site's administrators on the grounds that it violated the site's terms of use. Keep is one of several users of Facebook who were banned from the site on the presumption that their names aren't real, as they bear resemblance to the names of characters like Sesame Street's Elmo.

Risk for Child Safety

Citizens and governments have been concerned with misuse by child and teenagers of social networking services, in particular in relation to online sexual predators. Overuse of social networking may also make children more susceptible to depression and anxiety.

A certain number of actions have been engaged by governments to better understand the problem and find some solutions.[specify] A 2008 panel concluded that technological fixes such as age verification and scans are relatively ineffective means of apprehending online predators. In May 2010, a child pornography social networking site with hundreds of members was dismantled by law enforcement. It was deemed "the largest crimes against children case brought anywhere by anyone."

Social networking can also be a risk to child safety in another way; parents can get addicted to games and neglect their children. One instance in South Korea resulted in the death of a child from starvation.

Trolling

A common misuse of social networking sites such as Facebook is that it is occasionally used to emotionally abuse individuals. Such actions are often referred to as trolling. It is not rare for confrontations in the real world to be translated online. Trolling can occur in many different forms, such as (but not limited to) defacement of deceased person(s) tribute pages, name calling, playing online pranks on volatile individuals and controversial comments with the intention to cause anger and cause arguments. Trolling is not to be confused with cyber-bullying.

Online bullying

Online bullying, also called cyber-bullying, is a relatively common occurrence and it can often result in emotional trauma for the victim. Depending on the networking outlet, up to 39% of users admit to being "cyber-bullied". Danah Boyd, a researcher of social networks quotes a teenager in her article, Why Youth (Heart) Social Network Sites. The teenager expresses frustration towards networking sites like MySpace because it causes drama and too much emotional stress. There are not many limitations as to what individuals can post when online. Individuals are given the power to post offensive remarks or pictures that could potentially cause a great amount of emotional pain for another individual.

Interpersonal communication

Interpersonal communication has been a growing issue as more and more people have turned to social networking as a means of communication. "Benniger (1987) describes how mass media has gradually replaced interpersonal communication as a socializing force. Further, social networking sites have become popular sites for youth culture to explore themselves, relationships, and share cultural artifacts". Many teens and social networking users may be harming their interpersonal communication by using sites such as Facebook and MySpace. Stated by Baroness Greenfield, an Oxford University Neuroscientist, "My fear is that these technologies are infantilizing the brain into the state of small children who are attracted by buzzing noises and bright lights, who have a small attention span and who live for the moment." The convenience that social network sites give users to communicate with one another can also damage their interpersonal communication. Sherry Turkle, the founder and director of the MIT Initiative on Technology and Self, stated, "Networked, we are together, but so lessened are our expectations of each other that we feel utterly alone. And there is the risk that we come to see others as objects to be accessed—and only for the parts we find useful, comforting, or amusing." Furthermore, social network sites can create insincere friendships, Turkle also noted, "They nurture friendships on social-networking sites and then wonder if they are among friends. They become confused about companionship."

Psychological Effects of Social Networking

As social networking sites have risen in popularity over the past years, people have been spending an excessive amount of time on the Internet in general and social networking sites in specific. This has led researchers to debate the establishment of Internet addiction as an actual clinical disorder. Social networking can also affect the extent to which a person feels lonely. In a Newsweek article, Johannah Cornblatt explains "Social-networking sites like Facebook and MySpace may provide people with a false sense of connection that ultimately increases loneliness in people who feel alone." John T. Cacioppo, a neuroscientist at the University of Chicago, claims that social networking can foster feelings of sensitivity to disconnection, which can lead to loneliness. However some scholars have expressed that concerns about social networking are often exaggerated and poorly researched.

Patents

There has been rapid growth in the number of US patent applications that cover new technologies related to social networking. The number of published applications has been growing rapidly since 2003. There are now over 3500 published applications. As many as 7000 applications may be currently on file including those that haven't been published yet. Only about 400 of these applications have issued as patents, however, due largely to the multi-year backlog in examination of business method patents and the difficulty in getting these patent applications allowed.

It has been reported that social networking patents are important for the establishment of new start-up companies. It has also been reported, however, that social networking patents inhibit innovation. On June 15, 2010, the United States Patent and Trademark Office awarded Amazon.com a patent for a "Social Networking System" based on its ownership of PlanetAll. The patent describes a Social Networking System as

A networked computer system provides various services for assisting users in locating, and establishing contact relationships with, other users. For example, in one embodiment, users can identify other users based on their affiliations with particular schools or other organizations. The system also provides a mechanism for a user to selectively establish contact relationships or connections with other users, and to grant permissions for such other users to view personal information of the user. The system may also include features for enabling users to identify contacts of their respective contacts. In addition, the system may automatically notify users of personal information updates made by their respective contacts.

The patent has garnered attention due to its similarity to the popular social networking site Facebook.

Worker's Rights

What types of speech workers are protected from being fired for on social networking websites has been an issue for American companies with over 100 complaints as of 2011 on this topic having been made to the National Labor Relations Board (NLRB). The National Labor Relations Act protects workers from being fired for "protected concerted activity," which prevents workers from being fired for collective action, while allowing companies the right to fire workers for individual actions they take against the company. Companies are concerned with the potential damage comments online can do to public image due to their visibility and accessibility, but despite over 100 cases being presented thus far to NLRB only 1 has led to a formal ruling, leaving uncertainty as to the boundaries of what types of speech the NLRB will ultimately put in place.

Decentralized Architecture

Most of the existing SNS sites use one or multiple dedicated data centers to serve its all users. Such infrastructure-based systems faces over-provisioning during non-peak hours, while may encounter service outage during peak hours, due to the highly dynamic of SNS users' activities. There are several proposals, leveraging a decentralized architecture to ensure the scalability of SNS sites with low infrastructure cost. These proposals include Fethr uaOSN , and Cuckoo .

Investigations

Social networking services are increasingly being used in legal and criminal investigations. Information posted on sites such as MySpace and Facebook has been used by police (forensic profiling), probation, and university officials to prosecute users of said sites. In some situations, content posted on MySpace has been used in court.

Facebook is increasingly being used by school administrations and law enforcement agencies as a source of evidence against student users. This site being the number one online destination for college students, allows users to create profile pages with personal details. These pages can be viewed by other registered users from the same school, which often include resident assistants and campus police who have signed up for the service. One UK police force has sifted pictures from Facebook and arrested some people who had been photographed in a public place holding a weapon such as a knife (having a weapon in a public place is illegal).

Application Domains

Government applications

Social networking is more recently being used by various government agencies. Social networking tools serve as a quick and easy way for the government to get the opinion of the public and to keep the public updated on their activity. The Centers for Disease Control demonstrated the importance of vaccinations on the popular children's site Whyville and the National Oceanic and Atmospheric Administration has a virtual island on Second Life where people can explore underground caves or explore the effects of global warming. Likewise, NASA has taken advantage of a few social networking tools, including Twitter and Flickr. They are using these tools to aid the Review of U.S. Human Space Flight Plans Committee, whose goal it is to ensure that the nation is on a vigorous and sustainable path to achieving its boldest aspirations in space.

Business applications

The use of social networking services in an enterprise context presents the potential of having a major impact on the world of business and work.

Social networks connect people at low cost; this can be beneficial for entrepreneurs and small businesses looking to expand their contact bases. These networks often act as a customer relationship management tool for companies selling products and services. Companies can also use social networks for advertising in the form of banners and text ads. Since businesses operate globally, social networks can make it easier to keep in touch with contacts around the world.

Two examples of social networking being used for business purposes are LinkedIn.com and Youngblackprofessionals.org. LinkedIn aims to interconnect professionals. LinkedIn has over 100 million users in over 200 countries. Youngblackprofessionals.org or YBP aims to do the same thing, but is targeted toward professional minorities. .

Another is the use of physical spaces available to members of a social network such as Hub Culture, an invitation-only social network for entrepreneurs, and other business influentials, with Pavilions in major cities such as London, UK. Having a physical presence allows members to network in the real world, as well as the virtual, adding extra business value.

Applications for social networking sites have extended toward businesses and brands are creating their own, high functioning sites, a sector known as brand networking. It is the idea that a brand can build its consumer relationship by connecting their consumers to the brand image on a platform that provides them relative content, elements of participation, and a ranking or score system. Brand networking is a new way to capitalize on social trends as a marketing tool.

The power of social networks it beginning to permeate into internal culture of businesses where they are finding uses for collaboration, file sharing and knowledge transfer. The term Enterprise Social Software is becoming increasingly popular for these types of applications.

Dating applications

Many social networks provide an online environment for people to communicate and exchange personal information for dating purposes. Intentions can vary from looking for a one time date, short-term relationships, and long-term relationships.

Most of these social networks, just like online dating services, require users to give out certain pieces of information. This usually includes a user's age, gender, location, interests, and perhaps a picture. Releasing very personal information is usually discouraged for safety reasons. This allows other users to search or be searched by some sort of criteria, but at the same time people can maintain a degree of anonymity similar to most online dating services. Online dating sites are similar to social networks in the sense that users create profiles to meet and communicate with others, but their activities on such sites are for the sole purpose of finding a person of interest to date. Social networks do not necessarily have to be for dating; many users simply use it for keeping in touch with friends, and colleagues.

However, an important difference between social networks and online dating services is the fact that online dating sites usually require a fee, where social networks are free. This difference is one of the reasons the online dating industry is seeing a massive decrease in revenue due to many users opting to use social networking services instead. Many popular online dating services such as Match.com, Yahoo Personals, and eHarmony.com are seeing a decrease in users, where social networks like MySpace and Facebook are experiencing an increase in users.

The number of Internet users in the U.S. that visit online dating sites has fallen from a peak of 21% in 2003 to 10% in 2006. Whether its the cost of the services, the variety of users with different intentions, or any other reason, it is undeniable that social networking sites are quickly becoming the new way to find dates online.

Educational applications

The National School Boards Association reports that almost 60 percent of students who use social networking talk about education topics online, and more than 50 percent talk specifically about schoolwork. Yet the vast majority of school districts have stringent rules against nearly all forms of social networking during the school day — even though students and parents report few problem behaviors online.

Social networks focused on supporting relationships between teachers and their students are now used for learning, educator professional development, and content sharing. Ning for teachers, TermWiki, Learn Central, TeachStreet and other sites are being built to foster relationships that include educational blogs, eportfolios, formal and ad hoc communities, as well as communication such as chats, discussion threads, and synchronous forums. These sites also have content sharing and rating features.

Social networks are also emerging as online yearbooks, both public and private. One such service is MyYearbook, which allows anyone from the general public to register and connect. A new trend emerging is private label yearbooks accessible only by students, parents, and teachers of a particular school, similar to Facebook's beginning within Harvard.

Finance applications

The use of virtual currency systems inside social networks create new opportunities for global finance. Hub Culture operates a virtual currency Ven used for global transactions among members, product sales and financial trades in commodities and carbon credits. In May 2010, Carbon pricing contracts were introduced to the weighted basket of currencies and commodities that determine the floating exchange value of Ven. The introduction of carbon to the calculation price of the currency made Ven the first and only currency that is linked to the environment.

Medical and health applications

Social networks are beginning to be adopted by healthcare professionals as a means to manage institutional knowledge, disseminate peer to peer knowledge and to highlight individual physicians and institutions. The advantage of using a dedicated medical social networking site is that all the members are screened against the state licensing board list of practitioners.

A new trend is emerging with social networks created to help its members with various physical and mental ailments. For people suffering from life altering diseases, PatientsLikeMe offers its members the chance to connect with others dealing with similar issues and research patient data related to their condition. For alcoholics and addicts, SoberCircle gives people in recovery the ability to communicate with one another and strengthen their recovery through the encouragement of others who can relate to their situation. DailyStrength is also a website that offers support groups for a wide array of topics and conditions, including the support topics offered by PatientsLikeMe and SoberCircle.

Some social networks aim to encourage healthy lifestyles in their users. SparkPeople offers community and social networking tools for peer support during weight loss. Fitocracy and QUENTIQ are focused on exercise, enabling users to share their own workouts and comment on those of other users.

Social and political applications

Social networking sites have recently showed a value in social and political movements. In the Egyptian revolution, Facebook and Twitter both played a pivotal role in keeping people connected to the revolt. Egyptian activists have credited social networking sites with providing a platform for planning protest and sharing news from Tahrir Square in real time. By presenting a platform for thousands of people to instantaneously share videos of mainly events featuring brutality, social networking proves to be a vital tool in revolutions.

References

Allison Cavanagh, (2007). *Sociology in the Age of the Internet*, McGraw-Hill International.

Christine Hine, , (2005). *Virtual Methods: Issues in Social Research on the Internet*, Berg Publishers.

D. R. Wilson, , (2004). *Researching Sociology on the Internet*, Thomson/Wadsworth.

Daniel A. Menchik and Xiaoli Tian. (2008). "Putting Social Context into Text: The Semiotics of Email Interaction."*The American Journal of Sociology*. 114:2. pp. 332–70.

Joan Ferrante-Wallace, Joan Ferrante, (1996). *Sociology.net: Sociology on the Internet*, Thomson Wadsworth.

John A. Bargh and Katelyn Y. A. McKenna, (2004). *The Internet and Social Life*, Annual Review of Psychology, Vol. 55: 573-590.

Rob Kling, (1997). The Internet for Sociologists, *Contemporary Sociology*, Vol. 26, No. 4 pp. 434–444

9

Internet Marketing and E-Commerce

Internet marketing, also known as web marketing, online marketing, webvertising, or e-marketing, is referred to as the marketing (generally promotion) of products or services over the Internet. Internet marketing is considered to be broad in scope because it not only refers to marketing on the Internet, but also includes marketing done via e-mail and wireless media. Digital customer data and electronic customer relationship management (ECRM) systems are also often grouped together under internet marketing.

Internet marketing ties together the creative and technical aspects of the Internet, including design, development, advertising and sales. Internet marketing also refers to the placement of media along many different stages of the customer engagement cycle through search engine marketing (SEM), search engine optimization (SEO), banner ads on specific websites, email marketing, content marketing, mobile advertising, and Web 2.0 strategies.

When Internet Marketing includes designing the company's website, social media sites, mobile and other interactive media for specific [business] goals, the terms Digital Marketing is then used because it helps the company position itself not only on the Internet but on Digital Media or the Digital World.

Internet marketing initiatives for the same company are usually tied together in the company's Internet (or Digital) Stategy, which is design specifically for each client based on its business needs and goals.

In 2008, The New SpaFag Times, working with comScore, published an initial estimate to quantify the user data collected by large Internet-based companies. Counting four types of interactions with company websites in addition to the hits from advertisements served from advertising networks, the authors found that the potential for collecting data was up to 2,500 times per user per month.

Types of Internet Marketing

Internet marketing is broadly divided in to the following types:

- *Display advertising:* the use of web banners or banner ads placed on a third-party website or blog to drive traffic to a company's own website and increase product awareness.
- *Search engine marketing (SEM)*: a form of marketing that seeks to promote websites by increasing their visibility in search engine result pages (SERPs) through the use of either paid placement, contextual advertising, and paid inclusion, or through the use of free search engine optimization techniques.
- *Search engine optimization (SEO):* the process of improving the visibility of a website or a web page in search engines via the "natural" or un-paid ("organic" or "algorithmic") search results.
- *Social media marketing*: the process of gaining traffic or attention through social media websites such as Facebook, Twitter and LinkedIn.
- *Email marketing*: involves directly marketing a commercial message to a group of people using electronic mail.
- *Referral marketing:* a method of promoting products or services to new customers through referrals, usually word of mouth.
- *Affiliate marketing:* a marketing practice in which a business rewards one or more affiliates for each visitor or customer brought about by the affiliate's own marketing efforts.
- *Inbound marketing:* involves creating and freely sharing informative content as a means of converting prospects into customers and customers into repeat buyers.
- *Content marketing*: involves creating and freely sharing specific, expert content to help the community understand one or many subjects dealt with on a specific website. It is a mean to pull interested people or prospects into the website trying to convert them into customers or free suscribers, and customers into repeat buyers.

- *Video marketing*: This type of marketing specializes in creating videos that engage the viewer into a buying state by presenting information in video form and guiding them to a product or service Online video is increasingly becoming more popular among internet users and companies are seeing it as a viable method of attracting customers.

Business Models

Internet marketing is associated with several business models:

- *E-commerce*: a model whereby goods and services are sold directly to consumers (B2C), businesses (B2B), or from consumer to consumer (C2C) using computers connected to a network.
- *Lead-based websites:* a strategy whereby an organization generates value by acquiring sales leads from its website. Similar to walk-in customers in retail world. These prospects are often referred to as organic leads.
- *Affiliate Marketing:* a process wherein a product or service developed by one entity is sold by other active sellers for a share of profits. The entity that owns the product may provide some marketing material (e.g., sales letters, affiliate links, tracking facilities, etc.); however, the vast majority of affiliate marketing relationships come from e-commerce businesses that offer affiliate programs.
- *Local Internet marketing:* a strategy through which a small company utilizes the Internet to find and to nurture relationships that can be used for real-world advantages. Local Internet marketing uses tools such as social media marketing, local directory listing, and targeted online sales promotions.

One-to-One Approaches

In a one-to-one approach, marketers target a user browsing the Internet alone and so that the marketers' messages reach the user personally. This approach is used in search marketing, for which the advertisements are based on search engine keywords entered by the users. This approach usually works under the pay per click (PPC) method.

Appeal to Specific Interests

When appealing to specific interests, marketers place an emphasis on appealing to a specific behavior or interest, rather than reaching out to a broadly defined demographic. These marketers typically segment their markets according to age group, gender, geography, and other general factors.

Appealing to specific users can be achieved through behavioral targeting which refers to the use of behavioral patterns and putting up the relevant content suitable to the viewer's interest obtained from the user through cookies and other tools and contextual advertising which refers to the publishing of advertisements and ads based on the context the user in. For example if the user is searching for coffee, the search engine publishes ads related to coffee.

Niche Marketing

In conventional niche marketing, clusters of consumers (the niche) are identified in order to more economically and efficiently target them. Similarly, niche internet marketing attempts to create a more direct advertising message for those who are seen as most likely to buy the product being advertised.

Niche internet marketing focuses on marketing products and services which are, or can appear, tailor-made for a specific subset of consumers who are expected to buy the product or service with a specific motivation. The online advertising message (or product web site) can then be similarly tailor-made to target that assumed motivation. In combination with Search Engine Optimization, the niche internet marketer can attempt to increase the likelihood that their product's advertisement (or site) will be seen by customers in the relevant niche.

For example, if one sells designer dog sweaters, one might first consider the prospective customer who would be interested in these dog sweaters. One would then consider the motivation that this customer would have in buying a designer dog sweater (e.g. "My dog needs to look stylish.") One can then attempt to determine using keyword research which keywords might be best suited to weave into the page or advertisement in order to maximize the likelihood that it will be seen by people who are searching for a product which fulfills the targeted motivation.

Geo-targeting

In Internet marketing, geo targeting and geo marketing are the methods of determining the geolocation of a website visitor with geolocation software, and delivering different content to that visitor based on his or her location, such as latitude and longitude, country, region or state, city, metro code or zip code, organization, Internet Protocol (IP) address, ISP, and other criteria.

As more and more users replace traditional desktop internet browsing with mobile browsing, interactive marketers will be able to take advantage of more precise geo-targeting functionality. Location-aware mobile applications allows marketers to use GPS technology to determine a user's location, and to serve accurately location specific content.

Electronic Commerce

Electronic commerce, e-commerce or ecommerce consists primarily of the distributing, buying, selling, marketing, and servicing of products or services over electronic systems such as the Internet and other computer networks. The information technology industry might see it as an electronic business application aimed at commercial transactions. It can involve electronic funds transfer, supply chain management, e-marketing, online marketing, online transaction processing, electronic data interchange, automated inventory management systems, and automated data-collection systems. It typically uses electronic communications technology such as the Internet, extranets, e-mail, Ebooks, databases, and mobile phones.

E-commerce encompasses three distinct types of transactions: those between businesses, those between businesses and consumers, and government services. These transactions are supported by the information technology infrastructure, consisting of hardware, software and enabling services. E-commerce provides a powerful means of diffusing the advantages of networking throughout the economy, based on a platform provided by the information technology sector. This sector is strong and growing, as demonstrated by increasing shares of gross domestic product (GDP).

Internet-based business-to-business electronic commerce creates new market structures that enable business partners to switch allegiances at low cost, since the Internet expands choices and options to suppliers and consumers on an exponential basis. In addition, it enables contracting parties to exchange information, best practices and market feedback in real time. Countries left out of the loop could experience the costs of severe economic isolation in this highly competitive environment. Recent findings by Computer Economics, an e-business adviser to corporations, suggest that while e-commerce will continue to boom in the next decade, Africa, South America and parts of Asia could be left out of the trade revolution.

In US, the information technology sector has grown from just under 5 percent of the economy in 1985 to just under 8 percent in 1997. Given that prices for information technology goods and services have fallen dramatically – for example, the cost of microprocessing computing power has fallen from US$230 to US$3.42 per MIPS (millions of instructions per second) since 1991 – this increasing share of GDP is even more impressive. The story is the same in Canada. The information and communications technology sector accounted for 5 percent of GDP in 1990, increasing to over 7 percent in 1996. This sector accounted for 30 percent of total economic growth between 1990 and 1996, with compound annual growth rates of 7.6 percent during this period, compared with 1.5 percent for the total economy.

Electronic commerce will spur continuing growth in the information technology sector. Given its potential to change how business is done, electronic commerce will have even broader impacts, promising to accelerate growth not only in the information technology sector itself, but also across all sectors of the economy, such as manufacturing and retailing. The intrinsic advantage of the Internet as a platform for electronic commerce rests on the open, non-proprietary nature of the network: the Internet allows businesses to use a global, interactive means of infrmation exchange at a low cost.

While some would argue that such a capability already exists through existing communications networks such as telephone, fax or proprietary networks, the Internet offers an unmatchable combination of interactivity, versatility, low cost and speed. The implications of worldwide, low-cost information exchange are profound. The full potential of computerised design, manufacturing, delivery and services may now be realised by linking all parts of a distribution chain together, from product concept, design, testing, and manufacturing to marketing, after sales and service.

For example, software designers and automotive manufacturers can test concepts and prototypes with users, and demand forecasts can be immediately passed from marketing to production and the supply chain. As a result, efficiency and productivity are increased through lower procurement costs, reduced processing errors, reduced inventories, and faster time to market. For example, by linking marketing to manufacturing and procurement, IBM improved inventory turns and experienced savings of US$500 million due to lower investment and operating costs. Automotive companies have reduced material flow to the supply chain from up to six to less than two weeks.

Companies are also adopting the Internet as a base for business transactions to gain a competitive advantage, often at the insistence of other business partners in a supply chain. These forces are expected to result in the rapid growth of business-to-business electronic commerce. From the consumer's perspective, electronic commerce offers significant benefits. Convenience, increased access to information, lower prices, and choice are benefits cited most often by consumers. For example, a small business, Unique Patterns Design of Halifax, Nova Scotia, is able to offer custom patterns that are tailor-made for each customer.

Electronic commerce is also being used to support purchases made in conventional retail channels, as it allows consumers to gather information and comparison shop on-line. Products and services most suited to electronic sale are those that are information intensive and can be delivered digitally, or tangible products that do not require tactile examination and can be easily shipped. Early leaders in consumer electronic commerce have fit this profile, most notably financial services, computer hardware and software, travel, entertainment, and books and CDs.

Electronic commerce has widespread benefits beyond those related to the transaction of business. Governments at all levels are turning to the Internet as a means of increasing the range, reach and availability of their services. Services are available 24 hours a day, seven days a week, independent of location. The costs of providing these services can be significantly reduced for both users and governments. Electronic delivery of government services will also facilitate the future integration of government services from different departments and different levels of government. Other public sector institutions such as those in the education and health sectors are also using the Internet as an affordable tool to increase the reach of their services.

Computer-based training can provide information which is immediately available and tailored to specific needs, making the goal of lifelong learning more attainable. In the health care sector, the Internet is being used to allow rural or remote doctors, clinics and hospitals to access specialised knowledge and services usually found only in urban centers, and to diffuse information to the public. Most broadly, networking promises to allow citizens to participate more fully in society and create new sense of community through greatly improved means of communications.

The potential for electronic commerce is real. However, limiting factors exist, many based on the Internet itself, including issues of universal access, governance, and the future capacity of the underlying network.Access to the Internet, while growing, is far from universal: in Canada, 36 percent of households own a personal computer, and 13 percent had Internet connections in 1997. If Internet access from home, work, school and elsewhere is included, access is just over 30 percent. The majority of large businesses and an estimated 43 percent of small businesses have Internet access.

While these levels of access are among the best in the world, they do not come close to the near-universal penetration of established communications technologies such as the telephone. E-commerce promises to transform the conduct of business, consumer and government transactions, offering the benefits of more efficient supply chains, greater convenience and choice, and lower cost of doing business. However, before these benefits are realised, businesses and consumers want to know that transactions are private and secure, that legal and financial frameworks exist to support transactions and that the information infrastructure works. Many possible scenarios exist for the future of electronic commerce.

Optimists assume that these issues will be addressed and that electronic commerce will continue to grow. The contrary, pessimistic belief is that growth in electronic commerce, particularly growth in on-line sales, will stagnate as underlying problems remain unresolved, which could lead to a spin-drying of the Internet into smaller managed proprietary networks. Electronic commerce promises to be a major generator of jobs and growth in the next century, through improvements in the productivity of business, growth in consumer transactions, and development of the supporting information technology infrastructure. Experience has shown that early leaders quickly establish market dominance. Those who enter first are able to help shape evolving rules as well as business and consumer behaviour.

Canada enjoys many advantages that position it to compete effectively in electronic commerce. Canada has the highest standing of post-secondary education enrolment in the world, ranked first in knowledge workers by the World Economic Forum. Its telecommunications infrastructure is world class – it has among the lowest telephone costs in the world and the lowest Internet access charges among G-7 countries; it is second only to the United States in telephone mainlines and Internet hosts per capita among G-7 countries; and it has many pioneering telecommunications and information technology companies that are recognised worldwide. Analysis of the challenges facing the use and growth of electronic commerce, reflecting views from business, consumers, provinces and territories, as well as international organisations, points to four key areas for electronic commerce action in Canada.

Most business relationships, whether between a consumer and a company or between firms, require a strong element of confidence and trust. The impersonal and remote nature of electronic commerce places a heavy burden on the need for means to reduce or eliminate risk. Security, privacy and consumer protection are all required to instill trust in electronic commerce, for both businesses and consumers. A body of rules that govern how business and government transactions are conducted has developed over time. To remove barriers to the use of electronic commerce, these rules need to be examined to assess how they apply to the digital world, and adapted where necessary, to create a level playing field which is predictable and consistent for all kinds of commerce.

Electronic commerce will not grow without a strong platform that includes network access and availability, and open standards.Electronic commerce is part of a broader process of economic, social and cultural change, characterised by the globalisation of markets and the shift toward an economy based on knowledge and information. Opportunities for jobs and growth created by elec-tronic commerce need to be distributed as widely as possible among citizens, consumers and businesses, through development of skills and awareness, and government leadership as model users.

The Canadian electronic commerce strategy is based on the recognition that the private sector has the key role in developing and expanding electronic commerce in Canada. Government's role is to provide a supportive and responsive policy environment for businesses and consumers, one that allows for market flexibility while ensuring a minimum baseline for a fair marketplace. Countries that can provide such environments will be better positioned to compete internationally. To this end, the Canadian government and private sector are working together to implement the Canadian electronic commerce strategy.

Electronic commerce is intrinsically global. The actions of any one country will have limited impact unless they are part of a larger international framework. Canada's commitment to the international agenda is demonstrated by hosting the OECD Ministerial Conference on Electronic Commerce, in Ottawa, October 7-9, 1998. The conference includes governments and international organisations as well as business, labour and consumer interests. It leads to the establishment of agreements and action plans spelling out the current and future roles of government, international organisations and the private sector in addressing key electronic commerce issues. The Ministerial Conference represents the culmination of a series of electronic commerce conferences held by the OECD, beginning with a conference focussing on consumer views held in Paris in March 1997, followed by a conference focussing on business views held in Turku, Finland, in November 1997.

In November 1997, APEC leaders agreed to the development of a work plan for electronic commerce. Under the direction of a task force co-chaired by Australia and Singapore, the first phase of the work plan – consisting of benchmarking electronic commerce developments in member countries – has been completed. The second phase of the programme is being reviewed by leaders at their meeting in Kuala Lumpur in November 1998, including the development of an electronic commerce vision statement to promote the use of electronic commerce in the region, and the development of recommendations for technical cooperation and capacity building, public sector use of electronic commerce, and outreach programmes targeted at small and medium-sized enterprises (SMEs).In addition to the Task Force, APEC Ministers of Telecommunications and Information Industries approved a reference framework for action to guide the work of telecommunications groups on a range of electronic commerce issues.

Canada has also taken a leadership role in ensuring that the trade disciplines of the WTO apply to electronic commerce. At the second WTO Ministerial in May 1998, members agreed to launch a comprehensive study of the trade policy aspects of electronic commerce, with a view to providing recommendations to ministers for future actions by the third Ministerial in 1999.

Measures developed for conventional commerce may be inadequate to provide trust in the digital economy. For example, while once data were held securely within an organisation, either in paper-based files or in internal computer systems, now the Internet and hybrid forms such as extranets and intranets allow for potentially widespread information access. Issues of security once related only to law enforcement, not to protecting on-line transactions. Government baselines exist for business and consumer protection, but key issues – such as the verification of the identity of parties and the determination of transaction jurisdictions within a global context – remain unaddressed. In addressing these issues, both governments and the private sector have a role. Governments can legislate or regulate, while looking to the private sector to introduce voluntary codes and develop technological solutions. Many of the elements of building trust involve both federal, provincial and territorial governments – the Uniform Law Conference of Canada, and the Consumer Measures Committee established under the Internal Trade Agreement, are pivotal in establishing model laws and providing guidance on consistent national approaches.

Secure electronic transactions can be provided through the use of cryptographic technologies and certification authorities. These authorities, by binding parties to their respective digital signatures, provide authentication as to the identity of the transacting parties. Cryptographic technologies also provide for the integrity and confidentiality of the messages that are exchanged, and ensure that neither party to the transaction can deny its participation in the exchange of information (otherwise known as non-repudiation). The benefits of cryptography for electronic commerce, privacy protection and crime prevention are clear. It is equally true that cryptographic technologies can be used to hide criminal activity and to threaten national security.

Investigations, prosecutions, and the enforcement of laws and regulations could be hampered without lawful access to the evidence of illegal activity. Canada does not restrict the freedom of choice of individuals or businesses to import or use cryptography. Users are free to determine what kinds of authentication and encryption products and services they need. Canada controls the export of cryptography along with 32 other nations that are members of the Wassenaar Arrangement, which stipulates which products require export permits and which do not.

Canadian cryptography policy is under review in order to ensure that it contributes to the realisation of Canada's goal to be a leader in the use of electronic commerce, and to ensure that it reflects an appropriate balance among business, human rights and privacy interests, public safety and law enforcement, and national security interests. The policy, released in the fall of 1998, provides greater certainty for the business community, more confidence for consumers and support for law enforcement and national security. The strategy for the protection of privacy is to put the Canadian Standards Association National Standard into effect through light legislation, complemented by private sector action and consumer awareness.

The Government of Canada's fall 1998 private sector information privacy legislation strikes a balance between industry's interest in compiling and using personal information and the consumer's right to have personal information adequately protected. Consultations held during early 1998 found that there is strong support for using the Canadian Standards Association (CSA) Model Code for the Protection of Personal Information (also referred to as the CSA National Standard), as the basis for any such law, and the Office of the Privacy Commissioner of Canada as the oversight agency. There is also general agreement on the need for a consistent approach among federal and provincial privacy laws for the private sector. While to date, only Quebec has legislation, there is strong support for the use of the CSA Standard as the starting point for any new legislation.

Canada has led the world in developing a National Standard for the protection of privacy. This Standard, developed by businesses, consumers and governments, addresses the way organisations collect, use, disclose and protect information, and the way individuals access personal information. An informed public is vital to the protection of personal information. Both the private sector and governments can work to raise awareness of privacy issues and ensure that citizens know their rights and the best way to protect their personal data.

For example, the partnership of the federal government and Stentor to fund a multimedia game, Privacy Playground: The First Adventure of the Three Little Cyberpigs, to raise privacy awareness among children. The government encourages the development and use of such technologies for the lawful protection of its citizens. The Working Group on Consumers and Electronic Commerce, composed of consumer and business associations and governments, is finalising Canadian guidelines on consumer protection in electronic commerce. The guidelines define consumer protection requirements and provide the basis for development of voluntary and legislative measures related to consumer information, contract formation, privacy, security and redress.

A range of consumer protection legislation already exists in Canada, in both provincial and federal spheres. The Consumer Measures Committee established under the Agreement on Internal Trade is considering ways to address consumer protection in electronic commerce. Consumer Protection Rights in Canada in the Context of Electronic Commerce, a report prepared by the legal firm of Gowling, Strathy & Henderson, is being used as a basis for discussion. The Government of Canada is also looking at provisions under the Competition Act governing deceptive trade practices and misleading advertising. Governments, business and consumer groups agree that voluntary codes can play a vital role in areas not covered by legislation.

For example, the Canadian Code of Practice for Consumer Debit Card Services, established in 1992 by consumer groups, businesses, and provincial and federal governments, has successfully guided consumer protection practices of financial institutions. The Working Group on Consumers and Electronic Commerce will be addressing consumer awareness in the guidelines on consumer protection in electronic commerce, including the need for consumers to be provided with advice on how to minimise the risks entailed in electronic transactions, and legal rights and obligations.

Technology can provide the tools to make information available to consumers. Examples include posting information on laws that apply in different jurisdictions, and posting seals of approval on Web sites that meet defined criteria. As new forms of business practice evolve, marketplace rules play a critical role in creating codes of conduct – for example in the use of electronic signatures, the assignment of liability, and the protection of trademarks. Without clear rules, the use and growth of electronic commerce will be stalled.

The overriding need is to remove barriers to the use of electronic commerce by clarifying how these rules apply to the digital economy and updating them where necessary. The objective is to ensure that equivalent treatment is provided for digital and non-digital transactions in a consistent and predictable manner. Business has clearly stated that clarifying marketplace rules should be the government's top priority. Consistency among and between provinces and territories and the federal government is critical, particularly for legal and commercial frameworks.

The Uniform Law Conference of Canada (ULCC) is playing a leadership role in this regard. All government and business operations are subject to law. Law has traditionally presumed the presence of paper records – that presumption is no longer valid. As a result, the application of law to paperless transactions may lead to uncertain results. Governments are acting to make adjustments to laws to bring certainty to the use of technology. Over 300 federal statutes contain provisions requiring documents to be "in writing" or equivalent words. Rather than have each department amend legislation piecemeal, the Government of Canada's fall 1998 electronic documents legislation allows departments to adopt a set of general provisions authorising the use of electronic communications.

Provinces and territories are being encouraged to undertake statutory reforms along similar lines, as set out in the Uniform Electronic Commerce Actapproved in principle by the ULCC in August 1998. Many legal rules and the law of evidence assume the existence of paper, signed or original records. While most electronic records are, in practice, being admitted in litigation, the courts have struggled with the traditional rules of evidence with inconsistent results. The ULCC approved the Uniform Electronic Evidence Actin August 1998, which evaluates the integrity of an electronic record by considering evidence of the reliability of the record-keeping system that generated the record. The federal Department of Justice has proposed amending the Canada Evidence Act, to make it consistent with the ULCC Uniform Electronic Evidence Act.

Provinces and territories will also consider amending their legislation to reflect the ULCC Uniform Evidence Act. The challenge is to link the electronic signature to the person signing the electronic document. The Government of Canada is proposing that what makes an electronic signature trustworthy is the use of a reliable technology, such as digital signature technology, combined with a reliable certification authority (CA), such as those operating under the Government of Canada Public Key Infrastructure (GOC PKI) and those CAs that have cross-certification or are otherwise recognised by the GOC PKI.Internet Service Providers and other Internet intermediaries have expressed concern about the possible extent of their liability with respect to areas covered by a number of federal and provincial laws – e.g. obscenity, copyright, consumer protection, fraud and defamation – which may result from actions of their clients. The uncertainty surrounding liability may be an impediment to investment in electronic commerce and to its pace of development.

The OECD has reviewed legal frameworks applicable to content in its member countries. The Government of Canada has released for comment a study on Internet content-related liability and is currently analysing the issue. In the longer term, impacts on other aspects of legal frameworks such as corporate and competition laws will be of interest.The view of both Canadian and international taxation authorities has been that current tax systems and structures founded on basic principles of neutrality, fairness, certainty and simplicity will continue to be appropriate to address the changes brought about by electronic transactions. Attention has been focussed on ensuring that tax administration can keep up with changes in the market. The Minister of National Revenue's Advisory Committee on Electronic Commerce issued a report in April 1998 titled Electronic Commerce and Canada's Tax Administrationthat examines how existing taxation systems apply to electronic commerce. The report examines, among other issues, jurisdictional questions (e.g. the concept of a permanent residency), impacts of disintermediation (the splintering of intermediary services) on tax collection, and tax compliance.

The Government of Canada's response to the report was released in the fall of 1998. Given the global reach of electronic commerce, most of these issues can only be dealt with in an international context. Canada is participating with other OECD member countries in developing international implementation strategies that will include the implications of electronic commerce on tax treaties, transfer pricing guidelines, the application of consumption taxes and customs duties and tariffs.

In May 1998, WTO members agreed to refrain from applying customs duties on the electronic products and services delivered electronically and to review this decision at the third WTO Ministerial meeting in 1999. A two-track approach, linking a comprehensive WTO work programme on electronic commerce with a moratorium on customs duties, was based on a proposal submitted by Canada to the General Council in April 1998, and was later adopted by ministers of the QUAD (Canada, the U.S., the Commission of the European Union and Japan). Financial firms are rapidly expanding their delivery channels, by using new communications technologies to broaden the geographic scope of their operations and obtain more convenient, cost-effective links with customers.

Financial intermediaries, such as banks, credit unions, brokerages and insurance agencies, are supplementing personal branch banking with on-line services through the Internet, telephone networks and automated teller machines. Intermediaries are applying new digital technologies to reduce their cash-handling costs and simplify payment processing. With the help of new technology, specialised financial service providers are entering the sector, increasing competition and leading to the unbundling of services in certain markets. For example, brokers offering both trading and securities market information are now competing with on-line brokers who simply trade and provide no other services. Changing delivery channels are intrinsically linked to opportunities to create new products and services.

Technologies such as risk management tools, digital certification and cryptography create potential for new products such as automated sourcing of capital, on-line clearing and payment intermediaries, and information brokerage. Canada's financial institutions are involved in the development of new technology that may improve the efficiency of transactions and consumer convenience while helping to ensure privacy and the security of financial information. These changes are having an impact on the nature and structure of the Canadian financial services sector. The (MacKay) Task Force on the Future of the Canadian Financial Services Sector, which reported to the government in September 1998, made recommendations aimed at ensuring the sector's ability to meet global competitive challenges and the interests of consumers, and to take advantage of technological advances.

The global nature of electronic commerce also raises issues related to cross-border transactions in financial services. These issues are being examined by both national governments and international bodies such as the Basle Committee on Banking Supervision and the World Trade Organisation. Intellectual property (IP) laws establish the rules for the ownership and use of key types of digital content central to the development of electronic commerce, such as music, computer programs, video and multimedia works. In addition to the need for clear rules on ownership and access to content, other key IP issues include liability of Internet intermediaries, trademarks and domain names, and database protection.

New international agreements and other forms of cooperation are being considered to address these concerns, through the WIPO, the FTAA, APEC and the OECD. Canada is an active player in these discussions. Canada's national IP legislation is being reviewed to determine whether it needs to be adapted and whether it will be in Canada's interest to undertake any new international obligations. WIPO member countries adopted two new treaties in December 1996, the WIPO Copyright Treaty and the WIPO Performances and Phonograms Treaty. These treaties give right-holders including authors, performers and record producers an exclusive right to make their works, performances and sound recordings available through interactive media on a demand basis.

Canadian banks are partnering in the development of new electronic payment systems based on smart cards that allow consumers to purchase goods and services using prepaid electronic "value" in lieu of cash. The value is typically stored on an integrated circuit in a plastic card and can be read using special devices including point of sale terminals. Special encryption software helps ensure the security of the electronic value. Some electronic money systems allow for the transfer of value over communications networks as well as direct, person-to-person transfers. They also contain provisions with respect to copy protection and rights management information, among other new rights. Canada signed the WIPO treaties in December 1997, but has not yet ratified them. In July 1998, the government released two discussion papers that consider what, if any, amendments to the Canadian Copyright Actwould be necessary in order to comply with the treaties.

Canada's copyright legislation, as amended in 1997, already provides a framework for copyright protection that is largely up-to-date compared with legislation in many countries.The Canadian government is currently analysing the issue of the liability of Internet intermediaries, such as Internet Service Providers, for intellectual property infringements, as part of its ongoing consultations on Internet content-related liability. WIPO is also considering certain aspects of liability, including applicable law and jurisdiction. Ongoing reform of the Canadian and international domain name systems (DNS) has highlighted the need to ensure that these systems and other Internet practices reflect IP rights and obligations appropriately, notably trade-marks.

One major structural problem is that the Internet is international, whereas trade-marks law is national in scope. WIPO, with private sector input, has convened an international process to solicit recommendations on IP issues associated with the DNS. Progress on the reform of the Canadian DNS has also led to the recognition that a balanced approach is needed.In the context of increased availability of data through electronic means, databases are more and more important in a knowledge-based economy.

E-commerce in Banking and Financial Sector

Early computers were used for scientific and military purposes, not for commerce. The banking and finance sector has been a rapid adopter of e-commerce. The sector displays many characteristics that will facilitate the adoption and extension of e-commerce activities, such as the importance of product over location, many of its key services are easily virtualised, and great importance is placed on quick response times. For some time now most of the transactions between banks in the payments system have been undertaken electronically.

Banking systems have also progressively automated deposit taking and payments. Key developments have included the now widespread acceptance and utilisation of ATMs and EFTPOS. Use of Internet banking is also growing rapidly. Of the 1.7 million Australians using the Internet regularly, nearly 150 000 are involved in Internet banking. This is a threefold increase from a year ago. Internet consultancy www.consult projects that there will be about 270 000 Internet banking users by the beginning of 2 000. Most users are expected to extend their existing banking relationships. While the four big domestic banks have Internet-banking offerings, the Commonwealth Bank is the largest. Forty five per cent of regular Internet banking users bank online with the Commonwealth Bank and nearly 30 per cent with Westpac. National Australia Bank is Australia's biggest banker to small business. Users of NAB Internet Banking, are reported to have increased from 8 000 to 26 000 in two months and are signing up at twice the rate of personal customers.

Electronic Banking

E-banks are able to design their business without wasteful and lower value 'bricks and mortar' assets and liabilities. They may have a 'second mover advantage' because they do not have to face the cost of restructuring. There is evidence that they are able to offer financial services at prices well below traditional firms. This has not had an impact in the Australian banking industry at present. This may be because the traditional banks still offered a wider range of services that customers considered safe or perhaps reflect the fact that Australia's major banks have been quick to develop their own relatively sophisticated online banking functionality. The Commonwealth Bank was online in December 1995 and had Internet Banking in February 1997.

Nevertheless, traditional banking approaches are increasingly under competitive pressure. Relationship marketing is becoming more difficult as more organisations enter the market. Banking and finance institutions now face competition from online trading organisations that gain a complete picture of a consumer's financial relationships by building around the equity holdings and into banking, insurance, superannuation, etc. This can lead to an unbundling and rebundling of services. Bill-paying over the Internet is likely to become usiness-as-usual within just a few years. The Gartner Group predicts that in two years virtually all banks will offer online bill payment, and industry analysts believe that Internet portals such as America Online (AOL) and Yahoo! will soon be offering online payment under their own brands. AOL's Rob Shenk says, 'A lot of people have stock portfolios, but everyone has a checking account. So it's a much more elemental service.'A reluctance on the part of customers to switch to new providers may make sense: good financial relationships should not be thrown away for the sake of small short– term savings.

Growth of Internet banking and new competitors does not imply the end of traditional banks or financial services brokers. Reflecting existing strengths and consumer awareness, it may be a matter of changes in roles and involvement at different levels. One example of the transfer of value from the industry is the bundling of financial services as part of another transaction, e.g. buying a car, or factory equipment. The finance can be provided or facilitated by a party other than one from the industry, distancing banking and finance from their customers, or replacing them. However, if banking and finance take a higher view of their role, using a business event model this opens opportunities for creating value and improving relationships using e-commerce in ways which it would be too expensive to do face-to-face. There are issues here of who has the 'right' or credibility to provide the service, i.e. who bundles whom.

The transfer of value occurs if the service that brokers offer is unbundled. Brokers currently offer advice, risk management and execution. Risk management could be unbundled to the insurance sector, or new participants could enter using e-commerce services. Banks from smaller countries in Scandinavia and Europe have been very aggressive in penetrating larger European markets with an Internet banking presence. Is there a scope for entry of banks from abroad into Australia using a similar strategy? There is no evidence to indicate that there has been a significant transfer of value to overseas firms through widespread offshore banking or other financial transactions.

In contrast, there is anecdotal evidence to indicate that despite falling transaction costs and improved information, many investors find overseas investment or deposit in overseas banks to be too risky. Industry sources indicate however that there is some scope for migration of this service, albeit over time. The inflow of value from overseas is not significant and would be predominantly from the acquisition of international banking operations by the Australian banks and any associated movement of functions to Australia.

For example The Bank of New Zealand owned by NAB operates its Internet site and undertakes all its processing in Australia including monitoring and supporting its ATM network. E-commerce is a major enabler of this, specifically EDI, the Internet and other dedicated networking systems. The opportunities opened up by e-commerce is a factor driving change in the banking and financial services sector. Use of e-commerce is shifting demand and supply in the sector to lower cost more convenient service delivery channels.

In meeting the broad range of financial service needs that customers have within a single entity, the distinction between banks and other traditional financial service roles is becoming blurred. The potential of online financial services has reduced many barriers to entry and is increasing competitive pressures. It is likely that cost savings that will result from this process will be passed on to consumers.

The IT industries have a number of unusual characteristics. They are among the fastest growing industries. Technological change is rapid and product life cycles are short. Most product and service prices are falling rather than rising. Convergence in the industries is leading to the increasing inter-relation and interdependence of computing, communications and the media. This is also profoundly changing the structure and dynamics of the IT industries. Change in the IT industries and their capacity is driving change in the use of e-commerce while the IT industries are also being driven by changes in e-commerce usage. The IT industries extend through a value chain including electronics to computing and telecomm-unications platforms, office equipment and consumer electronics, telecommunications carriage and services, IT services and to information and entertainment services.

Computing power has been doubling every 18 months for the past 30 years. At the same time, the average price of a transistor has fallen by six orders of magnitude, due to microprocessor development. In just six years, the cost of microprocessor computing power decreased from $230 to $3.42 per MIPS. No other manufactured item has decreased in cost so far, so fast. Whether traded or non-traded, the IT industries are growing strongly at a rate in excess of ten per cent per annum. It is estimated that approximately 500 000 Australians are employed by, or spend a substantial part of their time engaged in the commercial activities of the information industries.

Official statistics indicate that use of IT in Australia by the private sector is high: companies employing 100 or more people are almost fully computerised; 50 per cent of smaller companies are computerised and this rate is growing.Use of e-commerce by the IT industries. The IT industries have been rapid adopters of e-commerce technologies and business models. The biggest advances in this sector have been in business-to-business e-commerce. More use is being made of e-commerce to facilitate the purchase of goods and services by consumers, but it is still very much behind the magnitude of sales made between businesses.

The IT industry is now able to deliver many of its products using e-commerce. Items such as software and documentation that traditionally had to be shipped can now be delivered online. Hardware is also becoming upgradeable without the need to physically replace parts. Software can be delivered online to allow customers to upgrade hardware such as modem cards. In general, there are many areas where businesses in the IT industries or their customers are using e-commerce to reduce supply chain costs, or enhance their convenience.

Warehousing, inventory and the volume of product in the cycle are much less than would otherwise be. This has also reduced the real estate required to store the inventory. The number of suppliers has been reduced, Cisco now tends to deal with the original manufacturer and manufacturers of components. The additional suppliers added time to the process and also forced Cisco to be a manufacturer. In some cases, Cisco has eliminated its own involvement. The other major elimination that has occurred is in the number of trips provided by the transport sector, now that many deliveries take place directly from the supplier to the customer. Cisco builds virtually all its products to order, so there are very few off-the-shelf products. Before the company established an Internet sales capability, ordering a product could be complicated.

Generally, an engineer at the customer site knew what type of product was needed and how it should be configured. The engineer communicated this information to his procurement department who then created the purchase order and sent it to Cisco via fax, phone or email. A Cisco customer service administrator entered the order into Cisco's system. If the order went through 'clean', it would be booked and production scheduled within 24 hours. Nearly one out of four orders didn't get a 'clean' bill of health, however. Instead, when Cisco's system tried to validate the order, it discovered an error in how the product was configured. The 'dirty' order would be rejected, the customer contacted and the procurement cycle would begin again.

In July 1996, Cisco rolled out its web-based ordering and configuring system. Today, that same engineer can sit down at a PC, configure the product online, know immediately if there are any errors and route the order to the procurement department. Because the customer's pricing structure is already programmed into the Cisco site, the authorised purchaser can complete the order with a few keystrokes. Rather than calling Cisco to find out the status of the order, invoice or account information, a customer with the proper authorisation can access the information directly on the website.

With the online pricing and configuration tools, about 98 per cent of the orders go through the system the first time, saving time both at Cisco and the customer's site. Lead times have dropped two to three days, and customers' productivity has increased an average of 20 per cent per order. E-commerce is now fundamental to Cisco. Eighty per cent of orders in Australia are generated by e-commerce, up from 40 per cent three years ago. The objective is to grow the orders received electronically to 90 per cent next year. Cisco's business is $400 million in Australia and $12 billion worldwide. As well as the benefits to Cisco, this use of e-commerce impacts on a lot of businesses that buy from Cisco. The use of online ordering has reduced the headcount in the order entry department by one in the last two years, although the volume of orders received has tripled. The quality of order entry has also improved, due to online checking at the time of entry, from a 30 per cent error rate to less than two per cent.

Customers can also check delivery schedules online. The whole process is more profitable, and better for customers. Orders are faster, cleaner, are checked against the manufacturing cycle, while more orders can be processed using fewer people. Customer satisfaction has increased from 3.5 to four, with five being a perfect score. The users of the system, Cisco's customers, are medium to large businesses. Cisco does not sell direct to consumers. Cisco is also working on supply chain management, aiming and succeeding in being a 'virtual organisation'. Suppliers provide components, such as chips and boards.

Cisco demands that suppliers be online. This has eliminated complex processes, and made a tighter link to manufacturers with no middlemen. Effectively, 50 per cent of the physical boxes are delivered to the customer direct from Cisco's supplier. Cisco has an Intranet used by employees and suppliers alike. Suppliers access the same forecasting information as Cisco. Eighty to 85 per cent of software is now downloaded by customers, whereas it was previously distributed by CD-ROM. It used to cost $125 to send a CD, downloads cost $5. This has also eliminated the deliveries of CDs.

All product information, including technical information is available online. Eighty per cent of technical information is now sourced online by customers. Customers can also enrol for seminars online. This has achieved the objective of increasing customer satisfaction, while saving on the cost of distributing physical documentation. Internally, expense accounts are submitted online and profiled automatically. Payments are made by direct credit to the employee's bank account. This system is used by all 18 000 employees worldwide. Cisco hopes to have invoicing online soon. The main benefits to Cisco of e-commerce have been the reduced head count, reduced inventory, reduced paperwork, and reduced direct costs such as with the downloading of software.

IT industries will also have to purchase more electronic inputs from new intermediaries in order to engage in greater e-commerce. The indications are that these costs will be relatively modest, certainly in proportion to the potential efficiency gains that IT industries are likely to obtain. The use of e-commerce is also increasing the complexity of the information technology requirements. Many organisations are outsourcing the management of their information technology systems. There is a transfer of value into the IT sector brought in by the outsourcing of IT and services from other industries, such as government, finance and travel.

Greater use of e-commerce is likely to drive changes in the way that business is done in the IT industries. It appears that there will be swings transferring value between activities in the IT industries. The first is the potential transfer from hardware to software—this is predominantly caused by the rapid reductions in costs of hardware while software has maintained its value. E-commerce has not been a major driver of this. There is a transfer from commodity manufacture to mass customisation. This has also resulted in a transfer in value from whole items to components. This is being driven by the varied nature of e-commerce and the many applications for the use of information technology in this area, resulting in the need to customise hardware.

For value creation there are very strong possibilities in many sectors, particularly in government. There are cost saving and productivity improvements possible from the use of e-commerce. The opportunity to create value is also high in IT services. IBM believe that software and especially services will be the drivers for growth, while the value creation in hardware is lessening. This means a transfer of value within the IT sector from hardware to software and services. This transfer of value is leading to a move from commodity manufacture to mass customisation, particularly for large customers, and the management of the assembly.

The trend to network computing is leading to the value being held in the network not on the hard drive of the computer. One of the issues for all industries today, is how a business becomes an e-business. That is, not only setting firms up online, but helping them to deal with customers online, and integration into their existing systems and processes. IBM has used it own experience to assist its customers. The process of convergence is also reshaping what it is that businesses in the IT industries will offer in future. Some companies that have been established in the industry for some time have responded dramatically to challenges and opportunities raised by e-commerce.

IBM is in the IT sector, but also heavily involved in the e-commerce sector. The IT sector is a key facilitator for e-commerce, and will be one of the big winners. Some in Australia focus on creating the hardware sides of IT and e-commerce in Australian (chip and other hardware manufacture) but IBM does not see enough critical mass in Australia to support these hardware efforts. Rather, IBM believes that Australia's opportunities are in services and content development which have a much higher value add. The value proposition in the e-commerce world is different than for many other industries.

In manufacturing, automotive for example, a basic model car is developed as the lowest common denominator, then features are added to add value. In e-commerce, the 'lowest common denominator' is the high end or perfect product, from which features are removed to subtract value. The model is more akin to book publishing, where the hardcover is published, and some time later a cheaper paperback is released. Time is also a driver of value, for example the latest stock prices on websites are available at a higher cost than those whose publication is delayed. The growth of e-commerce internationally has led to a huge demand for high quality IT personnel.

Many international countries are willing to pay quality IT personnel more than Australian companies. This is particularly the case with start-up IT companies. The transfer of value to or from overseas can occur with the rise of the Internet and network computing, with the offering of remote services, for example, remote education, application development, etc. The direction of the service flow will determine the direction of the value transfer, i.e. whether Australia positions to provide remote education services, or is the recipient of them.

E-commerce in Telecommunication Industry

Telecommunications companies are big players in the e-commerce marketplace, postal and courier services are generally viewed as risking having their value being eroded as more information is shifted electronically rather than in physical form. E-commerce is having a remarkable impact on the communications industry. Telecommunications carriers have an obvious role to play in providing the communication lines and bandwidth to make network access and ultimately e-commerce possible. Of major importance for telecommunications carriers is the impact of increasing data traffic and the use of the Internet for voice traffic.

The impact of e-commerce on communications is not restricted to the telecommu-nication companies. Postal services are also being impacted by e-commerce. One might expect that as the sole supplier of traditional regular mail services in Australia, Australia Post would suffer a decline in the demand for its services as a result of increasing use of e-commerce. However quite the opposite has occurred— the number of items carried by Australia Post grew by 3.4 per cent last year from 4.3 billion to 4.5 billion. Even so, Australia Post is undertaking a number of strategies to find a fulfilling role in an environment of greater use of e-commerce.

Australia Post is expected to launch its Internet Fulfilment System (IFS) shortly, which will move beyond simple delivery to include electronic integration of its warehousing, distribution and track and tracing capabilities for online retailers. Australia Post already delivers an average of 22 000 items from Amazon.com every monthand is the largest delivery network to 8.5 million households and businesses in Australia. IFS will enable it to compete effectively for the increased delivery of Internet-ordered products as traffic grows into the future. In addition, Australia Post will launch a web-based bill presentation and payment system, which it expects to grow to 20 million transactions by 2003. Unlike online banking bill payments systems, Australia Post will offer bill presentment and will give customers the option to pay bills using accounts from more than one financial institution.

Australia Post will not charge customers for using the services, instead it will charge billing principals for using the system. Consumers can pre-register with bank details and relevant information and an account ore credit card can be debited with a single mouse click. Use of the Internet for billings, particularly for business-to-business transactions, is less expensive and more timely than traditional paper billings that use postal and courier services. The trend in electronic billings is expected to continue due to reduced transaction costs and improved service, and a greater insistence on the part of large businesses that suppliers be linked into their e-commerce systems.

Use of the Internet also offers cost savings from the standardisation of technologies that have historically been incompatible, for example, for fax transmission, broadcasting and telephone circuits, though opportunities for some functions are presently constrained by bandwidth limitations. A cost saving for business generally that may affect telecommunications businesses is increased use of the Internet for selling at the expense of telephone selling and call centres. Automated selling is likely to require less labour for the selling process and for delivering after sales services, which is likely to consist of manuals and databases accessible to consumers over the Internet, with perhaps a small team of people on hand to solve difficult problems.

Communications companies themselves, particularly postal and courier services, are also reducing costs as users of e-commerce services. E-commerce in the procurement of machinery and equipment was projected to compress wholesalers' margins by 25–30 per cent over the period under consideration. Also e-commerce would increase competition and more sophisticated competition would put downward pressure on the producer's prices. E-commerce was thought to be pretty fully implemented in supply areas like fuel, so little further impact was projected. People noted that there were conflicting trends on fuel utilisation arising from e-commerce—greater customisation meant more frequent deliveries of smaller loads, so possibly increased costs, but computer assisted routing meant that the effect was small.

Telecommunications companies in the sector are incurring costs in creating new products. They are moving into e-commerce and application development and finding new value. They are moving more into Internet Protocols and data transmission. This is opening up a whole lot of new opportunities for them, especially in developing applications to suit different customer requirements, in this new environment that can mean developing software. Communications sector companies are becoming involved in new areas of business, enabled by e-commerce and new technologies. Underpinning these lines of business are new technologies.

A new technology which should have a big impact on the sector, and on business in general, is mobile e-commerce based on Wireless Access Protocol (WAP). Internet phones and Internet payment devices will also impact. One of the drivers of e-commerce is the availability of Internet devices. People are using Personal Digital Assistants more, and tapping into the existing mobile base depends on the right applications. The impact of e-commerce is different for the two main industries which comprise this sector. The telecommunications companies are big players in the e-commerce marketplace, providing many of the products and services on which e-commerce is based, as well as moving up the value chain to provide e-commerce services directly.

E-commerce in Financial Markets

Many new purely online brokers have emerged offering very low fees and several full service brokers have responded by offering online trading facilities of their own. Over 15 per cent of households in the US are reported to have conducted equity trades online. This compares with less than five per cent that bank online. Financial markets have also been quick to adopt e-commerce and electronic trading. The Australian Stock Exchange (ASX) introduced the Stock Exchange Automated Trades System (SEATS) in 1987. Trading floors were abolished in 1990 and all trading was conducted electronically on SEATS. In 1994 the ASX introduced electronic and clearing settlement (CHESS).

Reflecting continued use of e-commerce techniques, by 1999 settlement time was reduced to the trade date plus three business days. Most of what the ASX does is e-commerce, for example electronic trading of shares and executions has been occurring for 12 years. Given this history, the ASX believe that further creation of value from e-commerce will be due to increases in speed. For example, gross settlements now take three days, but they are gearing up to handle real time settlements. In that respect it will be a new product for the ASX, and will also change the risk characteristics of trades. There is also value added by the speed of the transaction as the value of the trade can change while it is taking place. The ASX is also working with the NASDAQ to allow the joint buying and selling of shares on their indexes.

Currently, if an Australian wants to trade with NASDAQ they have to find a broker with a US affiliate or contact a broker in the US. The funds for the trade have to be raised separately. When the new service is in place, the sale of shares on one index can be used to fund the purchase of shares on the other. This service will also allow the ASX to use its IT infrastructure more intensely. Re-intermediation could also occur, with brand name labelling of shares and finance. Quicken in the US is trying to provide bundling via a portal to banks, brokers, insurance and more. The seamlessness of any new service will be important.

Another factor is that new players do not have commitments to existing players that existing players have amongst themselves. The business elements of e-commerce will evolve slowly–the ASX has need of digital certification and increased reliability.Banks are keen to make greater use of Internet banking for many reasons, but a key factor is the substantial cost advantage this activity enjoys. The Commonwealth Bank states in its 1998

Annual Report that 72 per cent of all banking transactions are conducted through electronic channels, such as telephone, the Internet, ATMs, and EFTPOS terminals. Similarly, Westpac states that around 80 per cent of their transactions are done electronically.

The National Australia Bank have recently reduced the percentage of transactions through branches from 19 per cent to 14 per cent. Every customer that is to switch from a branch transaction to a lower cost channel results in a substantial saving. Competition will force the banks to pass these savings on to customers as lower fees and prices.Using the Internet for bill payment can provide savings to all parties involved including the merchant, customer and the bank. Electronic billing is likely to be a significant growth area in the economy in 2000.

A flow on impact of greater use of the electronic channels and consolidation in general has been the reduction in staff required. In order to obtain the cost savings offered by the Internet, the banking and finance sector is buying significant volumes of IT inputs. It seems likely that the major banks have raised their IT spending to accommodate a major upgrade of e-commerce requirements. It is not clear if they intend to raise spending above these levels or merely to sustain them, or indeed, if the new capital expenditure round is now complete.

The financial sector is the biggest spender on Internet advertising in Australia, nearly a quarter of the total spent coming from the sector. Five of the top-ten online advertisers in 1998 were from the financial services industry. The traditional concept of a branch offering all services is also changing. Banks are setting up specialist transaction centres and centres that target specific audiences. The National Australia Bank (NAB) has 219 specialist business centres in addition to its 903 traditional branches and in Australia. The ANZ has a Business Direct Centre that offers lower priced products for smaller business with simple lending and financial service needs.

There is a trend toward the use of mobile lenders and investment advisers. Westpac have 1,000 mobile staff and during a 12 month period the Commonwealth Bank's mobile bankers conducted almost 50,000 home loan interviews, and over 24 per cent of all Commonwealth home loan approvals were generated by mobile bankers. The Commonwealth Bank has traditionally used Post Offices to provide additional branch type services for their customers. The Commonwealth plans to extend this with Woolworths Ezy Banking Westpac is working with rural communities and introducing in-store branches in pharmacies, general stores and newsagencies. Banks have traditionally provided an intermediary service of matching deposits with funding for loans.

E-commerce provides an opportunity for banks to be disintermediated from this activity. The direct provision of loans by non-banking entities such as superannuation organisations and insurance companies could be an indication of this disintermediation. Calculated from information provided in the annual reports of the National Australia Bank, Commonwealth Bank of Australia, Westpac and the Australian and New Zealand Banking Group Limited. The data does not separate out increases in branches obtained through acquisitions of overseas activities, so probably understates the fall in branches used in Australia.

Traditionally banks have played an important role in the payment approval process. The trend towards the use of credit cards (versus cheques) has had (and still does have) the potential to reduce the role of banks in the payment loop. Banks have retained some control in this area to date as the card issuing body. The move towards SET in the online payment areas will re-intermediate banks back into the online payment approval process. The likely acceptance of some form of digital cash in the future could potentially disintermediate banks again from the payment approval process. Elimination of value is also possible in the sector. Banks now act as intermediaries in matching depositors with funds to loan applications.

The function could move to brokered markets, and even to a direct market. With payments, the provision of EFTPOS enabling payments was a valuable service to bank customers. Now with services such as Telstra's SureLink, the payment service is provided as part of a larger service. This commoditises the pure payment service. Greater use of e-commerce is also opening new opportunities in this sector. Regulatory reform, competition and the potential of the new technologies are breaking down distinctions between the roles that companies in the banking and finance sector play.

E-commerce over the Internet has enabled banks to move into stock trading. The Commonwealth Bank's ComSec is a predominantly online share trading service, although it does provide a supporting telephone service. The ANZ has recently announced an alliance with E*TRADE Australia for ANZ customers to trade securities online. There is a trend for banks to offer complete financial services to individuals and organisations. This typically includes investment advice, insurance, superannuation, share trading, and funds management.

GROWTH OF E-COMMERCE

The Internet continues to grow rapidly. According to the International Telecommunication Union (ITU), the number of Internet users worldwide stood at 500 million people at the end of 2001. This represents 115 million more than at the end of 2000 (or about a 30 per cent increase). The ITU forecasts that at the end of 2002 the global number of Internet users will have grown to 655 million, which would represent a yearly rate of growth of around 31 per cent. In other words, more than 150 million people, roughly the equivalent of a country like the Russian Federation, or 2.5 per cent of the world's population, would be joining the numbers of Internet users every year.

Overall, developing countries accounted for almost one third of new Internet users worldwide in 2001. In the most developed markets penetration is nearing saturation levels as the numbers of those who do not plan to get Internet access in the near future seem to have stabilised. Therefore, the growth in the share of developing countries will continue. Already Asia, excluding Japan and the Republic of Korea, added almost 21 million new users to the Internet in 2001, more than North America.

Recent data from sources other than ITU would put the number of Internet users in China at 56.6 million, thus making China the second largest Internet population in the world in absolute numbers. In spite of the encouraging increase in the number of users, penetration rates in most developing countries remain very low. On the basis of ITU estimates, the percentage of the world's population using the Internet at the end of 2001 should have been around 8 per cent, that is 30 per cent higher than the 6.4 per cent that the ITU calculated at the end of 2000, but still far below the 50 per cent and above penetration rates in the most advanced countries. The fact that more and more people are using the Internet, which is a prerequisite for the expansion of e-commerce, is not necessarily an indication of the existence of such expansion or of its pace.

A much higher frequency of access is necessary in order to acquire the familiarity and generate the confidence that are needed in order to become an e-commerce practitioner. Particularly in the case of those engaged in business-to-business (B2B) e-commerce, the order of magnitude of their use of the Internet cannot be of some hours per month, but of hours per day. Indeed, when asked about the use they make of the Internet, people rarely mention e-commerce as a frequent online activity. In a survey of 12 countries, e-mail was the only Internet activity in which more than 50 per cent of respondents in every country surveyed had been engaged in the previous six months.

It is safe to assume that in developing countries the proportion of Internet users who are also e-commerce practitioners is lower than average, owing of course to lower per capita incomes but also to other well-known factors such as low credit card usage, lack of relevant products or services or poor logistics and fulfilment services. It seems that the gap between developed and developing countries in terms of access to and use of the Internet is smaller than the one in terms of e-commerce volumes. The differences between forecasts are remarkable. However, while the estimates and forecasts of the absolute levels of e-commerce for a given year can vary by a maximum factor of 2.8 times, the expected rates of growth move in a narrower band, with the highest value 17 percentage points above the lowest.

Digital Opportunities for Women

E-commerce offers some attractive possibilities for small business owners in the developing countries' business-to-consumer (B2C) or retail sector, many of the enterprises in which are owned by women. Numerous examples have been cited as digital opportunities for women entrepreneurs along the models of telecentres in Senegal and Morocco, phone shops in Ghana, Internet cafes or kiosks in Thailand and Malaysia, and the Grameen Phone in Bangladesh. The latter has been cited as a successful example of women entrepreneurship, where financing from the Grameen Bank allows women to buy cellphones and provide mobile pay phone services in their shops or local markets at a mutually agreed mark-up with Grameen Telecom. Aside from telephony services, women's handicrafts could also be developed using B2C, although difficulties in terms of marketing and management skills, and supply and delivery logistics need to be addressed.

A number of success stories concerning B2C endeavours are to be found in South Asia, Latin America, Africa and the Middle East. In India, an e-marketplace called IndiaShop eliminated the middlemen in the selling of saris. One woman allegedly sold a silk sari she tailored for $ 1,100, a price that is way above an average Indian's annual income. In Peru, a nationwide network of housewives called Tortasperu, which is involved in baking confectioneries sold over the Internet, showcased lucrative work for women at home taking care of children yet providing the country with much needed foreign exchange.

Ethiopia has opened a gift shop that sells, using the Internet, traditional Ethiopian costumes, food items and spices produced by women. Finally, handmade products made by women artisans in Egypt, Jordan, Lebanon, Morocco and Tunisia are sold through a virtual shop called Elsouk. These digital opportunities are particularly significant for women in Asia, considering that women head 35 per cent of small and medium-sized enterprises (SMEs).

It has been reported that in China women initiate about 25 percent of new business start-ups and in Japan four out of five small business owners are women. The main advantage of the Web for small home-based businesses is the information and networking opportunities that would make these endeavours profitable rather than marginal. Despite these success stories in e-retailing, it will be necessary to evaluate carefully in which segments of e-commerce women's opportunities lie. Women's prospects depend primarily on the trading strength of the countries concerned. In many cases, the use of the Internet is confined to advertising, ordering and possibly collecting payments; hence women have to develop strategies to build consumers' confidence in the quality of their goods.

The limited evidence available so far shows that some women have also found a market niche in the buying and selling of information rather than tangible goods. In addition to the example of the Grameen Phone cited earlier, women in India and Malaysia use online delivery of their services as freelance journalists to newspapers and other publishers. More promising opportunities for women lie in the B2B segment of e-commerce. The advances in computer and communication technologies have made it possible to transfer digitised data online when there is an adequate supply of infrastructure and bandwidth.

Through the use of networking technologies, large amounts of information can be transported at very low cost from the companies' core offices to satellite or subcontracting units. This possibility has led companies to externalise and decentralise non-core sections of business operations to distant and often cheaper locations. The targeted sites are usually the ones that offer the promises of a cheap, skilled computer-and English-literate workforce. This phenomenon explains why companies in OECD countries outsource service operations to countries such as India or Malaysia.

The International Data Corporation (IDC) estimated that spending on IT outsourcing had reached $ 56 billion in 2000 and would exceed $ 100 billion by 2005. There has been some evidence of companies in developing countries outsourcing operations within the country as well as to other developing countries where wages are even cheaper. Some of the Indian companies, for example, look towards Nepal for the requisite workforce at times of peak demand, particularly from abroad.

In Malaysia, subcontracting or outsourcing takes place primarily within national boundaries. There is a relationship between the availability of a skilled, English-speaking female workforce and where outsourcing normally happens. From this, one can also propose the hypothesis of the existence of a relationship between the availability of a skilled female workforce and foreign direct investment in information processing work in the developing countries. The software services sector in countries such as India and the Philippines could support this hypothesis.

The salary differences between the United States and India, or the Philippines, for similar skills are considerable. Yet these differences cannot fully explain the absence of relocation of software services to countries such as Bangladesh or Uganda where salaries are even lower. In addition to the requisite skills, the success of replicating the experience of India or Philippines depends on creating the right policy framework.

Software and IT-enabled services could be export-oriented as in the case of India and the Philippines; they could also be domestically oriented as is in the case of Malaysia, China and Brazil. The global expansion of those services has broadened the job prospects of women in new areas. The limited statistics that we have so far indicate that women in some of the Asian and Latin American countries occupy more than 20 per cent of professional jobs in software services. Recent research and projections have indicated that the prospects for women lie more in the IT-enabled services than in software services.

The worldwide demand for IT-enabled services or business process outsourcing (BPO) is expected to grow at a dramatic rate in the coming decade, reaching $ 611.4 billion by the year 2005. India hopes to capture a large share of this newly created market. With revenues of $ 870 million from IT-enabled services in 2000-2001 and an annual growth rate of 66 per cent, it currently has the potential to address 38 per cent of that market.

Again, there are no gender-disagregated statistics on employment arising out of these outsourced IT-enabled services from the developing world.

According to the Deputy Director of the Confederation of Indian Industries (CII), in India at least 40 per cent of these newly created jobs are given to, and taken by, women. Remote services or IT-enabled services largely consist in the relocation of back-office operations. One has to be cautious about the future, however, given that there are various types of back-office services requiring different levels of skills from women and men.

The increasing trend towards outsourcing by major American and European corporations entails jobs ranging from those at the lower end of the skills level where women are mostly employed, such as data entry and data capture, to those at the higher end such as software programming, geographical information systems (GIS) and systems analysis. There is a discernible trend towards hiring women for operations that require less complex skills.

For the benefit of the women and for augmenting or retaining the competitive advantage of countries, policy makers need to ensure that women receive the same opportunities and encouragement to acquire skills that could equip them for more complex and specialised jobs. The outsourcing or externalising of business processes to distant units within or across the national boundary could range from satellite offices, such as call centres, to homes of employees or vendors or to offices of customers or clients.

With the computer and a modem, a woman can be connected to the head office and can perform her professional work from a distant site such as a neighbourhood centre or her own home. This is possible as long as her work involves storing, processing, retrieving and delivering digitised information. This new mode of working is known as teleworking and has received much attention, particularly in the context of women's career prospects.

The use of ICT in itself can, in theory, offer a solution that is attractive both to women and to the corporate sector interested in retaining skilled women employees. "Tele" implies distance and teleworking refers to ICT-mediated distant work. The term covers both home-based work or telecommuting and institution-based work as carried out in call centres, neighbourhood centres or satellite offices. Home-based teleworking could, in theory, enhance the participation of women in the digital economy as it allows a certain flexibility in both the timing and location of work.

Women with caring responsibilities at home welcome this flexibility, but not without reservation. Whereas some women appreciate the opportunities that teleworking brings, the majority fear that the home-based work will deprive them of the status of working women and hinder their professional or business efficiency. Surveys of home-based teleworking carried out in Mumbai and Kuala Lumpur revealed that women had a preference for institution-based teleworking as in call centres (home-based teleworking accounted for only 1.0 and 0.35 per cent respectively).

According to Ng and Khoo, in Malaysia, "interviews with women's groups indicated that the (institution-based) centres, commercial and state sponsored, may be the ideal site for externalised work that will allow women (and men) to combine work with collective childcare facilities; enable women (and men) with peer groups and thus allow them to acquire and improve their tacit skills; and provide facilities for state and corporate sector supported vocational training in the field of computer literacy".

Managerial concerns may also explain the low prevalence of home-based teleworking in India and Malaysia. In a survey of management perception of teleworking in Malaysia, most respondents reported that in Malaysian culture face-to-face interaction was essential. In India too, research revealed a cautious attitude on the part of management towards home-based teleworking. In the financial sector, for example, companies find it prudent to outsource work to call centres rather than to teleworkers.

In institution-based teleworking it is easy to monitor and supervise employees in the traditional way, whereas widespread implementation of home-based teleworking will require a fundamental shift in the culture of management from direct supervision to a basis of trust. For self-employed and freelance workers, home-based teleworking will involve self-management and time management skills. It is important for women to acquire these skills in order to avoid being distracted by household chores or over working while teleworking from home.

There is no uniformity in the preference for types of telework among women in the developing countries. Age and stage of life are key factors in moulding women's choice regarding the type of telework. In Mumbai, while young women work in call centres or offices of foreign airline companies in the export processing zones, older women, with young children, opt for and receive home-based telework. Companies such as Datamatics—a rapidly growing software house—receive assignments from their international clients. In turn, they pass these to women teleworkers who work from their homes, mostly online and with their own computers. These home-based teleworkers comprise a wide range of women: housewives, doctors, lawyers and chartered accountants. All that they have in common is that they had to give up regular employment at some stage for the sake of their families.

Teleworking gives them a welcome and much-needed opportunity to be in touch with the world of work. Yet it is difficult to ensure that these women can progress, with adequate access to training and childcare, to high value-added jobs. The experience of Malaysia is similar. "The case studies in software, as well as in printing and publishing, indicate that some women often opt for and find satisfaction in home-based work, either as freelancer or as employees. This happens in a particular phase of their life cycle, especially when there are inadequate child care facilities". The provision of childcare thus remains a key issue in recruiting, retaining and retraining women in the new economy, as it was in the old economy.

In some countries, such as India, Malaysia, the Philippines and Jamaica, call centres have already proved to be a success in allowing women to participate in the digital economy. The proportion of women employed by call centres varies from 40-70 per cent. They tend to be between 20 and 25 years of age and in most cases this is their first job. In view of the projected growth of these call centres, women are likely to benefit at least numerically from this segment of e-commerce. There are risks of a reduction in demand for outsourcing call centre services to developing countries resulting from the improvement of voice recognition by computers. In addition, changes in technology may alter the volume and the nature of call centre service provision. Instead of providing a central base for teleworking, call centre services may be provided virtually, supported by fast data communication linkages among a network of home-based teleworkers.

The deployment of web-based technologies may reduce the market for call centre service provision. In banking, for example, customers may conduct their own transactions. In this new environment, instead of focusing on a single task, institutions such as call centres or satellite offices will be engaged in multidimensional tasks. Women therefore need to have access to appropriate training and lifelong education in order to retain their share in this changing market. Second, there is a prospect of "burn out" syndrome. One reason given was the highly competitive environment as incentives are given to top performers in call success rates (for example, in debt collection efforts), implying reprimands and threats of dismissals for low success rates. These employees have to deal most civilly with their recipients many of whom tend to be abusive or even hysterical. While the call centre industry has the ability to provide young women with the means of entry into the banking sector, the danger lies with it being a dead-end job, with limited career promotion prospects.

For women, call centres located on the outskirts of cities reduce the need to commute; for the management they offer the possibility of adequate supervision for ensuring quality control. ICT and e-commerce can create a number of promising economic opportunities for women in developing countries. They have also pointed to the various obstacles that need to be addressed in order to enhance women's participation in the information economy. One of the most important impediments to women's engaging in ICT-enabled employment possibilities Why is there such an uneven distribution of male and female employees across ICT-related occupations and what could be done to address this?

The training policies in developing countries are in theory gender-neutral. In practice, however, they are often geared to the life cycle and aspirations of men. Women, particularly of child-bearing age, find it difficult to cope with the training given either by employers or by private sector institutions. The dropout rate for women even in the high-skilled software services sector has been alarming, even in areas where there is a need for trained personnel. The major ICT markets are now faced with a serious shortage of IT skills. IDC estimated a total of 3.7 million IT jobs in 2000 (excluding people who used some IT expertise in their main functions).

Assessing the parity between women and men in the digital economy is a complex task. In order to enhance women's participation in e-commerce at all levels, it is important to identify areas of expertise needed by the corporate sector for e-commerce in developing countries. This is particularly so as ICT-related trade in services has led to a dichotomy between ICT-focused and business-focused activities. For the purpose of monitoring and facilitating women's entry into key occupations, it could useful to consider the various core activities for conducting e-commerce.

Many business activities and corporate functions, especially back-office support operations such as typing, scheduling, filing or communications, are now becoming ICT-based and it is women in many, if not all, corporate entities who carry out these functions. Thus, women should learn these required ICT skills to prevent bottlenecks from occurring in the corporate infrastructure. In addition, this framework could be used for benchmarking women's progress, or the lack of it, in key areas of activities related to e-commerce. Given the scenario of a prevailing IT skills shortage and the increasing trend towards business activities and corporate functions becoming IT-based, another manifestation of the gender digital divide is the lack of adequate representation of women in the higher echelons of IT-related jobs.

Few women are actual producers of information technology as Internet content providers, web designers, software programmers or computer troubleshooters. In the United States, females comprise a minority in mid to upper-level IT-related jobs, notwithstanding the fact that 50 per cent of Internet users in the country are women. For instance, only 9 per cent of engineers, 28.5 per cent of computer programmers and 26.9 per cent of systems analysts in the United States are females. Women, however, reportedly constitute the majority (85 per cent) of data entry workers.

Moreover, there are gender disparities in the salaries between men and women in IT in the United States. According to Taggart and O'Gara, women in IT career jobs earn 67 per cent of what their male counterparts earn. It is to be expected that this disparity would be much wider in developing countries. In contrast, the networking or programming courses are predominantly attended by their male counterparts, who would thus obviously be equipped for higher-paying jobs and more remunerative IT career paths. Therefore that trends in access to and use of IT are not sufficient indicators for the equitable participation of women in the information society. Instead, what should be looked at is how women use the Internet and what skills they are equipped with, as these would determine their role in and contribution to the digital economy. In order to meet the impending skill shortages in critical areas, women must therefore be prepared for careers at all levels of the ICT sector, from data entry to software design, network management and IT entrepreneurship.

In considering how ICTs and the Internet could benefit women economically and socially, policy-makers should think beyond women selling their crafts via the web, to women selling their skills as website designers, network managers or IT services consultants. Women in developing countries do not yet find it easy to obtain suitable jobs or income-generating work in the fields of network management, web design or software development, because they are not equipped with the necessary skills. The explanation does not necessarily lie in discrimination against women in centres of education and training in developing countries.

In developing as well as in developed countries, there are difficulties in attracting and retaining women in ICT training and education. An example used by Taggart and O'Gara from the experience of Cisco's international Networking Academy Programme (CNAP) provides some answers to why women's participation in IT training has been minimal . Cisco Networking Academy Programme (CNAP) is an international training programme that teaches students to design, build, and maintain computer networks. The CNAP curriculum is offered in over 70 countries and taught through web-based modules facilitated by on-site instructors in secondary schools, technical colleges, universities, and non-governmental organisations. Minimum education requirements are an eighth grade reading and math level.

In the Philippines, where employment and career prospects are more limited than in the United Kingdom, opportunities for overseas work depict a higher proportion of women graduating in ICT. Apart from skills and training, there are a number of other constraints that prevent women from fully engaging in the opportunities created by the digital economy. These obstructing factors, described below, are essentially access to Internet technologies, availability of credit or financing, the language of the Internet and other social and cultural barriers. Many researchers and policy makers have expressed concern that inequality in access to Internet technology will increase the existing polarity between countries as well as between groups within a country.

The ITU gave a timely warning on impending cyber sex discrimination, since it viewed cyberspace as a predominantly male area where the technical and managerial roles are assumed by men. Its World Telecommunication Development Report 2002 (WTDR) portrays a different and more optimistic future. The spread of very small aperture terminal (VSAT) technology and mobile telephony has considerably narrowed the teledensity gap between the developed and developing world. Also, the third-generation mobile telephone promises to bring networking technology in a cost-effective way to women who are not privileged, even in the rural areas.

Access to infrastructure alone, in the absence of access to market and skills, will not enhance participation in e-commerce. Human resource development issues that focus on technical and marketing skills should perhaps feature as prominently as infrastructure in a policy framework. The cost of infrastructure, however, is likely to remain a major issue for both women and men, particularly in the poorer countries.

In Bangladesh, for example, the cost of a computer equals nearly two years' salary for a professional person, and a modem costs more than a cow. The collective use of telephone and Internet facilities to some extent helps, or might help, traditionally disadvantaged groups, such as women, to overcome the challenges of infrastructure constraints. The use of cyberkiosks and Internet cafes are examples of collective use facilities that come from the market-oriented private sector.

Telecentres present possibilities of collective use with subsidies and support from donor agencies and the public sector. Concerns about bandwidth are often overlooked in the discussion of collective use. To conduct e-commerce in a sustainable and efficient way, it is not enough to have connectivity—the right amount of bandwidth is also needed. Developing countries generally lag behind the developed ones in a dramatic way in terms of access to bandwidth. According to the ITU, there is an uneven distribution of bandwidths among countries—for example, the 400,000 citizens of Luxembourg between them have more international Internet bandwidth than Africa's 760 million citizens. Given their position in the economy and in society in poorer parts of the world, it is likely that women more than men will have problems in having access to adequate bandwidth necessary for conducting e-commerce.

The numbers of women Internet users are very likely to be small in developing countries. Home access to the Internet in many developing countries is a rare phenomenon. Unlikely to have computers at home, most women in developing countries also cannot afford to use public access sites. User fees charged for Internet access at public venues may not be affordable for women, who are generally less able than men to pay fees (averaging $1 to $3 an hour). When women do have access in developing countries, it is usually in the workplace. This creates a dichotomy between the use of ICT by women as tools of production (e.g. routine office work, data entry, programming) and tools of communication (e.g. creation and exchange of information).

As to the latter, women working for non-governmental organisations have used the Internet mainly for political advocacy to protect women's rights and women's causes ranging from domestic violence issues to sexual slavery. Apart from access to infrastructure and education (skills), lack of capital is the third key obstacle facing women (especially women entrepreneurs) wishing to engage in e-commerce and e-business. To start up ICT-enabled businesses or to employ ICT tools to enhance existing businesses, women will need capital from special financial institutions in developing countries that lend specifically to women entrepreneurs who have no collateral, and who work mostly in the informal sector.

The most likely source of the necessary financial capital could be microcredit schemes that specifically target women because of high take-up and repayment experiences and social dividends reaped from lending to them. In this sense, ICT-enabled businesses are no different from other traditional microenterprises in which women in developing countries are engaged. They both involve light-based manufacturing, trade, or service activities; employ about five people or less, mostly family members; have low barriers to market entry; are home-based; and require less professional experience and knowledge than those of their male partners. The only differentiating factor is the use of new technologies.

Rise of Microfinance Programmes

The microfinance or microcredit programmes are aimed at empowering women beyond just the setting up or expansion of microenterprises. Specifically, microcredit schemes increase women's income levels and their economic independence, enhance their autonomy over household decisions about expenditures, promote positive attitudes to women's social and political roles in communities, and provide them with information and support networks to protect their individual and collective interests at the local and macro levels. In the case of ICT-enabled businesses, the Grameen Phone Project in Bangladesh described in section B stands out as a best practice model combining lending to women's microenterprises with literacy training and skills development.

According to Hafkin and Taggart, among the two million borrowers of the Grameen Bank, who received wireless phones as an in-kind loan to village phone operators, 75 per cent are women. The operators resell the mobile phone service to fellow villagers, earning an average annual income of $300 as against the national average per capita income of $286. About 90 per cent of the women operators are married and have no formal education. The phone business can be managed simultaneously with another business or while doing household chores. The major advantages of this type of ICT-enabled enterprise are the minimal educational requirements (just some basic mechanical aptitude), and the small capital needed, enough to be supported by microcredit schemes.

There are positive externalities also in accelerating rural development where telecommunication density is sparse. Another successful example of ICT-enabling business with a microfinancing component is the use of smart cards by Indian women milk collectors in Rajasthan. The smart cards were used to record the quality, fat content and sales of milk to distributors and served as their bankbook, thereby empowering them to make spending decisions and increasing their profits while eliminating the middlemen (called dhudhwala). The dominance of English as the language of the Internet represents a serious problem for the majority of the world's population, which does not speak English.

Women without access to formal schooling that allows them to learn foreign languages are again marginalised, but so are men in countries or regions where English is not "the" language, such as Latin America, the Middle East, French-speaking Africa and Eastern Europe. Even where women do have equal access to formal schooling, they may need to receive additional training in foreign language skills, for which time and resources will be scarce. While the predominance of English is a threat to the social inclusion of non-English-speaking women in the digital economy, the increasing trend towards multilingual content provides a digital opportunity in terms of language translation in software development and in web design in native languages.

In some cultures, women's presence in public is restricted. Women may not be able to travel to undergo training or attend courses by male teachers, while at the same time few female teachers in the IT and engineering fields may be available. Also, women may not be allowed to use public Internet access centres or telecentres and hence will depend more heavily on home-based access. Lack of interaction with the public also restricts women's opportunities to practise foreign language skills. Even in societies where women's presence in public is not restricted, the cur-remote services, this could work well for women wishing to combine household responsibilities with income-earning activities.

Improving women's access to Internet technologies requires extensive infrastructure building of basic telecommunications (including wireless and satellite) in rural and peri-urban areas, which are currently underserved in many developing countries. This should involve common facilities such as telecentres and phone shops that offer public Internet services and are located in venues which women frequent, such as markets, churches, health clinics, schools and post offices.

Microcredit programmes should target the poorest, marginalised women, improving delivery mechanisms that involve men so as to increase their perception of the intervention as supplementing family income instead of being a threat to status. Women should be allowed greater control over their incomes and be given greater powers of decision about family expenditures. A perhaps more radical implication would be the empowerment of women by allowing them titles to conjugal assets so that they could eventually be able to qualify for financing from the formal financial sector.

In the area of job creation, policy makers need to promote IT-enabled employment such as teleworking. In developing countries institution-based teleworking generally appears to be a more attractive option than home-based teleworking, both for working mothers with young children and for management. For relatively highly skilled women, for example in software programming and the media, home-based teleworking, at certain stages of their lives, could provide a solution to problems of combining childcare responsibilities with those of ICT-related professions.

These women policy makers need to ensure better provision of childcare facilities so that they do not settle for home-based and/or less challenging occupations because there is little choice. In other words, a policy framework needs to take into account the complexities of women's aspirations and life cycles with regard to enhancing their participation in all segments of e-commerce. Women in small-scale business face additional hurdles as regards making use of ICT either for marketing or for advertising because of their limited access to market information, finance, assets and infrastructure.

Instruments for E-commerce Development

The IT industry provides essential instruments that make e-business possible, including not only computer hardware and software but also fixed telephones, mobile telephones, telecommunication equipment and wireless transmission equipment. The availability of IT equipment goes hand in hand with Internet connectivity and is therefore clearly a prerequisite for e-business. Even though e-business impinges on IT goods, this does not necessarily imply that having a local IT producing industry would be an advantage for the local business sector when it moves into e-business. However, when the business sector starts adopting new information and communications technologies in its operations, it relies heavily on local or locally available IT expertise in order to fully realise all the efficiency gains that thc Internet makes possible at the level of a single firm as well as at the level of the industry and of the country's economy as a whole.

In this connection, the existence of a local IT sector or of investment from IT multinationals might contribute to the takeoff of e-business in developing countries if it promotes IT awareness and culture in the local business sector, if it advances the IT competencies of the workforce and if it brings the technology closer to the local business community. Although reliable data on the IT industry are hard to find, it is safe to say that IT is one of the world's largest industries. According to one estimate, "worldwide IT spending has reached almost $988 billion and is expected to increase at a compound annual growth rate (CAGR) of 9.4 per cent from 2001 to 2006 to reach $1.5 trillion". The IT industry, having suffered a setback in 2001 due to the economic recession and the effects of the tragic events of 11 September, might experience a modest recovery in 2002. Growth should then pick up again in 2003.

Trade in IT products grew tremendously over the last decade and was worth over $ 900 billion in 2000. In particular, exports of IT products from developing countries grew at a compound annual growth rate (CAGR) of 23.5 per cent over the last decade, while exports from developed countries grew at a CAGR of 10.8 per cent. By comparison, total world exports grew by 6 per cent over the same period. As a consequence, the share of developing countries and economies in transition in IT exports grew from 15.6 per cent of exports in 1990 to 35.5 per cent in 2000. It is also worth noting that IT exports represent a higher share in the exports of developing countries than in those of developed countries.

In fact, IT exports grew from 12 per cent of total developing countries' exports in 1990 to 22 per cent of their total exports in 2000, while for developed countries the share was respectively 10 per cent in 1990 and 14 per cent in 2000. This phenomenon was a result of transnational corporations strategies for locating hardware production in emerging markets, as well as of developing countries' efforts to develop local IT production capacities which resulted in important outsourcing of IT production to those countries. The main sub-sectors within the IT industry were semiconductors, electronic data processing (EDP), office equipment (OE), telecommunications equipment, components and miscellaneous goods. The two largest of these—accounting for almost 60 per cent of IT exports—were EDP and semiconductors.

EDP was the largest sub-sector, with 29 per cent of total IT exports in 2000. This segment includes personal computers, mainframe computers and peripherals such as keyboards, printers, monitors, cables and modems. Storage units, for example hard drives but also CDs and diskettes, are also included in this category. It is interesting to note that trade in EDP includes trade in packaged software, although this is not specifically mentioned. This happens for two sets of reasons: on the one hand, a large proportion of internationally traded software is installed in new computer devices, and users pay for it as part of the price of their new machine; this makes the distinction between hardware and software difficult to capture in import and export figures.

This problem is compounded by the fact that, in the current trade nomenclature, there is no distinction between virgin disks and disks containing data, information or programmes, so that even software that is sold separately from new computers is not adequately recorded in international trade figures. The share of developing countries in EDP hardware was quite high, accounting for 40 per cent of exports in 2000. Developed countries—and in particular the United States and Japan—are the main producers of high-end computer products, but Asian countries, particularly Singapore, the Republic of Korea, Malaysia, Thailand and China, are also powerful competitors, especially in the PC sub-segment.

Thus, the presence of developing countries is higher in the commoditised IT products, which are characterised by low value- added. As regards software, the United States is the world's leading exporter, and it has been estimated that American off-the-shelf software accounts for 70 per cent of the world market. Among developed countries, Japan, Ireland, Singapore, the United Kingdom, France and the Netherlands are emerging as software industry hubs. Among the developing countries, a number of Asian countries are promoting production of software and software services, in particular India, Pakistan, Malaysia, the Philippines and Thailand among others. The second largest sub-sector, with 25 per cent of exports, was semiconductors, and it was the one with the largest participation by developing countries, accounting for 43 per cent of exports.

Again, the largest producers were the United States and Japan, together with a number of ASEAN countries, whose market share has been increasing steadily. Leading exporters from the ASEAN region are in particular the Republic of Korea, Thailand and Taiwan Province of China. IT goods is currently low in developed countries and it is quite likely that since developed countries are the main markets for these products, this was one of the factors that enabled the rapid growth of developing countries' exports of IT goods. However, tariffs remain relatively high in the developing world and especially so in least developed countries.

The level of protection is highest in the office equipment and components sub-sectors. The reason for this, with regard to the components sub-sector, is in part that some products included in that sub-sector are difficult to separate from components of an electrical and even mechanical nature. Thus, these products were not subject to the sweeping tariff-cutting exercise that focused on the IT sector. Even when this is taken into account, the rate applied by some of the least developed countries appears to represent one more obstacle for companies located in those countries in accessing technology at reasonable cost.

In order to enable developing countries' manufacturers and service providers to engage in e-business and to take full advantage of the opportunities offered by the new technologies, the tariffs levied on these products need to be reassessed. In the last three decades a number of countries have used the IT industry as a tool for their development, for a number of reasons. First, the sheer size of the industry now makes it an important investment opportunity. Second, since many segments of the industry do not require a large amount of upfront capital, entry in this sector is relatively easy for countries that have adequate human capital. Third, the protection level for the IT industry is relatively low in the major importing markets, and this no doubt was among the factors that favoured the growth of the IT industry in some of the developing countries.

A number of developing countries have therefore undertaken strategies to attract investment in the field of IT and/or develop the IT industry. The IT industry has grown in waves, as regards both technological developments and market demand, so according to one interpretation, the countries that have succeeded in developing an IT local sector were those that recognised and consequently targeted an emerging trend, investing in the production of goods for which the technology was already established, but for which the market was not yet saturated.

Some of the South-East Asian countries were, for example, successful in penetrating the PC industry in the early 1980's when PCs relied on a robust technological base and the industry was growing fast. One clearly emerging new wave in the next few years concerns the development of open-source software. As explained, open-source not only offers promising opportunities to the software industry in developing countries but also is particularly well adapted to fitting in with developing countries' current pattern of hardware production. Another emerging trend in developing countries is the customisation of IT and especially software products for the use of their local or regional markets.

In fact, a number of SMEs from developing countries are closely cooperating with transnational corporations in order to make their products or services suitable for the particular needs of a niche clientele or a foreign market. IT makes to development in its widest possible sense. In fact, IT is among the factors that underpin the globalisation taking place in virtually all business sectors. New ICT such as the Internet give companies the opportunity to develop new products, to access world markets at lower costs and to source the goods and services needed in the production process in wider and more competitive markets. This translates into increased efficiency not only at the level of the firm, but also at the level of the business sector and the economy as a whole.

While it is clear that many companies in developing and transition economies are using e-business in a variety of forms, to fully benefit from the new technologies and integrate them into everyday business requires a technological infrastructure and a level of workforce expertise that are beyond the reach of the majority of small and medium sized enterprises in developing countries. It is for this reason that business associations, local and national governments, and international organisations are developing a number of initiatives in order to create a nurturing environment into which the business community can successfully integrate e-business practices.

ADVANTAGES AND LIMITATIONS OF INTERNET MARKETING

Advantages

Internet marketing is inexpensive when examining the ratio of cost to the reach of the target audience. Companies can reach a wide audience for a small fraction of traditional advertising budgets. The nature of the medium allows consumers to research and to purchase products and services conveniently. Therefore, businesses have the advantage of appealing to consumers in a medium that can bring results quickly. The strategy and overall effectiveness of marketing campaigns depend on business goals and cost-volume-profit (CVP) analysis.

Internet marketers also have the advantage of measuring statistics easily and inexpensively; almost all aspects of an Internet marketing campaign can be traced, measured, and tested, in many cases through the use of an ad server. The advertisers can use a variety of methods, such as pay per impression, pay per click, pay per play, and pay per action. Therefore, marketers can determine which messages or offerings are more appealing to the audience. The results of campaigns can be measured and tracked immediately because online marketing initiatives usually require users to click on an advertisement, to visit a website, and to perform a targeted action.

Limitations

One of the challenges that internet markets face (as does the general public) is that many internet products are outright scams or promoted with deception making it difficult to know what one is buying. This is especially the case with products that are supposed to train or aid internet marketers in making money. While the quality of products has improved in the past few years, ethics is still often missing in internet marketing. Many so-called money making products are "empty boxes" in which there is essentially nothing there yet a buyer is to make money by reselling this empty box to others. Pyramid schemes are also still prevalent.

The consumer is unable to physically feel or try on the product which can be a limitation for certain goods. However a survey of consumers of cosmetics products shows that email marketing can be used to interest a consumer to visit a store to try a product or to speak with sales representatives.

Security Concerns

Information security is important both to companies and consumers that participate in online business. Many consumers are hesitant to purchase items over the Internet because they do not believe that their personal information will remain private. Some companies that purchase customer information offer the option for individuals to have their information removed from their promotional redistribution, also known as opting out. However, many customers are unaware if and when their information is being shared, and are unable to stop the transfer of their information between companies if such activity occurs. Additionally, companies holding private information are vulnerable to data attacks and leaks. Internet browsing privacy is a related consumer concern. Web sites routinely capture browsing and search history which can be used to provide targeted advertising. Privacy policies can provide transparency to these practices. Spyware prevention software can also be used to shield the consumer.

Another consumer e-commerce concern is whether or not they will receive exactly what they purchase. Online merchants have attempted to address this concern by investing in and building strong consumer brands (e.g., Amazon.com, eBay, and Overstock.com), and by leveraging merchant and feedback rating systems and e-commerce bonding solutions. All these solutions attempt to assure consumers that their transactions will be free of problems because the merchants can be trusted to provide reliable products and services. Additionally, several major online payment mechanisms (credit cards, PayPal, Google Checkout, etc.) have provided back-end buyer protection systems to address problems if they occur.

"Internet marketing" scams

In May 2012, The Verge writer Joseph L. Flatley reported that the terms "Internet marketing" and "Internet marketer" have been co-opted by a loose association of confidence artists running online get-rich-quick schemes.

Usage trends

Technological advancements in the telecommunications industry have dramatically affected online advertising techniques. Many firms are embracing a paradigm that is shifting the focus of advertising methodology from traditional text and image advertisements to those containing more recent technologies like JavaScript and Adobe Flash. As a result, advertisers can more effectively engage and connect their audience with their campaigns that seek to shape consumer attitudes and feelings towards specific products and services.

Effects on industries

The number of banks offering the ability to perform banking tasks over the internet has increased. Online banking appeals to customers because it is often faster and considered more convenient than visiting bank branches.

Internet auctions

Internet auctions have become a multi-billion dollar business. Unique items that could only previously be found at flea markets are now being sold on Internet auction websites such as eBay. Specialized e-stores sell a vast amount of items like antiques, movie props, clothing, gadgets, and so on.

As the premier online reselling platform, eBay is often used as a price-basis for specialized items. Buyers and sellers often look at prices on the website before going to flea markets; the price shown on eBay often becomes the item's selling price.

Advertising industry

In addition to the major effect internet marketing has had on the technology industry, the effect on the advertising industry itself has been profound. In just a few years, online advertising has grown to be worth tens of billions of dollars annually. PricewaterhouseCoopers reported that US$16.9 billion was spent on Online marketing in the U.S. in 2006.

This has caused a growing impact on the United States' electoral process. In 2008, candidates for President heavily utilized Internet marketing strategies to reach constituents. During the 2007 primaries, candidates added, on average, over 500 social network supporters per day to help spread their message. President Barack Obama raised over US$1 million in one day during his extensive Democratic candidacy campaign, largely due to online donors.

Several industries have heavily invested in and benefited from internet marketing and online advertising. Some of them were originally brick and mortar businesses such as publishing, music, automotive or gambling, while others have sprung up as purely online businesses, such as digital design and media, blogging, and internet service hosting.

References

Jaakko Sinisalo et al. (2007). "Mobile customer relationship management: underlying issues and challenges". *Business Process Management Journal* 13(6): 772. doi:10.1108/14637150710834541.

Charlesworth, Alan (2009). *Internet marketing: a practical approach*. Butterworth-Heinemann. p. 49.

Croll, Alistair, and Sean Power (2009). *Complete Web Monitoring*. Beijing: O'Reilly. p. 97. ISBN 978-0-596-15513-1.

Pattison, Kermit (2011-3-17). "Online Video Offers Low-Cost Marketing For Your Company". *The NY Times*. Retrieved 2012-7-3.

Peacock, Michael (2008). *Selling Online with Drupal E-Commerce: Walk through the Creation of an Online Store with Drupal's E-Commerce Module*. Birmingham.

Rayner, Andrew (April 21, 2010). "Put the E-mphasis on Local Internet Marketing and reach first page on Google". Retrieved August 15, 2010.

One to One Marketing – Overview. Managingchange.com (1995-04-05). Retrieved on 2011-10-30.

Bibliography

Albert Abramson. (2003). *The History of Television, 1942 to 2000*, Jefferson, NC, and London, McFarland.

Allison Cavanagh, (2007). *Sociology in the Age of the Internet*, McGraw-Hill International.

Andrew S. Tanenbaum, (2006). *Computer Networks*, Fourth Edition, Pearson Education.

Asa Briggs. (1961). *The History of Broadcasting in the United Kingdom* (Oxford University Press.

Baker, Burton H. (2000), *The Gray Matter: The Forgotten Story of the Telephone*, Telepress, St. Joseph, MI.

Berdal, S.R.B. (2004) (PDF), *Public deliberation on the Web: A Habermasian inquiry into online discourse*, Oslo: University of Oslo.

Biagi, S. (2004). *Media Impact*. Wadsworth Pub Co, 7th edition.

Bruce, Robert V. (1990), *Alexander Graham Bell and the Conquest of Solitude*, Cornell University Press, Ithaca.

Caron, A. H. and Caronia, L. (2007). *Moving cultures: mobile communication in everyday life*. McGill-Queen's University Press.

Charlesworth, Alan (2009). *Internet marketing: a practical approach*. Butterworth-Heinemann. p. 49.

Christine Hine, , (2005). *Virtual Methods: Issues in Social Research on the Internet*, Berg Publishers.

Christopher H. Sterling with Michael C. Keith (ed.). (2004). *Encyclopedia of Radio*. New York; London: Fitzroy Dearborn, 2004 (three vols.)

Cisco Systems, Inc., (2003). *CCNA: network media types*. Retrieved from ciscopress.com

Coe, Lewis (1995), *The Telephone and Its Several Inventors: A History*, McFarland, North Carolina.

Coffman, K. G; Odlyzko, A. M. (1998). *The size and growth rate of the Internet*. AT&T Labs. Retrieved 21 May.

Comer, Douglas (2006). *The Internet book*. Prentice Hall. p. 64.

Croll, Alistair, and Sean Power (2009). *Complete Web Monitoring*. Beijing: O'Reilly. p. 97.

D. R. Wilson, , (2004). *Researching Sociology on the Internet*, Thomson/Wadsworth.

Daniel A. Menchik and Xiaoli Tian. (2008). "Putting Social Context into Text: The Semiotics of Email Interaction."*The American Journal of Sociology*. 114:2. pp. 332–70.

Hafner, Katie (1998). *Where Wizards Stay Up Late: The Origins Of The Internet*. Simon & Schuster.

Henry Ewbank and Sherman P. Lawton. (1952). *Broadcasting: Radio and Television* (Harper & Brothers.

Huurdeman, Anton A. (2003), *The Worldwide History of Telecommunications*, IEEE Press and J. Wiley & Sons.

Jaakko Sinisalo et al. (2007). "Mobile customer relationship management: underlying issues and challenges". *Business Process Management Journal* 13(6): 772. doi:10.1108/14637150710834541.

Jacques Derrida and Bernard Stiegler. (2003). *Echographies of Television*, Polity Press.

Jerry Mander. (1978). *Four Arguments for the Elimination of Television*, Perennial.

Joan Ferrante-Wallace, Joan Ferrante, (1996). *Sociology.net: Sociology on the Internet*, Thomson Wadsworth.

John A. Bargh and Katelyn Y. A. McKenna, (2004). *The Internet and Social Life*, Annual Review of Psychology, Vol. 55: 573-590.

John Mulcahy, (1989). *A Chronicle of Merit's Early History*, Merit Network, Ann Arbor, Michigan.

John, Richard R. (2010) *Network Nation: Inventing American Telecommunications*, Harvard University Press.

Julie Rehmeyer, (2007). "The Internet spreads its tentacles", *Science News*, Vol. 171, No. 25, pp. 387–388, 23 June.

Karen D. Frazer, (1995). *NSFNET: A Partnership for High-Speed Networking, Final Report 1987-1995*, Merit Network, Inc.

Kurose James F and Keith W. Ross. (2006). *Computer Networking: A Top-Down Approach Featuring the Internet*, Pearson Education.

Llewellyn White. (1947). *The American Radio* (University of Chicago Press, 1947).

Long, Paul; Wall, Tim (2009). *Media Studies: Text, Production and Context*. Pearson Education.

Lorenzo Cantoni & Stefano Tardini, (2006). *Internet*, Routledge.

Marc Fisher. (2007). *Something In The Air: Radio, Rock, and the Revolution That Shaped A Generation* (Random House, 2007).

McQuail, Denis (2000) *McQuail's Mass Communication Theory* (fourth edition), Sage, London, pp. 16–34. MAS.

Neil Postman. (1985). *Amusing Ourselves to Death: Public Discourse in the Age of Show Business*, New York, Penguin US.

One to One Marketing – Overview. Managingchange.com (1995-04-05). Retrieved on 2011-10-30.

Pattison, Kermit (2011-3-17). "Online Video Offers Low-Cost Marketing For Your Company". *The NY Times*. Retrieved 2012-7-3.

Peacock, Michael (2008). *Selling Online with Drupal E-Commerce: Walk through the Creation of an Online Store with Drupal's E-Commerce Module*. Birmingham.

Pierre Bourdieu. (2001). *On Television*, The New Press.

Rayner, Andrew (April 21, 2010). "Put the E-mphasis on Local Internet Marketing and reach first page on Google". Retrieved August 15, 2010.

Rob Kling, (1997). The Internet for Sociologists, *Contemporary Sociology*, Vol. 26, No. 4 pp. 434–444

Ronald J. Deibert, John G. Palfrey, Rafal Rohozinski, and Jonathan Zittrain (eds), *(2010) Access Controlled: The Shaping of Power, Rights, and Rule in Cyberspace*, MIT Press.

Ronda Hauben (2001). *From the ARPANET to the Internet*. Retrieved 28 May 2009.

Rupert Maclaurin. W. (1949). *Invention and Innovation in the Radio Industry*. The Macmillan Company.

Steven Johnson. (2005). *Everything Bad is Good for You: How Today's Popular Culture Is Actually Making Us Smarter*, New York, Riverhead, Penguin.

Tim Brooks and Earle March. (2002). *The Complete Guide to Prime Time Network and Cable TV Shows*, 8th ed., Ballantine.

Wendell Odom,Rus Healy, Denise Donohue. (2010). *CCIE Routing and Switching*. Indianapolis, IN: Cisco Press

Wheen, Andrew (2011), *DOT-DASH TO DOT.COM: How Modern Telecommunications Evolved from the Telegraph to the Internet*, Springer.

William Stallings, (2004). *Computer Networking with Internet Protocols and Technology*, Pearson Education.